New York Yankees

An *Interactive* Guide to the World of Sports

SB

Savas Beatie

New York and California

Printed in the United States of America

Cataloging-in-Publication Data is available from the Library of Congress.

ISBN 13: 978-1-932714-41-8

10 09 08 07 06 05 04 03 02 01
First edition, first printing

Cover photo used wih permission National Baseball Hall of Fame Library Cooperstown, N. Y.

SB
Published by
Savas Beatie LLC
521 Fifth Avenue, Suite 3400
New York, NY 10175
Phone: 610-853-9131

Editorial Offices:

Savas Beatie LLC
P.O. Box 4527
El Dorado Hills, CA 95762
Phone: 916-941-6896
(E-mail) editorial@savasbeatie.com

Savas Beatie titles are available at special discounts for bulk purchases in the United States by corporations, institutions, and other organizations. For more details, please contact Special Sales, P.O. Box 4527, El Dorado Hills, CA 95762. You may also e-mail us at sales@savasbeatie.com, or click over for a visit to our website at www.savasbeatie.com for additional information.

In Memory of

Joe D. Walden

Also by Daniel J. Brush, David Horne,
and Marc CB Maxwell

University of Oklahoma Football:
An Interactive Guide to the World of Sports
(Savas Beatie, 2007)

NASCAR
An Interactive Guide to the World of Sports
(Savas Beatie, 2008)

Major League Baseball
An Interactive Guide to the World of Sports
(Savas Beatie, 2008)

Also by Marc CB Maxwell

Surviving Military Separation: 365 Days
An Activity Guide for Family Members of Deployed Personnel
Illustrated by Val Laolagi
(Savas Beatie, 2007)

"I'd like to thank the good Lord
for making me a Yankee."

— Joe DiMaggio

Contents

Contents (continued)

Photos, illustrations, charts, and tables have been placed
throughout the book for the benefit of our readers.

Foreword

*M*ost of the time, if you are a fan of a sports team, you root for that team. You cheer for that team. Maybe you wear a sweatshirt with their logo on the front, or a hat with team colors splashed prominently on it. If you wander a little close to the frenzied fringe, perhaps you paint your face in the appropriate hues.

Sports fans, they care about their teams. They care deeply.

And then there are Yankees fans.

"Yankees fans," Derek Jeter told me once, with a look of wonder swimming in his eyes, "belong in a separate category all their own."

OK: we know what you're doing now, if you happen to reside in a distinctly non-Yankee precinct of this country, in which there are many. You are rolling your eyes. You are shrugging your shoulders. The Yankees take themselves so seriously, and their fans take themselves even *more* seriously, and this is all supposed to only be about baseball games, right?

See, that's where you're wrong. And that's what you miss out on if you don't fall under the umbrella of Yankee fandom. There is responsibility attached to being a Yankee fan. There is a sense of history, and a sense of belonging. What others see as entitlement, Yankee fans interpret as an almost sacred kind of duty, one that reaches across generations and stretches all the way back to the Harding Administration.

"When you manage the Yankees," says Joe Torre, who managed them with great distinction for 12 seasons from 1996 through 2007, "you aren't only managing this year's team, you're managing for 1996 and 1977 and 1956 and 1941. You aren't only managing players, you're managing ghosts. And I suspect that's what it means to root for the team as well. It's a fascinating thing."

That fascination has likely brought you to this book. If you are a Yankees fan, that makes perfect sense, because what you're going to find in the coming pages is an absorbing collection of facts, of figures, of trivia, and of history. Some of it you'll already know, because Yankees fans are nothing if not ardent students of history. Much of it will add to your knowledge. Some of it will surprise you. All of it will delight you.

And if you aren't a Yankees fan?

Then you are proving the very point that all Yankees fans make whenever they present their valedictories for why the Yankees are the most important team in American sport. Because even if you swear to loathe the pinstripes, even if the thought of a 27th championship banner flying high above the Bronx someday makes you somewhat queasy, you certainly understand the Yankees. You certainly appreciate them, even if you may be slow to use that word.

For it is impossible to tell a tale of baseball across the last century and not include the Yankees. Similarly, it is impossible to be a fan of the game and not be, even silently, even cryptically, a fan of who the Yankees are, what they've done, the excellence they've maintained, fairly regularly, for 87 years.

The Yankees *matter*.

But you already knew that. You've already started perusing this wonderful book. And soon, you'll dive into this wonderful yield by the good folks at Sports by the Numbers™ and you will lose yourself in baseball, in history, in numbers, and in the New York Yankees. I envy you. I can't think of a better way to pass the next couple of hours. Enjoy.

Mike Vaccaro
Sports Columnist
New York Post

Preface

"Americans love numbers—they just don't like arithmetic," writes political analyst and noted author Mark Penn. "We are fascinated by the mathematical underpinnings of our daily lives," he continues. "We may have fewer numbers experts, but we have more Numbers Junkies."

Of course Numbers Junkies—as he calls them—have been around for a long time, and we know that the vast majority of them are also baseball fans. Baseball is a great sport for Numbers Junkies because there are so many things you can count and figure statistics for: games, wins, losses, innings, extra-innings, runs, earned runs, unearned runs, at bats, hits, homeruns, strikeouts, walks—and the list just goes on and on, and we are Numbers Junkies because we love all of it, and we can't get enough of it. This is especially true when your team happens to also be the greatest franchise in professional sports history, the team with the most storied history, the greatest legends, and the most championships, and the team that hails from the greatest city in the world—New York.

No other franchise can generate such passion or raw emotion from both its own fans and those who look at the numbers and find their personal team lacking. Bill Veeck, the long time owner of the Chicago White Sox and executive member of the Baseball Hall of Fame, famously said, "Hating the Yankees is not part of my act. It is one of those exquisite times when life and art are in perfect conjunction."

The sentiment expressed by Veeck is not limited to owners.

Bob Feller, the Hall of Fame pitcher for the Cleveland Indians who pitched three no-hitters during his career, is quoted as having said, "I would rather beat the Yankees regularly than pitch a no-hit game."

It may be vogue in other major league cities to hate the Yankees, but the truth is people come out to watch the Yankees play in far greater numbers than they do for other franchises—and knowing the reasons for such venomous sentiment from their opponents only serves to make those who make up the fan base for the most successful professional sports franchise in the world enjoy being a Yankees Numbers Junkie just a little bit more: 15 American League East Division titles, 39 American League pennants, and 26 World Series titles.

To borrow a line from *Good Will Hunting* that was scripted by a couple of well-known Red Sox fans and Academy Award winning writers, "How do you like them apples?"

Well, most likely not so much.

It is not that other franchises have no worthy accomplishments, legends, or great numbers—but rather, no other major league franchise can boast so many extraordinary moments, legends, and numbers. Just a partial list of the iconic men who wore pinstripes reads like the roll-call at the Hall of Fame: Berra, Boggs, Chesbro, Clemens, Combs, Dickey, DiMaggio, Ford, Gehrig, Gomez, Griffith, Guidry, Howard, Hoyt, Huggins, Hunter, Jackson, Jeter, Lazzeri, Mantle, Maris, Martin, Mattingly, McCarthy, Munson, Pennock, Rivera, Rizzuto, Ruffing, Ruth, Stengel, Torre, Williams, and Winfield—and the list could easily go on, and on, just like the concept behind Sports by the Numbers™, because with the Yankees, it literally does not end.

It is for all these reasons and more that our quest to use numbers to tell the stories behind every major league franchise begins with the Bronx Bombers. The numbers in this book tell the stories of every team captain, every retired jersey number, every member of the Hall of Fame, every season, every post-season, every Cy Young Award recipient, every Most Valuable Player, every Rookie of the Year, and every World Series title. The numbers you are about to read will also tell you the stories of players you may have forgotten, or never even heard of, but because of the numbers you will soon come to know them—and that is only one of the many great things our readers have come to love about the Sports by the Numbers™ series.

One thousand numbers are in this book—and every one of them tells the story of the New York Yankees. The format is unique, intriguing, and compelling, because as baseball fans we all love the numbers, and in these pages the numbers celebrate records, lore, trivia, personalities, anomalies, championships won, championships lost, the good and the bad, and all that is great about baseball and the New York Yankees.

Sit back, reminisce, and we hope you enjoy reading this book as much as we enjoyed writing it. Be on the lookout for some of our favorite numbers too. We tag them with our logo and call them Hall of Fame and All Star numbers. On our website you can access more content on these numbers using our SBTN Locker. You can also find some of our favorite SBTN Memories on our site: www.sportsbythenumbers.com.

Check them out, and take a look at some of our weekly SBTN Stats too—and then come back often as we will be posting new Yankee numbers throughout the first season of the post-Torre era.

Acknowledgments

It is pretty standard to thank the people who are most responsible for bringing to a successful conclusion any project, much less one as large as writing a book—but the truth is, it can be difficult to say thank you in a way that does not come off sounding like the standard when you rely so heavily on as many people as we do.

So with that in mind, we begin our lengthy list with Joe Torre. We echo the sentiment of Yankee fans everywhere when we say thank you for six pennants, four World Series titles, and more than a decade of being the consummate professional. It is a pretty impressive feat to end your tenure with an equal number of spring trainings and post-seasons under your belt, and you gave us an amazing run for which Yankee fans will forever be grateful.

Joe is a vital part of this book, of course, because of his numbers and his stature among Yankee fans. He did not have any knowledge that he was supporting our efforts though; we merely observed his performance and told his story using the numbers available.

But Yankee fans are truly grateful for Joe, because after nearly two decades of wandering in the proverbial desert he brought home four titles—and Yankee fans everywhere came to rely on his steady hand to guide the club in the proper direction, confident that with his leadership all would be well.

So Joe is on our list.

The rest of it, well, think of it like this—these people are to us what Joe Torre has been to Yankee fans, only more. We need them to keep us steady and going in the proper direction. Plus, they are on a list that includes Joe Torre.

Our list continues:

Our publisher who makes all this possible, Theodore P. "Ted" Savas, and the fine team of professionals he assembled in California: Sarah Keeney, Savas Beatie director of marketing; Val Laolagi, artist, logo designer, and webmaster; Jim Zach of zGrafix, cover design; and Lee Merideth, layout.

Our new friends in New York, Mike Vaccaro and Patricia Kelly— Mike is a senior sports columnist for the *New York Post* who took time from his busy writing schedule to pen the foreword to our book. He is an exceptional talent with numerous awards and two highly successful books, and we are honored to have him on our team. Pat is the photo archivist at the Baseball Hall of Fame in Cooperstown, which has got to be one of the coolest jobs in the world, but she was never too busy to work with us and for that we are grateful.

Our friends, colleagues, and supporters in Norman: Lisa, Yira, Jay, Doctor Jay, Bill, Al, Tara, Gabi, Tina, Joe, Trent, Keith, Bob, Barry, and Rudy's "Country Store" and Bar-B-Q.

Our friends, colleagues, and supporters who serve overseas: Tammie, Ericka, Mark, Teresa, Adele, Barriett, Zac, and Heather.

Military brats who serve overseas with their parents and prove their love for baseball in general and the Yankees in particular by watching games at 2 am on school nights: James, Jimmy, Alex, Jon, Andrew, Cookie, Agustin, Lindsey, Kaite, Jamie, Chelsi, Frankie, and Wayne.

Our friends and family members scattered throughout the world: Ben and Celina in Seoul; Dwin and Kelly in Jacksonville; Travis and Gracie in Keystone; Cayden, Lillian, and Jade in Seoul; Steve and Sandy in Keystone; David and Jesi in Santiago; Willy in Quito; Irma and Luis in Salt Lake; Joshua in Las Cruces; Moo-Moo in Copenhagen; GiGi in Heidelberg; Brother Mooney in Ansbach; Brother Mark and Kim in Fort Walton Beach; Brother Ken and Helen in Keystone; Daddy and Mama Dale in Odum; Edgar and Denise in Keystone; Derryl and Betty in Cary; Boyd and Jane in Richmond Hill; Billy and Nana in Gainesville; and Grandmaw in Charleston.

Joe Walden, who bought his grandson a 1984 Donruss Don Mattingly rookie card at the Swamp Fox hobby shop in Charleston, South Carolina back in 1985—and who also taught his grandson to drive a Mustang. He paid eight bucks for the card, but the memory is priceless.

Our parents who brought us into this world: Bill and Dorthe Brush, Larry and Connie Horne, and Richard and Deanna Maxwell.

And the ones who make our world complete: Paulina, Lisa, and Christine.

Daniel J. Brush, David Horne,
and Marc CB Maxwell

Norman, Oklahoma
October 26, 2007

The Locker

Welcome to Sports by the Numbers™ and our Interactive Guide to the World of Sports. In compiling our first 1,000 numbers that we used to tell stories in our debut title, *University of Oklahoma Football*, it was apparent to us that for one reason or another some of the numbers resonated more deeply with us than did others—they were special.

The numbers were all great, but there were some numbers that we were drawn toward and felt the need to expand on more than the others. Our website provided us with the opportunity to do just that in an area we call The Locker.

The team of authors for this title on the New York Yankees has used special logos to designate five Hall of Fame numbers and ten All Star numbers that you will come across as you read the stories that unfold within these pages.

Numbers designated as Hall of Fame or All Star lets you know that they are among our favorites from this book—and once in the locker room, you will find out why.

Our website is: www.Sportsbythenumbers.com

Use the tab at the top of our homepage or the locker on the bottom right-hand corner of our homepage to enter our locker. Once there you will see the covers of all the SBTN titles that are currently available.

Click on the cover of your favorite SBTN title to view the Hall of Fame and All Star numbers that the SBTN authors have selected for that book.

You can then click on any number in the locker room to gain access to additional information that may come in the form of pictures, video, audio, text, or random musings from one of the SBTN authors, but regardless, it will enhance the story told by the number, and it will let you know why we feel the number is so significant.

Creating an Interactive World of Sports that combines the best of the traditional book world with the unlimited potential of the Internet is an exciting and fluid process—and we are constantly working on new and better ways to bring together the book world and the cyber world with one goal in mind, to give sports fans the ultimate experience when it comes to reminiscing about their favorite numbers, players, teams, and memories.

Enjoy the experience.

George Steinbrenner

"Winning is the most important thing in my life,
after breathing. Breathing first, winning next."

— George Steinbrenner

Chapter One

Mr. Steinbrenner

On the day George Steinbrenner was born the Yankees lost both ends of a double-header against the Washington Senators and fell 4.5 games out of first in the race for the American League pennant. The losses were numbers three and four of a season high seven game losing streak, and despite a roster consisting of nine future Hall of Fame players, the Yankees never got any closer to first the rest of the season.

Some old-timers in the Bronx today will tell you a tale not quite true, but probably not too far off either.

On July 4, 1930, the date Henry and Rita Steinbrenner celebrated the birth of their firstborn child in a suburb of Cleveland, Ohio, a cold chill set in on first-year skipper Bob Shawkey. It was a chill felt by many who have dared to take the helm of the Bronx Bombers, and it has been the undoing of more than a few. It grew deeper for Shawkey the next day. In desperate need of a victory to break the losing streak, he turned to a roster full of legends: Bill Dickey, Lou Gehrig, Tony Lazzeri, Babe Ruth, Earle

Combs, Red Ruffing, Herb Pennock, Lefty Gomez, and Waite Hoyt. All nine of those players made it to Cooperstown, and if there is something more impressive, it would probably be that those same nine players combined to win 45 World Series during their playing days.

But having lost four in a row, the Yankees impressive roster meant nothing to the Senators.

Washington secured a 3-2 victory over New York on July 5. The streak was at five, and the chill grew deeper because the Yankees were now 5.5 games out of first. On July 6, the Yankees fell to the Senators again by a score of 3-2. After a day off, the Yankees began play 6.5 games out on July 8, having lost six straight. The Athletics beat the Yankees 4-0 to run the losing streak to seven, and the club fell 7.5 back in the standings.

The streak ended at seven, but the chill surrounding skipper Bob Shawkey never let up.

So then, as to the origin of the chill, and with respect to those old-timers, one has to agree it could not have been caused by the birth of a young Steinbrenner, though foreshadowing is often more clear in hindsight and there is certainly a substantial amount of irony to be found here, but rather it is more intuitive to assert it came from a franchise already bent on building traditions and attaining championships—and Shawkey understood as well as anyone the tradition being built in the Bronx, because he was already a part of it.

In 1923, Shawkey beat the New York Giants in game four of the World Series.

He tossed seven plus innings in front of 46,000 screaming fans at the Polo Grounds and secured an 8-4 victory to draw the series even at two games apiece. It was his only appearance of the series, but he was there to celebrate with his teammates when the Yankees won the first World Series title in franchise history just two days later. So Shawkey understood the importance of the winning tradition in the Bronx, but he donned the managerial cap beneath the long shadows of some of the greatest legends in franchise history anyway—and this, more than anything, has always been the curse of being the Yankees skipper.

In addition to having nine Hall of Fame players on his roster, it was never really his team—the team belonged to Hall of Fame manager Miller Huggins.

The New York Yankees claimed the first pennant in franchise history in 1921 under the guidance of Huggins. In 1923, Huggins led the club to victory in the World Series for the first time. In a span of only eight years, Huggins and the Yankees claimed six pennants and three World Series titles, and as a result the Yankees fan base began to grow, and so did their expectations.

In 1929, the club began play a bit sluggish. It took an eight game winning streak in early May before the Yankees gained a share of the lead. So accustomed to the Yankees' success, fans, players, and the media alike assumed Huggins and the Yankees would cruise the rest of the season. Unfortunately, the Yankees' lead lasted less than a week. On June 1, the Yankees fell to eight games out. On July 1, the deficit was nine. By the end of August, the Yankees trailed the Philadelphia Athletics by 12.5 games.

It was a disappointing season for Yankee fans. It became tragic though when Huggins resigned in September due to a rare skin disease, only to die one week later.

Art Fletcher managed the club in a caretaker status for the final 11 games of the season.

And then the managerial reign of Bob Shawkey began.

If you go back and look through the American League leaders for 1930 you will find Gehrig, Ruth, Combs, Lazzeri, Pennock, and Ruffing prominently placed in several statistically significant categories.

But with a record of 86-68, the Yankees came up 16 games short in the standings.

The media, fans, and the New York baseball establishment found it convenient to ignore the Yankees' 1929 record and instead blame the demise of the club in 1930 on Shawkey. The franchise began play as the Orioles in 1901, became the Highlanders in 1903, and finally took the name Yankees beginning in 1913. Huggins led the Yankees 12 consecutive seasons from 1918-29 and set the standard by which all other skippers are measured against—Shawkey was simply the first to fall victim to it. Huggins cast a long shadow, and when Shawkey could not rise to the challenge immediately he was replaced with Joe McCarthy by owner Jacob Ruppert. The irony, of course, is Shawkey became the first manager since the club began play as the Yankees to last only one season at the helm (if you discount captain and player-manager Roger Peckinpaugh, who was skipper for 20 games in a caretaker role after

Frank Chance left in 1914)—and the longest losing streak of his one season, the one the Yankees could not recover from, coincided with the birth of the Yankees owner who would become synonymous with managerial change.

Jacob Ruppert took ownership of the Yankees when the club was in chaos and in danger of falling into obscurity. He turned the club around by getting Babe Ruth, spending money, building a stadium, and expecting success—and he got it, too.

Ruppert also set a standard, and today people often criticize The Boss for living up to it.

Mr. Steinbrenner gets blamed for skyrocketing salaries in the free agent market. He gets maligned for being too involved with the team, and for being too emotional. He has made his fair share of mistakes, the worst of which led to public embarrassment and criminal charges, being banned from baseball, being reinstated, and receiving a presidential pardon. But he has also done something lacking all too often in our society today, and for all his faults, on this one thing he has always been consistent—he refuses to accept mediocrity.

His obsession with winning is notorious, and the casualties have been numerous. He changed managers 20 times during his first 23 seasons as owner, including Billy Martin on five different occasions. He replaced his general manager 11 times during his first 30 years. His feuds with players, managers, league officials, and the media are at the same time both infamous, and the stuff legends are made of.

When Jacob Ruppert took ownership of the Yankees in 1914, the franchise was a second tier club with a .479 winning percentage the previous 12 seasons. By 1921, the club won the first of three consecutive pennants, culminating in the first World Series title in franchise history.

When Mr. Steinbrenner and a group of investors bought the franchise from CBS in 1973, the Yankees were in the midst of an eight year playoff drought, the last World Series title was more than a decade in the past, and the traditions and expectations established long before by Ruppert, Huggins, and a long list of Hall of Fame legends were almost extinct.

In only his fourth season, the Yankees won the pennant.

In his fifth and sixth seasons, the club won back-to-back World Series titles. In his first 34 seasons, the Yankees made the playoffs 17 times, claimed ten pennants, and won six World Series titles—and today, the Yankees franchise is the most successful in all of professional sports.

People may choose to fault Mr. Steinbrenner for his methods and question the demands he puts on members of the Yankees organization, but they must also admit he enables them to be successful because he holds nothing back, and he gets results.

Bob Shawkey may have been the first managerial casualty in franchise history, brought about because of high standards and a storied tradition, but the longest shadow to work under will be the one left by Mr. Steinbrenner when he is no longer in place leading the club, and the success of The Boss will be the standard all others will be held to.

The jersey number (1) for Billy Martin retired in 1986. One of the Yankees best known personalities, Martin earned four World Series rings as a player in the 1950s. He often clashed with owner George Steinbrenner as manager, resulting in five different stints in the most prestigious managerial job in baseball. Martin managed the club to a World Series title and earned his fifth overall ring in 1977.

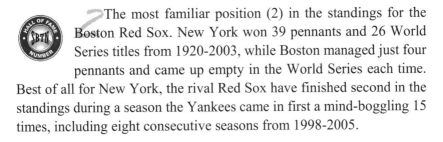

The most familiar position (2) in the standings for the Boston Red Sox. New York won 39 pennants and 26 World Series titles from 1920-2003, while Boston managed just four pennants and came up empty in the World Series each time. Best of all for New York, the rival Red Sox have finished second in the standings during a season the Yankees came in first a mind-boggling 15 times, including eight consecutive seasons from 1998-2005.

The jersey number (3) for Babe Ruth retired in 1948. A member of the inaugural class of players inducted into the Hall of Fame, Ruth is one of the greatest names in the history of sport. He is the Yankees all-time leading homerun hitter and he won 12 homerun titles in his career, but most importantly, he led the Yankees to victory in the World Series four times.

The jersey number (4) for Lou Gehrig retired in 1939. He played in 2,130 consecutive games and won six World Series titles before amyotrophic lateral sclerosis (ALS) forced him to retire from baseball in 1939. On July 4, 1939, the Yankees honored him with Lou Gehrig Day at Yankee Stadium. He became the first player in the history of baseball to have his jersey number retired, and he was elected membership into the Hall of Fame later that same year.

The jersey number (5) for Joe DiMaggio retired in 1952. He is considered by many as the best all-around player in baseball history. He gave three seasons during the prime of his career to serve in the military during World War II, and yet he still posted career numbers that place him among the top echelon of the game. DiMaggio earned three MVP awards and led the Yankees to a staggering nine World Series titles. Ted Williams, Hall of Fame legend for the Boston Red Sox, said, "Joe DiMaggio was the greatest all-around player I ever saw. His career cannot be summed up in numbers and awards. It might sound corny, but he had a profound and lasting impact on the country."

The number of World Series at bats (6) for Chad Curtis. They all came against the Braves in 1999, and he made the most of them. Atlanta led by four runs in game three when Curtis hit a homerun off Tom Glavine to cut into the deficit. New York rallied to tie the score in the eighth, and the stage was set for Curtis to be a hero in the tenth. He hit a walk-off shot to win the game, and the Yankees swept the series the next day. The bat used by Curtis to win game three is on display at the Hall of Fame.

The jersey number (7) for Mickey Mantle retired in 1969. He is the greatest switch-hitter in the history of baseball. Mantle won three MVP awards and led the club to seven World Series titles. Billy Martin, the legendary manager of the Yankees, once said, "No man in the history of baseball had as much power as Mickey Mantle. No man. You're not talking about ordinary power. Dave Kingman has power. Willie Mays had power. Then when you're talking about Mickey Mantle, it's an altogether different level—it separates the men from the boys."

The jersey number (8) for Bill Dickey and Yogi Berra retired in 1972. Dickey was the Yankees catcher from 1929-46, and he won seven World Series titles. Berra took over behind the plate from 1947-61, and he won ten World Series titles. Both players are in the Hall of Fame, and they are the only players in franchise history to have a shared number retired in their honor.

The jersey number (9) for Roger Maris retired in 1984. He earned back-to-back MVP awards in 1960 and 1961. Maris also won back-to-back World Series titles in 1961 and 1962, but he is best known for his assault on the record book when he broke Babe Ruth's homerun record in 1961. In light of recent steroid scandals, many baseball purists still consider Maris to be the rightful owner of the season homerun record.

The jersey number (10) for Phil Rizzuto retired in 1985. He batted .324 and earned MVP honors in 1950. Rizzuto earned another MVP award in 1951, this time in the World Series. He played 13 seasons for the Yankees, won nine pennants, and seven World Series titles. Rizzuto, a slick-fielding shortstop affectionately known by the Yankee faithful as "Scooter," was just as successful in his second career as a broadcaster for the club. He also took special care to mentor a young Derek Jeter back when Jeter was a rookie, and upon Rizzuto's passing on August 14, 2007, Jeter said, "He played with a lot of heart, he exemplified what it means to be a Yankee and I always will remember the relationship we had."

The number of sacrifice flies (11) for Lou Piniella in 1974. He hit only 61 during 18 seasons, but his 11 in 1974 are tied for the fifth highest season total in franchise history. Roy White set the team record with 11 in 1969. Graig Nettles did it in 1975, but by then it was only the third highest total. Paul O'Neill did it in 1995, but by then it was the fifth highest total in club history. O'Neill also hit 11 sacrifice flies in 1998, and again in 2000.

The record number of homerun titles (12) for Babe Ruth. He hit only 11 homeruns for the Red Sox when he won his first title in 1918, and he won his second title when he hit 29 the next season. His numbers surged when he joined the Yankees. Ruth hit 54 for the club in 1920, and then he hit 59 in 1921 for his fourth consecutive title. He led the league an unprecedented six consecutive seasons from 1926-31, and was among the top three league leaders every season from 1918-33.

The number of triples (13) for Earle Combs in 1925. He batted .342 and led the club in triples. He also picked up 203 base hits, scored 117 runs, and reached base at a .411 clip. His numbers are more impressive when you consider he was a rookie, he led the club in each of those categories, and his teammates included guys like Ruth and Gehrig.

The number of triples (14) for Tony Lazzeri in 1926. He batted .275 and was fifth among league leaders in triples. Lazzeri was also second in the league with 114 RBI and he placed among the top ten in MVP balloting, all during his rookie season. Only three years earlier Lazzeri quit baseball—for a total of ten days—after becoming frustrated with the Salt Lake City minor league club he was playing for. Then in 1925 he hit 60 homeruns and drove home a staggering 222 runs during a minor league season—and he was immediately purchased by the Yankees for $75,000 in preparation for the 1926 season.

The jersey number (15) for Thurman Munson retired in 1979. Munson was a first-round draft pick out of Kent State University in 1968, and only two years later was named ROY for the big club. He batted .300 with 100 or more RBI three consecutive seasons from 1975-77, a feat no Yankees catcher had done since Bill Dickey in the 1930s. Munson died in a plane crash in 1979, prompting owner George Steinbrenner to immediately retire his jersey number.

The jersey number (16) for Whitey Ford retired in 1974. He was the staff ace from 1953-65, and he won six World Series titles before he retired in 1967. Ford is the franchise leader in wins, innings, strikeouts, starts, and shutouts, and the ten games he won during World Series play are the most in baseball history.

The number of sacrifice flies (17) for Roy White in 1971. He only had 69 sacrifice flies during 15 seasons with the club, but he led the league in 1969 and again in 1971, when he also set the franchise record.

The number of times (18) Bert Daniels was hit by a pitch in 1911. He set a team record at the time, and then matched it when he was hit 18 times in 1912, and again in 1913. Daniels played only 455 games for the Yankees, but was hit by a pitch 70 times, the fourth highest total in club history.

The number of triples (19) for Wally Pipp in 1924. His triples total is the tenth highest in franchise history, but he hit only three more for the Yankees after 1924. On June 2, 1925, Pipp took the day off because of a headache, and a young Lou Gehrig got the start at first base, beginning his streak of 2,130 consecutive games (and the Yankees sold Pipp to the Cincinnati Reds prior to the 1926 season).

The number of strikeouts (20) for Yogi Berra in both 1951 and 1955. Yogi had more homeruns than strikeouts both seasons. He hit 27 homeruns in 547 at bats in 1951, and he hit 27 homeruns in 541 at bats in 1955. Both times he won the MVP.

The number of times (21) Babe Ruth was caught stealing in 1923. He also stole 17 bases to tie his career high, but he was caught the second highest number of times in the league. It was probably a better idea for Ruth to swing for the fence than to try and manufacture a run. He was caught stealing 117 times for the Yankees, the highest total in team history and one of the top 60 totals all-time. Ruth was also caught stealing for the final out of a 3-2 loss in game seven of the 1926 World Series.

The number of triples (22) for Birdie Cree in 1911. He set a franchise record that stood until HOF outfielder Earle Combs hit 23 triples in 1927. Combs posted season totals of 23, 21, 15, and 22 from 1927-30, giving him the record and a share of the second and third highest totals in franchise history.

The jersey number (23) for Don Mattingly retired in 1997. Mattingly became just the tenth captain in team history because of his relentless pursuit of perfection and the respect he earned from his teammates. He earned MVP honors in 1985 and was a six-time All-Star, but he had the misfortune of playing during the Yankees longest post-season drought since the club's first pennant in 1921. Mattingly got one shot at a title in 1995. He batted .417 and hit a homerun against the Mariners in the division series, but the Yankees lost in five games, and then he retired.

The number of times (24) Don Baylor was hit by a pitch in 1985. His total set a franchise record, and it was the second of four consecutive seasons from 1984-87 that he led the league. Baylor was hit by a pitch 267 times in his career, the fourth highest total all-time.

The number of games (25) Whitey Ford won in 1961. It is the fourth highest total in franchise history, and he shares it with Ron Guidry, who won 25 games in 1978. Ford led the league in wins in 1961, and he won both CYA and 1961 World Series MVP honors. Guidry led the league in wins in 1978, and he also won CYA and Major League Player of the Year honors.

The number of World Series titles (26) for the Yankees from 1923-2000. The Yankees beat the New York Giants to claim the first title in 1923. Babe Ruth hit three homeruns in that series, and it was the first of three titles for manager Miller Huggins. Joe McCarthy managed the Yankees to six titles from 1932-43, but Casey Stengel managed the most championship teams, earning seven titles from 1949-58. Joe Torre won the last four from 1996-2000. The Yankees have the most championship titles of any franchise in any major professional sport.

The number of games (27) Al Orth won in 1906. It is the second highest total in franchise history, and he shares it with Carl Mays, who won 27 games in 1921. Orth led the league in wins for the Highlanders in 1906, and Mays also led the league in wins for the Yankees in 1921. Jack Chesbro owns the franchise record with 41 wins in 1904.

The number of shutouts (28) for Lefty Gomez. He tossed six shutouts in a season twice. Gomez did it the first time in 1934, when he posted a 26-5 record. He did it the second time in 1937, when he posted a 21-11 record. Gomez led the league in shutouts three times, and his career total is the fourth highest in franchise history.

The number of times (29) Cardinals batters struck out during the 1928 World Series. It took only three arms for the Yankees to sweep St. Louis. Waite Hoyt went the distance in games one and four, and struck out 14 batters; George Pipgras struck out eight batters and completed the second game of the series; and Tom Zachary struck out seven batters as he completed game three of the series. Cardinals pitchers struck out only 13 Yankees in the series, but gave up 37 hits and 27 runs. Yankees pitchers struck out 29 batters, but gave up only 27 hits and ten runs.

The number of times (30) Dave Winfield grounded into a double-play in 1983. He set a franchise record in a dubious category, eclipsing the previous record of 27 set by Billy Johnson in 1943. Hideki Matsui, Paul O'Neill, and Jorge Posada have all come close with totals of 25, 25 and 24 respectively. Since someone has to own the record, it may as well be a HOF player of Winfield's caliber. Winfield also led the club with 32 homeruns and 116 RBI in 1983.

The number of saves (31) for Dave Righetti in 1987. He tossed 95 innings out of the bullpen and posted an 8-6 record. Righetti was second in the league in saves, but earned his second consecutive Rolaids Relief Award.

The jersey number (32) for Elston Howard retired in 1984. Howard began his playing career as a teammate of Ernie Banks for the Kansas City Monarchs in the Negro Leagues. His coach was the legendary Buck O'Neil. In 1955, Howard became the first African American to make the big club for the New York Yankees. He got a hit in his first major league at bat. Howard won four World Series titles with the Yankees, and in 1963 he became the first African American to win MVP honors in the American League.

The number of complete games (33) for Jack Chesbro in 1903. Chesbro made 36 starts for the Highlanders and posted a 21-5 record. He pitched 324 innings, and his complete games total is the fifth highest in franchise history.

The number of Hall of Fame players (34) who wore a Yankees uniform. Babe Ruth became the first in 1936, and Wade Boggs became the most recent in 2005. The Yankees are the only franchise with at least one player from every position in the Hall of Fame.

35 The number of homeruns (35) for Don Mattingly in 1985. He dominated opposing pitchers to the tune of a .324 average and a .567 slugging percentage. Mattingly led the league with 370 total bases and 145 RBI, and earned MVP honors.

36 The age in years (36) for Lou Gehrig upon his induction into the Hall of Fame. He was only 35 years old when doctors diagnosed him with ALS. On July 4, 1939, New York honored Gehrig with a ceremony at Yankee Stadium and celebrated not only his career, but the strength of his character. Gehrig was elected to the HOF later that year, and a ticket stub from Lou Gehrig Day at Yankee Stadium is among the memorabilia on display at the Hall of Fame.

37 The jersey number (37) for Casey Stengel retired in 1970. Stengel played all or parts of 14 seasons in the majors, but it was as manager of the Yankees that he left his mark on the game. He won 1,149 games, and owns one of the most impressive feats in managerial history—he led the Yankees to ten pennants and seven World Series titles from 1949-60. Stengel, when asked about his success, once quipped that, "Managing is getting paid for homeruns someone else hits."

38 The number of complete games (38) for Jack Powell in 1904. His total is the third highest in franchise history, but it was only the second highest on the club that season. Powell completed 38 of 41 starts, but his teammate Jack Chesbro completed a franchise record 48 of 51 starts.

39 The number of pennants (39) for the Yankees from 1921-2003. No team in history has won more pennants than New York. The Yankees have also repeated as pennant winners more than any other team, and have won at least three consecutive pennants nine times.

40 The number of saves (40) for Mariano Rivera in 2003. He converted 40 of 46 chances and posted a 5-2 record. Rivera gave up only 13 earned runs in 70 innings for a salty 1.66 ERA, but he did not receive any votes in the CYA balloting. Sportswriters may not have cast their ballots for Rivera, but they paid him high accolades in print. Buster Olney, a columnist for *New York Magazine*, wrote, "A summer afternoon of baseball ought to be nothing if not relaxing, and no other player can instill calm in his team's fans as reliably as Mariano Rivera, the game's dominant closer and arguably the best relief pitcher of all time."

The number of homeruns (41) for Babe Ruth in 1923. His three-run homerun against the Boston Red Sox on opening day was the first in Yankee Stadium history. Ruth batted .393 on the season and earned MVP honors. He also hit three homeruns against the New York Giants in the World Series, and he led the Yankees to the first World Series titles in franchise history.

The jersey number (42) for Jackie Robinson retired in 1997. He did not play for the Yankees, but he did play in New York. The Brooklyn Dodgers star became the first African American to break baseball's color barrier in 1947. Robinson also became the first African American inducted into the Hall of Fame in 1962. On the 50th anniversary of his major league debut, every major league franchise retired his jersey number to honor his legacy.

The number of stolen bases (43) for Mickey Rivers in 1976. Rivers led the league with 70 steals for the Angels in 1975, but was traded to the Yankees for Bobby Bonds in the off-season. His 43 steals for the Yankees was only the seventh highest total in the league, but the tenth highest total in franchise history. Steve Sax also stole 43 bases in 1989, and again in 1990. Alfonso Soriano stole 43 bases in 2001, and shares the tenth position in the franchise record book with both Sax and Rivers.

The jersey number (44) for Reggie Jackson retired in 1993. He is one of the top 15 homerun hitters in baseball history, but his prodigious blasts mean much more than that to true Yankees fans. Mr. October blasted three homeruns in game six of the 1977 World Series as he powered the Yankees to victory over the Los Angeles Dodgers. Jackson is fifth all-time with ten World Series homeruns, and he won two of his four rings wearing pinstripes.

The number of doubles (45) for Babe Ruth in 1923, Bob Meusel in 1928, and Hideki Matsui in 2005. Ruth led the club but only placed third among league leaders in 1923. Bob Meusel, who also placed third among league leaders, was only second on the team behind the 47 doubles hit by Lou Gehrig in 1928. Matsui at least led the Yankees in 2005, but he was second in the league behind the 50 doubles hit by shortstop Miguel Tejada of the Baltimore Orioles.

The number of doubles (46) for Red Rolfe in 1939. His total set a career high, led the league, and is the eighth highest in franchise history. Rolfe did quite a few things well that season, as he also led the league with 213 hits, 139 runs, and 295 times on base—not to mention, he won his fourth career World Series title. He got one more of those with the club in 1941.

The number of doubles (47) for Lou Gehrig in 1926, Bob Meusel in 1927, and Lou Gehrig again in 1928. Gehrig only placed fifth among league leaders in 1926, and Meusel also placed fifth among league leaders in 1927. Gehrig did manage to lead the league in 1928, and both players share the fifth highest total in franchise history.

The number of doubles (48) for Don Mattingly in 1985. He led the league in doubles, total bases, and RBI. His doubles total is also the fourth highest in franchise history, and to be honest, the man could just flat out hit. In the clubhouse at Yankee Stadium, Mattingly once requested his locker be moved to a new location, because as he said, "I like being closer to the bats."

The jersey number (49) for Ron Guidry retired in 2003. He won the 1978 CYA after posting a 25-3 record and leading the Yankees to one of the greatest comebacks in the history of division play. New York trailed Boston by 14 games on July 19, but Guidry pitched a four-hit shutout on July 20 to improve his own record to 14-1, and the Yankees began to make a move. On July 28, the lead was down to only eight games. When Guidry pitched a two-hit shutout against the Red Sox on September 9, the lead was only one. They ended the season tied, and Guidry got the call for a one game playoff at Fenway Park. He picked up win number 25, and the Yankees went on to defeat the Dodgers in the 1978 World Series.

The number of saves (50) for Mariano Rivera in 2001. He set a franchise record when he converted 50 of 57 save opportunities. Rivera broke his own record in 2004, when he converted 53 of 57 save opportunities.

The number of doubles (51) for Alfonso Soriano in 2002. His total is the third highest in franchise history, but he trailed the 56 doubles hit by league leaders Garrett Anderson of the Anaheim Angels and Nomar Garciaparra of the Boston Red Sox.

The number of doubles (52) for Lou Gehrig in 1927. His total is the second highest in franchise history, and it was the first of back-to-back seasons he led the league.

The number of doubles (53) for Don Mattingly in 1986. It was the third consecutive season Mattingly led the league in doubles, and he not only set a career high, but he also set the franchise record for most doubles in a season.

The number of homeruns (54) for Mickey Mantle in 1961. He set the major league record for most homeruns in a season by a switch-hitter, and he tied Babe Ruth (who hit 54 in 1920, and again in 1928) for the fourth highest total in franchise history.

The number of stolen bases (55) for Snuffy Stirnweiss in 1944. He set a career high and led the league in steals during his sophomore season, and his total is the sixth highest in franchise history. Stirnweiss also led the league with 33 steals in 1945. The infielder stole 99 bases his first three seasons, but stole only 134 total during nine full seasons.

The number of consecutive games hitting streak (56) for Joe DiMaggio in 1941. He batted 91 for 223 in the streak for a .408 average. DiMaggio's hitting streak is not only a major league record, but it is also one of the greatest feats in the history of sports.

The number of intentional walks (57) for Jorge Posada from 1997-2006. He was walked intentionally ten times in 2000, and again in 2001, coinciding with Posada earning consecutive Silver Slugger awards. His total is among the top ten in the franchise record book, but it is the highest among all active Yankees players in 2007.

The number of sacrifice flies (58) for Thurman Munson from 1969-79. He hit a career high ten sacrifice flies three times from 1975-78, and his career total is among the top ten in franchise history.

The number of homeruns (59) for Babe Ruth in 1921. Harry Stovey hit 14 homeruns for the Philadelphia Athletics in 1883 to set the professional record. His team hit only 20 homeruns on the season, and his record lasted only one year as Ned Williamson hit 27 homeruns for the Chicago White Stockings in 1884. Williamson hit only 64 homeruns in his career, and never hit more than nine in any other season, but his record stood until Babe Ruth hit 29 for the Boston Red Sox in 1919. Ruth shattered his own record with 54 homeruns for the Yankees in 1920, and his 59 homeruns in 1921 set yet another record. It is the only time in history the homerun record was broken in three consecutive seasons, and Ruth did it each time.

The number of homeruns (60) for Babe Ruth in 1927. He broke his own record of 59 homeruns set in 1921, and the bats used by Ruth when he connected for homeruns 58, 59, and 60 can be seen on display at the Hall of Fame.

The number of homeruns (61) for Roger Maris in 1961. He set the homerun record, earned MVP honors for the second time, and won his first World Series title. Maris said during the season, "I don't want to be Babe Ruth. He was a great ballplayer, but I'm not trying to replace him. The record is there and I want to break it—but that isn't replacing Babe Ruth."

The number of sacrifice flies (62) for Graig Nettles from 1973-83. He hit a career high 11 in 1975, and his career total is the fifth highest in franchise history.

63 The number of games (63) the Yankees lost in 1978. Billy Martin lost 42 games as manager before owner George Steinbrenner replaced him. Dick Howser was interim manager for one game, and lost. Bob Lemon came on board and guided the club to a 48-20 record the rest of the way, and the Yankees beat Boston in a one game playoff to win the division and close out the season 100-63.

64 The number of sacrifice flies (64) for Bernie Williams. He hit a career high nine sacrifice flies in 2001, but produced only 94 RBI for his lowest output from 1996-2002. His nine sacrifice flies also placed him among the top ten league leaders for the only time in his career, but his career total ranks him fourth all-time in franchise history.

65 The number of games (65) the Yankees won at home in 1961. The Tigers led the Yankees by six games on May 24, but New York began September with a season long 13 game winning streak, and by the end of the month it was the Yankees that carried an eight game lead. The key for New York was playing in the Bronx. On the road, the club posted a modest 44-37 record, but at home the record soared to 65-16 for an incredible .802 winning percentage. The Yankees closed out the season at 109-53, and set a franchise record for most wins at home.

66 The number of intentional walks (66) for Roy White. He drew a career high 11 intentional walks in 1970, the same season he set career highs with 22 homeruns and 94 RBI. White was among the top ten league leaders for intentional walks three times, and his career total is the fifth highest in franchise history.

67 The number of games (67) finished for Mariano Rivera in 2005. He led the league with the third highest total in franchise history, only two short of his team record 69 games finished in 2004. Rivera also saved 43 games, giving him 40 or more for the sixth time in nine seasons.

68 The number of games (68) finished for Dave Righetti in 1986. His total is the second highest in franchise history. Righetti came out of the bullpen 74 times, and led the league with a career high 46 saves.

The number of sacrifice flies (69) for Roy White. He led the league in sacrifice flies twice, and set a franchise record with 17 sacrifice flies in 1971. White is tied with Paul O'Neill for the second highest career total in franchise history. O'Neill never led the league, but he did post four of the top 11 seasons on record for the team. Don Mattingly is the franchise leader with 96 sacrifice flies.

The number of extra-base hits (70) for Derek Jeter in 1999. He was second in the league with a .349 batting average. Jeter was also second with 134 runs, nine triples, and 149 singles, and his 346 total bases were only fourth in the league. Jeter did lead the league by reaching base 322 times, and his extra-base hits, average, runs, triples, singles, and total bases all led the Yankees. He also won his third World Series title.

The number of games (71) for closer Mariano Rivera in 2005. He was 7-4 and converted 43 saves. Rivera recorded 80 strikeouts in 78 innings, but gave up just 50 hits. He placed second in CYA balloting, but earned his fourth Rolaids Relief Award.

The number of triples (72) for Bill Dickey and Mickey Mantle. Dickey hit a career high ten triples in 1931, and had at least one triple in 16 consecutive seasons. Not bad at all, considering the strain on his body from catching 120 games a year. Mantle hit a career high 12 triples in 1954, and then led the league with 11 triples in 1955. Both players share the tenth highest career total in franchise history.

The number of triples (73) for Tommy Henrich. He led the league with 13 triples in 1947. Henrich also led the league with a career high 14 triples in 1948, and his career total is the ninth highest in franchise history.

The number of stolen bases (74) for Fritz Maisel in 1914. He was a light-hitting infielder who played only six seasons in the majors. Maisel batted only .239 with two homeruns in 1914, but he also led the league in steals and set a franchise record that stood until 1985. His 74 steals in 1914 are the fourth highest total in franchise history, and the highest total by any player other than Rickey Henderson.

The number of wild pitches (75) for Whitey Ford. He never threw more than nine in any one season, well short of the team record 23 wild pitches thrown by Tim Leary in 1990. Ford did throw the most career wild pitches in franchise history though, but he is also the franchise leader for innings pitched.

The number of hits (76) for Bernie Williams in 1991. He batted just .238 as a rookie during 320 at bats. Of course, after 16 seasons he closed out his career fourth in franchise history with 2,336 base hits.

The number of games (77) for pitcher Jeff Nelson in 1997. He faced 327 batters in late relief, but gave up only 53 hits in 78 innings. Nelson was used by manager Joe Torre to set up closer Mariano Rivera, and his games total is the seventh highest in franchise history.

The number of games (78) for pitcher Steve Karsay in 2002. He was 6-4 out of the bullpen during his first season in the Bronx. Karsay also saved 12 games as closer Mariano Rivera spent substantial time on the disabled list, and his games total is the sixth highest in franchise history.

The number of hits (79) for Don Mattingly in 1983. He batted .283 during 91 games his rookie season. Mattingly batted .307 for his career and his 2,153 hits are the sixth highest total in franchise history.

The number of stolen bases (80) for Rickey Henderson in 1985. He led the league in steals and scored a career high 146 runs during his first season in the Bronx. Henderson's 80 steals are the third highest total in franchise history, but he also holds the top two spots. Bill James, who is widely known for his *Bill James' Baseball Abstract* that revolutionized statistics in baseball, wrote recently, "Some people have asked me whether or not Rickey Henderson belongs in the Hall of Fame. I've replied that if you could somehow split him in two, you'd have two Hall of Famers."

The number of games (81) Jack Chesbro won from 1903-05. The HOF legend set a modern era record when he won 41 games in 1904. Chesbro made 51 starts and pitched a staggering 454 innings that season.

He won 21, 41, and 19 games respectively from 1903-05, and was on the mound for 1,082 innings.

82 The number of times (82) Yankees base runners were caught stealing in 1920. Babe Ruth and Ping Bodie led the club, both getting caught 14 times. Ruth also led the team with 14 steals, but the club was successful only 64 times and set a franchise record for most times getting caught.

83 The number of games (83) for pitcher Scott Proctor in 2006. He was 6-4 and pitched 102 innings in relief during his third season in the Bronx. Proctor's game total is the second highest in franchise history.

84 The number of walks (84) allowed by Roger Clemens in 2000. His total may have been the highest on the team, but it was not a problem. Clemens allowed two walks against the Mariners during game four of the league championship series. Of course, he only gave up one hit and he struck out 15 batters en route to a complete game shutout. Clemens also got the call for game two of the World Series. He only pitched eight innings against the Mets, but gave up just two hits, no walks, and he struck out nine batters.

85 The number of games (85) for Bernie Williams in 1991. He was a rookie, and he hit only three homeruns in 320 at bats. He played only 62 games in 1992, but his numbers steadily began to improve until he became one of the most popular players in franchise history. Williams played 2,076 games for the Yankees in 16 seasons. Only four players took the field in pinstripes more often: Mickey Mantle, Lou Gehrig, Yogi Berra, and Babe Ruth.

86 The number of games (86) for pitcher Paul Quantrill in 2004. He was 7-3, and he faced 424 batters out of the bullpen. Quantrill pitched 95 innings, and set a franchise record for games. He made his big league debut with Boston in 1992, but he was a 35-year-old journeyman playing for his fifth team—none of which had ever made the post-season—when he put on pinstripes for the first time in 2004, and he finally got a ticket to play in October. He earned a win in the division series, but unfortunately, he will forever be known as the guy who gave up the game-winning homerun to David Ortiz during game four of the league championship series. His former club went on to win the World Series for the first time in (86) years—and Quantrill never got a ring.

The number of triples (87) for Bob Meusel during ten seasons in the Bronx. Meusel began a streak of five consecutive seasons with ten or more triples when he hit a career high 16 in 1921. His career total is tied with Jimmy Williams for the seventh highest in franchise history.

The number of RBI (88) for Yogi Berra in 1951. He batted .294 and won his first career MVP. In 1950, Berra batted .322 with 124 RBI, but only placed third in MVP balloting. Berra, who is famous for his off-beat sayings, once commented on his ability to hit by saying, "I never blame myself when I'm not hitting. I just blame the bat, and if it keeps up I change bats. After all, if I know it isn't my fault that I'm not hitting, how can I get mad at myself?" Luckily for Yankee fans, Berra was hitting just fine most all of the time.

The number of strikeouts (89) for pitcher Dave Righetti in 1981. He was a rookie, and he gave up only 75 hits in 105 innings. Righetti was 8-4 with a 2.05 ERA, and he earned ROY honors.

The ratio (9.0) of at bats per homerun for Babe Ruth in 1927. He hit a record 60 homeruns and his ratio was the best in the league, a feat he accomplished 13 times in his career. Ruth also posted an 8.5 ratio in 1920, a record that stood for 76 years until Mark McGwire surpassed it in 1996. Barry Bonds set the current record with a homerun every 6.52 at bats in 2001, but Ruth still holds the top three homerun ratios in franchise history.

The number of times (91) the Yankees offense grounded into a double-play in 1963. Catcher Elston Howard led the team with 17, but Hector Lopez and Joe Pepitone were the only other players on the team to reach double-digits. It was the lowest team total in franchise history.

The number of extra-base hits (92) for Alfonso Soriano in 2002. Soriano hit 51 doubles and 39 homeruns, and he led the league in extra-base hits. He also joined some pretty elite company, as he tied Babe

Ruth and Lou Gehrig for the tenth highest extra-base hits total in franchise history. Only four names are in the top ten on that list: Ruth, Gehrig, Joe DiMaggio, and Soriano.

The number of stolen bases (93) for Rickey Henderson in 1988. It was the eighth time he led the league in steals, a feat he accomplished a record 12 times before he hung up his spikes for good. It was also the third time he led the league as a member of the Yankees, and his 93 steals are the second highest total in franchise history.

The number of earned runs (94) allowed by Catfish Hunter in 1975. He led the league with 328 innings pitched during his first season in the Bronx. Hunter also faced a league high 1,294 batters, but gave up only 248 hits. It was the fifth consecutive season he won 20 or more games, but Hunter came in second in CYA balloting.

The number of extra-base hits (95) for Lou Gehrig in 1934. His total is the eighth highest in franchise history. Gehrig won the Triple Crown in 1934, but he only placed fifth in league MVP balloting. Mickey Cochrane won his second career MVP as his Tigers won the pennant, but Cochrane only had 35 extra-base hits on the season—and only two of those were homeruns. The top six in MVP balloting were: Cochrane, Charlie Gehringer, Lefty Gomez, Schoolboy Rowe, Lou Gehrig, and Hank Greenberg—all six players were a Tiger or a Yankee that season, and only Rowe is not a member of the Hall of Fame.

The number of games (96) for Mickey Mantle in 1951. He was a rookie, and he came to bat only 341 times. Of course, Mantle went on to play 2,401 games for the Yankees, and he batted 8,102 times. Both totals are franchise records.

The number of extra-base hits (97) for Babe Ruth in 1927. His total is the sixth highest in franchise history, but was only the second best on the team that season. Lou Gehrig led the majors with 117 extra-base hits, though Ruth did hit a record 60 homeruns.

The number of RBI (98) per 162 games for Bernie Williams. His career high 121 RBI came in 2000, and five times he drove in 100 or more runs. Bernie's 1,257 RBI are the sixth highest total in franchise history.

99 The number of extra-base hits (99) for Babe Ruth in 1920 and 1923. Both times he led the league, a feat he accomplished seven times in his career. Six of his league leading totals came from 1918-24, and Ruth is fourth in baseball history with 1,356 extra-base hits.

100 The number of walks (100) for Bernie Williams in 1999. His total set a career high and led the club that season. Bernie ranks among the top 80 in baseball history with 1,069 walks, but his total trails only Babe Ruth, Mickey Mantle, and Lou Gehrig in franchise history.

Derek Jeter

"I have the greatest job in the world. Only one person can have it. You have shortstops on other teams—I'm not knocking other teams—but there is only one shortstop on the Yankees."

— Derek Jeter

Chapter Two

Jeter

Phil Nevin, Paul Shuey, B.J. Wallace, Jeffrey Hammonds, and Chad Mottola are the only members of a very select group of ball players. They share something in common with each other so prestigious that no other player in the game today can boast they too belong. On June 1, 1992, Nevin, Shuey, Wallace, Hammonds, and Mottola were chosen as the top five picks in the annual amateur draft—and all were chosen ahead of the Yankees first-round selection and the overall number six pick, Derek Jeter.

Nevin was taken by the Astros after a solid career at Cal State Fullerton, and though he was often injured and well-traveled (he played for seven different teams), he did hit 208 homeruns and played 12 years in the majors. He only played in one post-season game though, and did not get a hit, or a ring.

Shuey was taken by the Indians as the second overall pick and the first pitcher in the draft after closing out games for the University of North Carolina during a stellar collegiate career. He put together a nice professional career for the Indians as well. He spent nine seasons pitching out of the bullpen and earned 45 career victories. Shuey also pitched in 16 post-season games, but never made it to the World Series (the Indians made it in 1997, but left him off the active roster). Injuries shut him down in 2004, and he did not make another big league appearance until landing with the Orioles in June of 2007.

B.J. Wallace was also a pitcher, drafted third overall by the Montreal Expos out of Mississippi State University. He never pitched in the majors.

Jeffrey Hammonds was the first outfielder taken, drafted fourth overall by the Orioles out of Stanford University. He also put together a nice career. He made the All-Star team for the Colorado Rockies in 2000, but spent all or parts of his 13 seasons playing for six different ball clubs. Hammonds hit 110 career homeruns and made two trips to the post-season. He batted only 3 for 16 with no homeruns in October though, and he never made it to the World Series.

Chad Mottola was drafted fifth overall out of the University of Central Florida by the Cincinnati Reds. He made his big league debut on April 22, 1996. He last appeared in the majors in 2006, but his career totals consist of only 125 at bats and four big league homeruns. He got a cup of coffee five times in a decade, with four different clubs.

And then the Yankees selected Derek Jeter.

The sixth man and first high school player taken in 1992, he's going to the Hall of Fame.

Andy Stankiewicz started at shortstop and batted leadoff for the Yankees on the day Jeter was drafted. Stankiewicz batted 1 for 4 and scored a run in a 7-1 victory over the Texas Rangers, but he knew his days in New York were numbered. The club used four players at shortstop in 1992, with Stankiewicz getting the most playing time at 81 games. Randy Velarde, Mike Gallego, and Dave Silvestri also saw limited action. Jeter, who was only the third shortstop in franchise history to be drafted in the first-round, was clearly the shortstop of the future for New York.

Jeter batted .557 and hit seven homeruns as a high school junior in 1991. In his senior year he batted .508 and hit four homeruns, but struck out only once in 23 games. Jeter was named the 1992 High School Player of the Year by the American Baseball Coaches Association, but he spent little time relishing his accomplishments. Instead he set out immediately to create new ones. He began his professional career playing Class-A ball in both Tampa and Greensboro. In 58 games his first season, Jeter batted .210 and hit four homeruns.

Spike Owen, a veteran shortstop who spent more than a decade playing for the Mariners, Red Sox, and Expos, became the primary caretaker for the Yankees at the shortstop position in 1993. Gallego, Velarde, Silvestri, and Stankiewicz were all on the roster, but the franchise was focused clearly on the man tearing up the South Atlantic League in his second professional season. Jeter was voted the Most Outstanding Major League Prospect by the managers of the South Atlantic League after batting .295 with five homeruns, 71 RBI, and 18 stolen bases. He also made the All-Star team and was named the Most Exciting Player and Best Defensive Shortstop in the South Atlantic League by *Baseball America.*

In 1994, Gallego, Velarde, Silvestri, Kevin Elster, and Robert Eenhoorn all fielded balls at short for the Yankees. Also in 1994, Jeter went from Class-A Tampa to Double-A Albany, all the way to Triple-A Columbus, and combined for a .344 average, five homeruns, 68 RBI, and 50 stolen bases. He was named the Minor League Player of the Year by *Baseball America*, *The Sporting News*, *USA Today*, and *Baseball Weekly*.

The Yankees signed veteran All-Star Tony Fernandez to anchor the middle of the infield in 1995 so Jeter could have one more season to get ready—but Fernandez was placed on the disabled list with a strained muscle in his rib cage on May 29, and Jeter became a major league player for the first time.

Jeter made 13 starts in his mid-season call-up in 1995. He batted only .234 with no homeruns, but he drove in six runs before going back to Triple-A Columbus. He got the call again in September, and raised his average to .250 for the season, batting 12 for 48 overall in 15 games.

In 1992, Stankiewicz led the club with 81 games at shortstop. Owen led the club with 96 games at short in 1993. Gallego played only 72 games at short in 1994, but led the team. Fernandez played 103 games for the Yankees at shortstop in 1995, but was one of six players to see innings at the position. The Yankees parted with Fernandez, Velarde, Elster, and Silvestri during the course of 1995 or shortly after the season ended.

Stankiewicz, Owen, Gallego, and Eenhoorn had already left—and for the Yankees, Jeter was going to be the shortstop from then on.

In 1996, Jeter played 157 games at shortstop for the Yankees.

Of course, the media, pundits, and even some fans complained during spring training in 1996 about the chances being non-existent for winning a championship with a rookie at shortstop. Joe Torre, in his first year as skipper, patiently suggested a wait-and-see approach. On opening day, Jeter became the first rookie shortstop to get the start for the Yankees since 1962 Rookie of the Year recipient Tom Tresh. Jeter batted ninth in the line-up on the road against the Cleveland Indians. In the top of the fifth inning, Jeter hit a solo shot to left against pitcher Dennis Martinez for his first career homerun.

And yet, many in the media remained skeptical Jeter could be an impact player over the course of a full major league season, much less into the post-season.

Jeter responded by hitting .314 with ten homeruns and earned Rookie of the Year honors. He led the club with 183 hits and 156 games started. He tied for the club lead with 49 multi-hit games—and during the post-season push in September when the club saw their one-time double-digit lead in the standings shrink to only 2.5 games over the Baltimore Orioles, Jeter hit in a season high 17 consecutive games. The last rookie to hit in so many consecutive games for the Yankees was a guy named Joe DiMaggio back in 1936.

In the post-season, and with no World Series titles for the club since 1978, the media continued to assert no major league team could win a World Series with a rookie for a shortstop.

Joe Torre again suggested patience.

In the division round of the playoffs, the Yankees lost game one of the series to the Texas Rangers. Facing a two game deficit at home, Jeter scored the winning run in the twelfth inning of game two to even the series. The club went on to win the series in four games.

In game one of the league championship series against the Wild Card Orioles, and trailing in the bottom of the eighth, Jeter hit a game-tying homerun. So maybe he did get some help from a 12-year-old Richie Garcia, who leaned over the fence to catch the ball, but so what—good for Garcia. Good for the Yankees too, because Bernie Williams hit a walk-off shot in the eleventh, and the Yankees went on to take the series in five games.

Jeter was chosen by the Yankees in the first-round of the 1992 draft because the scouts and front office personnel believed there was something special about him, and 1996 proved they were right.

In game six of the 1996 World Series against the defending world champion Atlanta Braves, Jeter singled home a run in the second inning to give the club a 2-0 lead against future Hall of Fame pitcher Greg Maddux. Jeter stole second, and scored the third and final run of the game for the Yankees when Williams singled to center. His run proved to be the game-winner, as the Yankees held on for a 3-2 victory to capture the 23rd World Series title in franchise history.

Jeter has since solidified his place in Yankees history.

He is a legend, but he is not done yet. In 2003, Jeter became the first team captain for the Yankees since Don Mattingly retired in 1995. Of course, by then Jeter already had won three more World Series titles—one more, and he will have one ring for each player taken before him in the 1992 draft.

101 The number of times (101) Lou Gehrig was caught stealing. His total is the fourth highest in franchise history. Gehrig only stole 102 bases, and he got caught 11 times or more in five seasons. Of course, his career is not defined by his success, or lack thereof, on the bases. Gehrig is a legend because he came to play every day, and he excelled at every other facet of the game.

102 The ratio (10.2) of at bats per homerun for Mickey Mantle in 1956. He led the league with 52 homeruns in only 533 at bats. His ratio is the seventh best in franchise history, and he also won the Triple Crown.

103 The number of games (103) the Highlanders lost in 1908. The team offense was last in the league, and so was the pitching staff, and it led to the most defeats in franchise history.

104 The number of saves (104) as a member of the Yankees for Johnny Murphy. His total is the fifth highest in franchise history. Murphy saved a career high 19 games in 1939, he led the league in saves four times, and he won six World Series titles.

105 The ratio (10.5) of at bats per homerun for Babe Ruth in 1926. He led the league with 47 homeruns in only 495 at bats, and his ratio is the eighth highest in franchise history. The attitude he brought with him to the ballpark helps explain why fans loved to see him play. "I swing big, with everything I've got," Ruth once said. "I hit big or I miss big—I like to live as big as I can."

106 The number of triples (106) as a member of the Yankees for Babe Ruth. It might be difficult to imagine Ruth dashing around the bases, legging out a three-bagger, but counting his time in Boston, Ruth is among the top 75 all-time for triples. Ruth hit 11 triples or more four times for New York, and his total with the club is the sixth highest in franchise history.

107 The number of pitches (107) thrown by Roger Clemens on September 19, 2001. Clemens beat the White Sox to improve his record to 20-1. It was only the second game for the Yankees since play resumed following the tragedy of 9/11. The Hall of Fame asked Clemens to sign a ball he used in that game. He signed his name under the words "God Bless the USA," and today the ball is on display in Cooperstown.

108 The ratio (10.8) of at bats per homerun for Babe Ruth in 1929. He led the league with 46 homeruns in only 499 at bats, and his ratio is the tenth highest in franchise history.

109 The ratio (10.9) of at bats per homerun as a member of the Yankees for Babe Ruth. His ratio is the best in franchise history. Ruth came to bat 7,217 times and hit 659 homeruns for New York. His career ratio of 11.8 is second only to Mark McGwire.

110 The number of walks (1.10) per nine innings for Tiny Bonham in 1945. He made 23 starts and posted an 8-11 record. Bonham only walked 22 batters in 180 innings though, giving him the best ratio in the league and the fourth best ratio in franchise history.

The number of earned runs (111) allowed by Andy Hawkins in 1989. His total was the highest on the team, but the reason he gave up so many runs is because he was good enough to stay on the mound and face more batters than any of his teammates. Hawkins also led the team in innings, wins, strikeouts, and complete games.

The ERA (1.12) for Mariano Rivera during the 2003 league championship series. He pitched in four games against Boston, and was on the mound for eight innings. Rivera gave up only five hits and one earned run, but struck out six batters. He got one win and two saves to lead the Yankees to the pennant, and Rivera earned series MVP honors.

The WHIP (1.13) for Lefty Gomez in 1934. WHIP is the ratio of walks plus hits per innings pitched. The lower the ratio, the better a pitcher is at not allowing base runners. Gomez led the league in WHIP in 1934, and he also led the league in wins, strikeouts, and ERA to win the pitching Triple Crown.

The number of earned runs (114) allowed by Randy Johnson in 2006. His total is tied for the tenth highest in franchise history. Johnson pitched 205 innings and struggled to a career worst 5.00 ERA, but he was still 17-11 on the season. Carl Mays and Vic Raschi also gave up 114 earned runs for the Yankees in 1921 and 1950 respectively. Mays tossed 336 innings though. He also won 27 games and posted a 3.05 ERA. Raschi pitched 258 innings, and he won 21 games with a 4.00 ERA.

The number of triples (115) for Tony Lazzeri. His total is the fifth highest in franchise history. Lazzeri hit a career high 16 triples in 1932, and six times he hit 11 or more in a season. The Hall of Fame legend is actually better known for some of his long ball exploits—and for good reason. On May 24, 1936, he became the first player to hit a pair of grand slams in the same game, and his 11 RBI in that game set a league record. Lazzeri also hit four homeruns in a game, five total homeruns during back-to-back games, a total of six homeruns during a three game stretch, and seven homeruns during a four game stretch.

116 The number of earned runs (116) allowed by Red Ruffing in 1931 and 1936. His total is the seventh highest in franchise history. Ruffing pitched 237 innings in 1931, and was 16-14 with a 4.41 ERA. He fared much better in 1936, when he pitched 271 innings and was 20-12 with a 3.85 ERA. In 1931, the Yankees came in second 13 games back of the Athletics. In 1936, the Yankees came in first 13 games ahead of the Tigers, and won the World Series.

117 The number of extra-base hits (117) for Lou Gehrig in 1927. His total led the league, and is the second highest in baseball history. Gehrig's total is not the franchise record though, because Babe Ruth set both the franchise and baseball record with 119 extra-base hits in 1921.

118 The WHIP (1.18) for Whitey Ford in 1961. Roger Maris and Mickey Mantle were not the only Yankees dominating the league in 1961. Ford made 39 starts and pitched 283 innings, but he gave up only 242 hits and 92 walks. His ratio was only the seventh best in the league, but his 25-4 record was the best, and he won the CYA.

119 The number of walks (119) for Willie Randolph in 1980. He led the league, but it was the only time he surpassed the century mark for a season. Randolph did work 1,243 walks in his career. His total is among the top 50 all-time, but he is among the top five in franchise history. Randolph was in dire need of the patience he once demonstrated at the plate for the Yankees during 2007, his third season as manager of the cross-town Mets. His club was on top of the N.L. East for 140 days and held a seven game lead as late as September 12—but they blew it. Randolph, after losing to the Marlins on the final day of the season to let the Phillies claim the division title, later said it was "probably the most pain I've felt since I've been in baseball."

120 The number of pitches (120) thrown by David Wells on May 17, 1998. Baseball tradition is that when a pitcher is flirting with a no-no the players in the dugout leave him alone—but Wells is not that kind of guy, so on that day in 1998, when he was perfect through seven against the Minnesota Twins, his teammate David Cone broke the tension by suggesting to Wells that he try breaking "out the knuckleball" in the eighth. Wells set the Twins down in order in the eighth, but upon returning to the dugout, Cone told him, "You showed me nothing out there, you wimp!" Inspired to keep going, Wells was perfect that day. He set down 27 batters in a row—11 on strikes, ten in the air, and six on the ground—he gave major league hitters 120 chances to get on base, but none could do it, and for that, the cap he wore during the game is on display at the Hall of Fame in Cooperstown.

121 The number of triples (121) as a member of the Yankees for Wally Pipp. He hit a career high and league leading 19 triples in 1924, and eight times he hit ten or more in a season. His career total of 148 is among the top 60 in baseball history, and his total for the Yankees is the fourth highest in franchise history. In yet another of the many ironies to be found in baseball, the man who hit more triples in pinstripes than any other player was Lou Gehrig—who hit a total of 163, all of which, except for one, came after Pipp's infamous headache that let Gehrig into the starting line-up. Pipp, who was sold to the Reds for $7,500 a few months later, famously said, "I took the two most expensive aspirins in history."

122 The number of walks (1.22) per nine innings for David Wells in 1998. He pitched 214 innings but gave up only 29 walks for the best ratio in the league, and the fifth best ratio in franchise history. Wells also struck out 163 batters, giving him a league leading 5.62 strikeouts to walk ratio.

123 The number of walks (1.23) per nine innings for Fritz Peterson in 1968. He gave up only 29 walks in 212 innings, and he led the league with the sixth best ratio in franchise history. It was the first of five consecutive seasons that Peterson posted a league leading ratio, but his record was only 12-11.

124 The number of games (124) Red Ruffing lost as a member of the Yankees. Mel Stottlemyre and Bob Shawkey are the only pitchers to lose more games. Ruffing lost 14 games in 1931 and 1933, his highest total for the Yankees, but he also won 15 or more games 11 times, including 1936-39 when he posted four consecutive 20 win seasons. Ruffing pitched 15 seasons for the Yankees and he is a member of the HOF, and only Whitey Ford won more games for New York.

125 The number of walks (1.25) per nine innings for Scott Sanderson in 1991. He led the club with the seventh best ratio in franchise history. Sanderson struck out 130 batters in 208 innings during his first season in the Bronx, but he gave up only 29 walks.

126 The number of intentional walks (126) for Mickey Mantle. His career high 23 IBB came in 1957. Mantle won his second consecutive MVP that season, and it is easy to understand why opponents would pitch around him. He only led the league in IBB twice, in 1958 and 1965, but his career total is among the top 75 all-time.

127 The number of earned runs (127) allowed by Sam Jones in 1925. Joe McGinnity gave up 151 earned runs in 1901 to set the franchise record, but the total for Jones in 1925 is the second highest. Jones made 31 starts and 14 relief appearances, and was on the mound for 246 innings. He lost 21 games, and posted a 4.63 ERA. Just two seasons earlier Jones won 21 games, and posted a 3.63 ERA.

128 The WHIP (1.28) for Don Larsen in 1956. He was 11-5 with a 3.26 ERA during the regular season. On October 8, he did a touch better. Larsen pitched the only perfect game in World Series history. No hits, walks, or base runners for the Brooklyn Dodgers, and the mitt used on that historic day by HOF battery mate Yogi Berra is on permanent display in Cooperstown.

129 The WHIP (1.29) for Javier Vazquez in 2004. His ratio was the best on the club. Vazquez struck out 150 batters in 198 innings, but he gave up only 195 hits and 60 walks.

130 The number of RBI (130) for Mickey Mantle in 1956. His career total of 1,509 RBI is among the top 50 all-time, but Mantle drove home 100 runs only four times. His 130 RBI in 1956 set a career high, and also set a franchise record for switch-hitters.

131 The number of triples (131) for Joe DiMaggio. He hit a career high 15 triples twice, during his rookie and sophomore seasons of 1936-37. He hit 13 triples in a season twice, in 1938 and again in 1942. DiMaggio hit 11 triples in a season twice, in 1941 and again in 1948; and he also hit ten triples in a season twice, in 1947 and again in 1950. All total, he led the league just once, but placed among the top ten leaders for triples nine times, and his career total is the third highest in franchise history.

132 The number of walks (132) for Lou Gehrig in 1935. His total is the tenth highest in franchise history, and it was also the first of three consecutive seasons he led the league in walks. Gehrig is among the top 15 all-time with 1,508 career walks.

133 The number of RBI (133) for Bill Dickey in 1937. His total set a career high, as did his 140 games, 530 at bats, 176 hits, 35 doubles, and 29 homeruns. Dickey only placed fifth in MVP balloting, though the Yankees did win the World Series.

134 The number of runs (134) for Derek Jeter in 1999. He led the league with 127 runs in 1998, but his total in 1999 was second behind Roberto Alomar of the Cleveland Indians. Jeter scored 100 or more runs ten times from 1996-2006, and his career total is among the top 15 for active players in 2007.

135 The ratio (13.5) of at bats per homerun for Tino Martinez in 1997. He hit a career high 44 homeruns in 594 at bats for the fifth best ratio in the league. Martinez is among the top 100 in baseball history with 339 career homeruns.

136 The number of intentional walks (136) for Don Mattingly. He was among the top ten league leaders every season from 1985-91. Mattingly is also the franchise leader for IBB, and his career total is among the top 60 in baseball history. He got a lot of respect from his opponents, especially for a guy who reportedly once said that, while growing up in Indiana, he thought, "Babe Ruth was a cartoon character."

137 The number of walks (137) for Babe Ruth in 1927 and 1928. His total is the seventh highest in franchise history. Ruth led the league both seasons in walks, homeruns, runs, OPS (on-base plus slugging percentage), and slugging percentage.

138 The number of walks (1.38) per nine innings for Fritz Peterson in 1970 and 1971. Peterson pitched 260 innings but gave up only 40 walks in 1970, and it was the third consecutive season his ratio led the league. The next season he pitched 274 innings but gave up only 42 walks, and his ratio led the league for the fourth consecutive season. He made it five in a row in 1972, and his career ratio is one of the top 50 all-time.

139 The number of strikeouts (139) for Alex Rodriguez in 2005 and 2006. He led the club both seasons, and his total is the ninth highest in franchise history. Of course he also hit 48 homeruns in 2005, and he led the club in RBI both seasons.

140 The number of strikeouts (140) for Jason Giambi in 2003. He led the club with 41 homeruns and 107 RBI, but he also led the league in strikeouts with the eighth highest total in franchise history.

141 The number of strikeouts (141) for Jack Clark in 1988. He led the club with 28 homeruns during his only season in the Bronx, but he was fifth in the league in strikeouts and his total is the seventh highest in franchise history.

142 The number of walks (142) for Babe Ruth in 1924. His total is the sixth highest in franchise history. Ruth also won his only batting title when he hit .378, and his league leading walk total gave him a .512 on-base percentage that is the fifth highest in franchise history.

143 The number of strikeouts (143) for Jorge Posada in 2002. He made the All-Star team and won the Silver Slugger award for the third consecutive season, but his strikeout total was the fourth highest in the league and the sixth highest in franchise history.

144 The number of walks (144) for Babe Ruth in 1926. He led the league with the fifth highest total in franchise history. Ruth and Barry Bonds are the only players in history to post 11 league leading walk totals in their careers.

145 The number of RBI (145) for Don Mattingly in 1985. Donnie Baseball won MVP honors after posting a career high and league leading RBI total. Mattingly is ninth in franchise history with 1,099 RBI.

146 The number of walks (146) for Mickey Mantle in 1957. His career high total led the league and is also the third highest in franchise history. Mantle batted .365, and his walk total gave him a .512 on-base percentage that tied Babe Ruth for the fifth highest in franchise history.

147 The number of walks (1.47) per nine innings as a member of the Yankees for David Wells. He played four seasons during two tours of duty in the Bronx from 1997-2003, and he posted a league best ratio three times. Wells walked a career high 62 batters in 1999, but his 2.41 ratio was still sixth best in the league. He pitched 213 innings in 2003, but only walked 20 batters for a franchise record .85 ratio.

148 The number of strikeouts (148) for Roberto Kelly in 1990. His total was the sixth highest in the league, but the fifth highest in franchise history. Kelly was third in the league with 42 steals, but he only reached base at a .323 clip because of his contact issues.

149 The number of runs (149) for Lou Gehrig in 1927 and Babe Ruth in 1931. Gehrig and Ruth share the tenth highest total in franchise history, but neither player led the club when they posted that total. Ruth scored 158 runs in 1927 to beat out Gehrig, and Gehrig scored 163 runs in 1931 to beat out Ruth.

150 The number of runs (150) for Babe Ruth in 1930. He was second in the league with the ninth highest total in franchise history. Ruth is the Yankees all-time leading scorer, and he is among the top five all-time in baseball history.

151 The number of runs (151) for Babe Ruth in 1923 and Joe DiMaggio in 1937. It is the seventh highest total in franchise history, shared by two of the greatest legends the game has ever known. Ruth led the club to victory in the 1923 World Series, and DiMaggio led the club to victory in the 1937 World Series.

152 The number of singles (152) for Don Mattingly in 1986. His total is the tenth highest in franchise history. Mattingly also set a club record with 238 base hits, and a league leading 86 went for extra-bases.

153 The number of stolen bases (153) for Mickey Mantle. He stole a career high 21 bases in 1959, and he stole ten or more bases in six consecutive seasons from 1956-61. Mantle was never among the league leaders in steals, but his career total is the ninth highest in franchise history.

154 The number of triples (154) for Earle Combs. He set a franchise record with 23 triples in 1927, and was the league leader for triples three times. Combs ranks among the top 50 all-time for triples, but only Lou Gehrig with 163 triples hit more for the Yankees.

155 The number of RBI (155) for Joe DiMaggio in 1948. His total was the best in the league, and the tenth highest in franchise history. DiMaggio only played 13 seasons, but his 1,537 RBI is the third highest total in franchise history behind Babe Ruth and Lou Gehrig, and the way he carried himself both on and off the field commanded the respect and admiration of his fans, opponents, and teammates. Mickey Mantle once said, "Heroes are people who are all good with no bad in them. That's the way I always saw Joe DiMaggio—he was beyond question one of the greatest players of the century."

156 The number of strikeouts (156) for Danny Tartabull in 1993. His total was the second highest in the league and the second highest in franchise history, but he also led the club with 31 homeruns and 102 RBI.

157 The number of strikeouts (157) for Alfonso Soriano in 2002. He led the league with 209 hits during his second season in the Bronx, but he also set the franchise record for most strikeouts. Soriano spent only one more season with the club after 2002, and then in February of 2004 he was traded to the Texas Rangers, along with Joaquin Arias and a sizable amount of cash, for Alex Rodriguez.

158 The number of runs (158) for Babe Ruth in 1920 and 1927. He led the league with the fifth highest total in franchise history, twice. Ruth owns four of the top six runs totals in the team record book.

159 The number of RBI (159) for Lou Gehrig in 1937. His total was only third best in the league, but it is the ninth highest in franchise history. Gehrig drove home 150 or more runs seven times, and he holds three of the top six RBI totals in major league history.

160 The number of singles (160) for Hal Chase in 1906. He batted .323, but did not hit a homerun all season. His singles total was second in the league and the fifth highest in franchise history, but it was not even the highest on the team in 1906. Willie Keeler led both the team and the league that season when he hit 167 singles, the second highest total in franchise history.

161 The number of walks (1.61) per nine innings as a member of the Yankees for Fritz Peterson. He led the league in this category five consecutive seasons from 1968-72, including a career best 1.23 ratio in 1968. His career ratio is among the top 50 all-time, and only Tiny Bonham and David Wells posted a better ratio during their tenure with the Yankees.

162 The number of singles (162) for Willie Keeler in 1904. Keeler batted .343, but picked up only 24 extra-base hits. His singles total led the league and is also the fourth highest in franchise history. Keeler led the league in singles seven times during his career, and his 2,513 singles are the fifth highest total all-time.

163 The number of games (163) for Hideki Matsui in 2003. On September 18, Hurricane Isabel forced the Yankees and Orioles to a 1-1 tie in a five inning game at Camden Yards. Matsui got credit for a game played, though the game was rescheduled as part of a double-header in New York on September 26. When Matsui played out the rest of the schedule, he became the only player in team history to play 163 games in one season.

164 The number of RBI (164) for Babe Ruth in 1927. His total is the 17th highest in baseball history, but was only second on the team behind the 175 RBI for Lou Gehrig.

165 The number of RBI (165) for Lou Gehrig in 1934. It was the fifth and final time he led the league in RBI. His total is tied for the 13th highest in baseball history, but it is the sixth highest in franchise history.

166 The number of singles (166) for Earle Combs in 1927. He led the league with the third highest total in franchise history. Combs also set career highs with a .356 average and 231 hits.

167 The number of runs (167) for Lou Gehrig in 1936. He led the league with the second highest total in franchise history. Gehrig scored 1,888 runs in 17 seasons, giving him the second highest career total in franchise history as well.

168 The at bats per strikeout ratio (168) for Joe Sewell in 1932. He struck out only three times in 503 at bats for the best ratio in franchise history. Sewell struck out only 15 times in three seasons with the Yankees from 1931-33, and he produced the top three season ratios in franchise history.

169 The number of hits (169) for Willie Keeler in 1905. His total led the club and was fourth in the league. Keeler also led the Highlanders that season with a .302 average and a .357 on-base percentage, and his .341 career average is among the top 15 in baseball history.

170 The number of walks (170) for Babe Ruth in 1923. He led the league and set a franchise record for walks. Ruth also holds the franchise record for career walks with 1,852.

171 The number of RBI (171) for Babe Ruth in 1921. He broke the previous record of 166 RBI set by HOF outfielder Sam Thompson of the Detroit Wolverines in 1887, and his total remains the seventh highest in baseball history.

The number of hits (172) for Babe Ruth in 1920. He batted .376 during his first season in New York, and led the league with a .533 on-base percentage and a .849 slugging percentage.

The at bats per strikeout ratio (17.3) for Nick Etten. He was an All-Star first baseman who struck out only 118 times in 568 games for the Yankees, and his ratio is the ninth best in franchise history.

The number of RBI (174) for Lou Gehrig in 1930. His total is the sixth highest in baseball history, but it was only the second highest in baseball that season. Hack Wilson drove home a record 191 runs for the Chicago Cubs.

The number of RBI (175) for Lou Gehrig in 1927. Babe Ruth set a record with 171 RBI in 1926. Ruth then hit a record 60 homeruns in 1927, but Gehrig broke the RBI record with a total that remains the second highest in franchise history.

The strikeouts to walk ratio (1.76) for Tommy John in 1988. He was a 45-year-old veteran who struck out only 81 batters, but he posted the best strikeouts to walk ratio on the club.

The number of runs (177) for Babe Ruth in 1921. He led the league and set a franchise record with the second highest total in baseball history. The major league record belongs to Billy Hamilton, who scored 192 runs in 1894.

The number of games (178) finished as a member of the Yankees for Joe Page. His total is among the top ten in franchise history. Page pitched 14 complete games, but he was primarily a reliever during his seven seasons in the Bronx. He set career highs with 48 games finished and 27 saves in 1949, and he also won two World Series titles in New York.

The number of walks (179) allowed by Tommy Byrne in 1949. He was 15-7 with a respectable 3.72 ERA, but he also set the franchise record for most walks in a season.

180   The ERA (1.80) for the Yankees during the 1941 World Series. Red Ruffing pitched a complete game 3-2 victory against the Brooklyn Dodgers in game one, Marius Russo pitched a complete game 2-1 victory in game three, and Tiny Bonham pitched a complete game 3-1 victory to clinch the series in game five. In total, Yankees pitchers gave up only 29 hits and nine earned runs during 45 innings.

181   The number of hits (181) for Bobby Richardson in 1964. He led the team in hits despite a .267 average. Richardson was a catalyst for the second highest scoring offense in the league, and the Yankees won their seventh pennant in eight seasons.

182   The ERA (1.82) for Jack Chesbro in 1904. He led the club with the fourth best ERA in franchise history. Chesbro started 51 games and made four relief appearances. He faced 1,778 batters and pitched 454 innings, but he gave up only 92 earned runs.

183   The number of stolen bases (183) as a member of the Yankees for Fritz Maisel. He led the league with a career high 74 steals in 1914, and he stole 25 or more bases four times in five seasons with New York. Maisel only played 502 games for the Yankees, but his stolen bases total is the eighth highest in franchise history.

184   The number of RBI (184) for Lou Gehrig in 1931. His total led the league, set a franchise record, and set a major league record for left-handed hitters.

185   The at bats per strikeout ratio (18.5) for Joe DiMaggio. His ratio is the seventh best in franchise history. DiMaggio nearly hit as many homeruns as times he struck out. He hit 361 homeruns, but struck out only 369 times in 13 seasons.

186   The number of games (186) finished as a member of the Yankees for Lindy McDaniel. He closed out 19 games after coming to the club in a mid-season trade in 1968, and then he closed out 25 or more games in each of his five full seasons in the Bronx. He set career highs when he closed out 51 games and saved 29 in 1970, and his games finished total is the sixth highest in franchise history.

The number of hits (187) allowed by Ron Guidry in 1978. He was on the mound for 273 innings and he faced 1,057 batters. Guidry struck out a career high 248 batters, and only 53 opponents reached base and scored an earned run against him. He led the league with a 1.74 ERA, and he won 25 games on his way to the CYA.

The ERA (1.88) for Joe Lake in 1909. He led the club with the sixth best ERA in franchise history. Lake won 14 games and gave up only 45 earned runs in 215 innings, but he played only two seasons for the Highlanders and his entire career consisted of just six seasons with three different clubs.

The ratio (18.9) of at bats per homerun for Joe DiMaggio. He led the league only once, in 1948 when he hit 39 homeruns in 594 at bats, but his career ratio is the eighth best in franchise history.

The at bats per strikeout ratio (19.0) as a member of the Yankees for Whitey Witt. He only played four seasons with the club, but his ratio is the sixth best in franchise history. Witt struck out only 93 times during 464 games. He also batted 43 times for the Yankees in the post-season. He got ten hits, struck out only three times, and won one World Series title.

The number of times (191) Don Mattingly grounded into a double-play. He was one of the toughest batters to strike out, and his ability to put the ball into play translated into a high number of double-plays. His career total is among the top 100 in baseball history, but it is the second highest in franchise history. Of course, it was this same ability to put the ball into play that gave him the highest number of sacrifice flies in franchise history.

The number of walks (1.92) per nine innings as a member of the Yankees for Herb Pennock. His ratio is the sixth best in franchise history. Pennock led the league three times for New York, including his career best 1.15 ratio in 1930.

The number of walks (1.93) per nine innings as a member of the Yankees for Steve Kline. His ratio is among the top ten in franchise history. Kline won a career high 16 games in 1972, when he gave up only 44 walks in 236 innings for the third best ratio in the league.

The ERA (1.94) for Ray Caldwell in 1914. He was only fourth among league leaders, but he led the club with the seventh best ERA in franchise history. Caldwell pitched 22 complete games and five shutouts that season.

The number of hits (195) allowed by David Wells in 1998. He tossed 214 innings and struck out 163 batters, but gave up only 29 walks. Wells was 18-4 and led the league with a 1.05 WHIP, but only placed third in CYA balloting. His post-season performance made up for it. He made two starts against Cleveland in the league championship series. Wells gave up only 12 hits in 15 innings, but struck out 18 batters. He won both starts, and earned series MVP honors.

The ratio (19.6) of at bats per homerun as a member of the Yankees for Tino Martinez. He hit 192 homeruns during seven seasons in the Bronx and his ratio is among the top ten in franchise history.

The number of innings (197) for Rick Rhoden in 1988. He made 30 starts and posted a mediocre 12-12 record, but with the Yankees bullpen one of the worst in the league, he gave the Yankees some much needed innings. Rhoden completed five games, and led the team in innings pitched.

The number of walks (1.98) per nine innings as a member of the Yankees for Ramiro Mendoza. His ratio is among the top ten in franchise history. Mendoza was primarily a relief pitcher, but his best season came in 1998 when he started 14 games and posted a 10-2 record. He gave up only 30 walks in 130 innings that season, and won the first of two rings with the club.

The number of innings (199) for Bob Grim in 1954. He was 20-6, and won ROY honors. Grim was third among league leaders in wins and winning percentage, but he played only seven more seasons and was just 41-35 the rest of his career.

200 The ratio (20.0) of at bats per homerun as a member of the Yankees for Charlie Keller. He was an All-Star outfielder who hit only 184 homeruns in ten seasons with the club, but his ratio is among the top 15 in franchise history.

Thurman Munson

"We wanted to win that game for Thurman—because that was Thurman's game."

— *Bobby Murcer*

Chapter Three

Munson

Bobby Murcer grew up in Oklahoma and was signed to play for the Yankees by the same scout who also signed fellow Oklahoman Mickey Mantle. He made his big league debut as a teenager on September 8, 1965, and was briefly teammates with the legendary Mantle. In fact, Mantle pinch-hit for Murcer during a game on September 15.

Murcer did not make the big club for good though until 1969, the year after Mantle retired, and by then he experienced the added pressure of having been labeled "the next Mickey Mantle." He inherited the title as much for his roots as for his skill, but for one additional reason as well—the most recent World Series title for the club came in 1962, and the most recent pennant came in 1964. The post-Mantle era began with the team already in decline in the minds of the New York faithful, and so Murcer was labeled the next Mickey Mantle to reassure fans that the future of the club was not in doubt, that more pennants were on the way. It is never fair to label a young player in such a way, especially in a city like

New York, and with a name like Mantle no less. If Murcer was going to be a part of the Yankees reasserting their dominance in baseball, he was going to need some help from the players around him.

The Yankees began acquiring some much needed talent in the 1968 amateur draft. The cross-town Mets chose shortstop Tim Foli with the first pick of the draft. Oakland made pitcher Pete Broberg the number two selection, and the Houston Astros chose catcher Martin Cott with the third overall pick. The Yankees used their first selection, and the fourth overall pick, to draft Thurman Munson out of Kent State University.

Munson was born in Akron, Ohio, and grew up nearby in Canton. He was a star in football, basketball, and baseball at Lehman High School in Canton, and he attended Kent State on an athletic scholarship. Upon being drafted, Munson signed and reported to the Yankees farm team in Binghamton, New York, where the catcher made quick work of the minor leagues. It took Munson only 13 months before he got the call.

On August 8, 1969, he made his major league debut in the second game of a double-header against the Oakland Athletics. He walked against Catfish Hunter in his first major league at bat. In his second at bat, Munson grounded out to shortstop Bert Campaneris. His first big league hit came in his third at bat, a single to left field against Hunter. Two batters later, he came around and scored his first run when Horace Clarke singled up the middle. Munson singled again in the eighth inning, but this time he picked up two RBI as Bobby Murcer and Jimmie Hall came around and scored the final runs of a 5-0 victory.

Munson picked up two hits, two RBI, and scored a run in his debut. He played 26 games in 1969. New York was only 80-81 on the season and placed fifth in the division, but fans who saw Munson play caught a glimpse of the team's future.

Munson won Rookie of the Year honors in 1970. He batted .302 to lead the club, and the man who was fast becoming his closest friend, Bobby Murcer, the same man who once was touted as the next Mickey Mantle, led the club with 23 homeruns. It was becoming clear that the Yankees were close to something special. Munson, Murcer, and Roy White led a resurgent offense that propelled the club to a 93-69 record, but the Orioles won the division by a large margin, and the Yankees were sitting at home in October for the sixth consecutive season.

Murcer posted big numbers in 1971. He led the club with a .331 average and 25 homeruns. Munson struggled though in his sophomore campaign, and so did the Yankees. Only a few months earlier the Yankees looked to be on the verge of making a breakthrough, but 1971 saw the club go the wrong way, and the season ended in disappointment.

Munson and Murcer grew closer as friends and teammates the next three seasons, and on September 22, 1974, they found themselves in first place with eight games left on the schedule. Just two days later though, they lost both ends of a double-header to the Boston Red Sox, and they never recovered. Baltimore won the division by two games, and in the off-season, the Yankees traded Bobby Murcer to the San Francisco Giants.

Thurman Munson batted a career high .318 in 1975, but in the second half of the season the Yankees never got close to catching the Red Sox for the division title. All of that changed though on April 17, 1976, when Munson was designated team captain—a title last held by Lou Gehrig.

New York lost the first game of the season, but then won five in a row and never looked back. Munson batted .302 with a career high 105 RBI, and when he was named the 1976 American League Most Valuable Player he became the first player in franchise history to win both ROY and MVP honors. Munson led the club to its first pennant in 12 years. He batted .529 in the 1976 World Series against the Cincinnati Reds, but despite his efforts the Yankees got swept, and once again the season ended in disappointment.

Lou Piniella came over to the Yankees from the Kansas City Royals in 1974, and his temperament and desire to win were a good fit on a club led by Thurman Munson. Piniella became close friends with both Munson and Bobby Murcer.

Murcer, of course, was gone after 1974.

He was in San Francisco when the Yankees won the pennant in 1976, and he was in Chicago playing for the Cubs when Munson, Piniella, and the Yankees broke through and won back-to-back World Series titles in 1977 and 1978. The long dry spell was over, and the fans who a decade earlier lamented the end of the Mantle era could once again celebrate, as the long awaited return to glory had finally arrived. But in their quest for a third consecutive championship, and a fourth consecutive pennant, the Yankees found themselves down ten games to the Baltimore Orioles in late June, 1979. Piniella and Munson could not have been happier when the club brought Murcer back to the Bronx, picking him up in a trade with the Cubs in preparation for a summer run at the post-season.

It never happened though. Murcer would eventually play in one World Series for the Yankees, but by then his friend, and team captain, was gone.

Only five weeks after being reunited with Munson, the club was in Chicago playing the White Sox. Murcer owned a house in Chicago, and Piniella and Munson stayed there with him during the series. The club had an off day on August 2, the day after the series ended, and Munson planned on flying his plane down to Canton to spend it with his family. Murcer was there when Munson took off on August 1, and it was the last time he ever saw his teammate. Munson died in a plane crash the following day.

The Yankees played on August 3, but Murcer was not in the line-up. He did not start on August 4, but came in the game as a pinch-runner, and he did not play at all on August 5. Only five days earlier, Munson had tried to convince Murcer to fly to Canton with him, but now on August 6, the entire team flew to Canton to bury their captain.

It was a long day, as the team returned to New York to play that night against the Orioles. Murcer started for the first time since the tragedy, but when he came to bat in the bottom of the seventh, the Yankees trailed 4-0. It was a game he wanted to win for his friend, and it would mean more to him than winning a championship. He hit a three-run homerun to cut the lead to one, but when he batted in the ninth the Yankees still trailed 4-3. Murcer batted with two men on base, and he delivered the game-winning hit. It was a moment that rivals all others in franchise history, and this for a club with a long history of great moments. Murcer came through in the clutch because there was nothing else he could do for his friend.

He gave the bat to Diana Munson, Thurman's widow.

The club immediately retired Munson's number 15 jersey, but to this day, an empty locker with the number 15 on it remains in the Yankees clubhouse as a tribute to one of the club's greatest legends.

The ERA (2.01) for Whitey Ford in 1958. It was the second time in three seasons he led the league in ERA, and he did it with the eighth best ERA in franchise history. Ford also pitched 15 complete games, and seven shutouts.

The number of hits (202) for Derek Jeter in 2005. His total was the third highest in the league, and it was the fourth time in eight seasons he got 200 or more hits. Jeter came right back with 214 hits in 2006, and his career total is among the top 15 for all active players in 2007.

The number of homeruns (203) as a member of the Yankees for Roger Maris. His first three seasons in the Bronx, Maris posted totals of 39, 61, and 33 homeruns. Maris led the league in extra-base hits in 1960 and 1961, and his 203 homeruns for New York are the tenth highest total in franchise history.

The number of hits (204) for Bernie Williams in 2002. He batted .333, and set the franchise record for most hits in a season by a switch-hitter.

The number of homeruns (205) as a member of the Yankees for Dave Winfield. He hit a career high 37 homeruns in 1982, and he hit 20 or more homeruns seven times during his tenure in New York. Winfield is one of the top 30 homerun hitters in baseball history with 465 big flies, and his total for the Yankees is the ninth highest in franchise history.

The ERA (2.06) for Allie Reynolds in 1952. In his tenth full season in the majors, Reynolds put together the best year of his career. He posted a 20-8 record to lead the team in wins, and he led the league with a career best ERA.

The at bats per strikeout ratio (20.7) for Earle Combs. He struck out only 278 times in 5,746 at bats, and he never struck out more than 43 times in any one season. Combs is one of the toughest batters to strike out in baseball history, with a career ratio that is the fifth best in franchise history.

208 The ERA (2.08) for John Wetteland during the 1996 World Series. He appeared in five games against the Braves, and saved all four of the Yankees' wins to give manager Joe Torre his first championship. Wetteland gave up just four hits and one run during four innings of work, and he struck out six batters as he earned series MVP honors.

209 The number of strikeouts (209) for pitchers David Cone in 1998, Whitey Ford in 1961, and Russ Ford in 1910. All three pitchers led the club in strikeouts during their respective seasons, and collectively, they share the tenth highest strikeout total in franchise history.

210 The number of strikeouts (210) for pitcher Bob Turley in 1955. He was second in the league, but he led the club with the ninth highest total in franchise history. Turley was 17-13, and he also led the club with six shutouts during his first season in the Bronx.

211 The number of hits (211) for Lou Gehrig in 1931 and Don Mattingly in 1985. Gehrig batted .341 and led the league in hits, but was only fifth in the batting title race. Mattingly batted .324 and was second in the league in hits, but only placed third in the batting title race. Both players share the ninth highest hit total in franchise history.

212 The number of hits (212) allowed by Tommy John in 1987. He was a 44-year-old veteran who gave up the most hits on the staff. But that is not meant as a criticism, as John posted a 13-6 record and led the team with 187 innings on the mound.

213 The number of hits (213) for Red Rolfe in 1939. His total is the eighth highest in franchise history, but it was only the sixth highest in the league. Rolfe batted a career high .329, and won his fourth consecutive World Series title.

214 The number of hits (214) for Derek Jeter in 2006. His total is the seventh highest in franchise history, but it was only the third highest in the league. Jeter batted .344, but lost the batting title by .003 to Joe Mauer of the Minnesota Twins.

The number of hits (215) for Joe DiMaggio in 1937. He did not lead the league, but he set a career high with the sixth highest total in franchise history. DiMaggio batted .346, but was only third in the race for the batting title.

The number of hits (216) allowed by Stan Bahnsen in 1968. He pitched 267 innings in 34 starts, and his ratio of hits per nine innings was the best on the team. Bahnsen won 17 games and led the club with 162 strikeouts, and he also earned ROY honors.

The at bats per strikeout ratio (21.7) as a member of the Yankees for Mark Koenig. He was a light-hitting infielder who struck out only 103 times in 2,233 at bats, and his ratio is the fourth best in franchise history.

The number of hits (218) for Lou Gehrig in 1927. His total was second in the league behind teammate Earle Combs. Gehrig was also second in the league with 18 triples, 47 homeruns, and a .765 slugging percentage. He hit .373, but was third in the race for the batting title. Of course, he did win the MVP and a World Series title.

The number of hits (219) for Derek Jeter in 1999. He led the league with the fourth highest total in franchise history. Jeter batted .349, but lost the batting title to Nomar Garciaparra of the Boston Red Sox.

The number of hits (220) for Lou Gehrig in 1930. His total was second in the league, but it is the third highest in franchise history. Gehrig batted .379, but lost the batting title by .002 behind Al Simmons of the Philadelphia Athletics.

The number of innings (221) for Andy Pettitte in 1996. He led the team in innings, and he led the league with a 21-8 record in his second season. Pettitte also made his first All-Star team, and placed second in CYA balloting.

The number of homeruns (222) for Don Mattingly. His total is the eighth highest in franchise history. Mattingly hit a career high 35 homeruns in 1985, the first of three consecutive 30-homerun seasons.

The number of times (223) Bernie Williams grounded into a double-play. His total is one of the top 50 in baseball history, but it is the highest in franchise history. Williams hit into a career high 21 double-plays in 2003, and for all his consistent play, the twin-killing proved to be his Achilles heel.

The at bats per strikeout ratio (22.4) as a member of the Yankees for Frank Baker. His ratio is the best in franchise history. Baker struck out only 114 times during 676 games.

The strikeouts to walk ratio (2.25) for Andy Pettitte in 1996. He led the team with 162 strikeouts and 221 innings, but gave up only 72 walks. His ratio also led the team, and was the tenth best in the league.

The number of homeruns (226) allowed by Ron Guidry. His total is the second highest in franchise history, but Guidry is also seventh in shutouts, sixth in innings, fourth in wins, fourth in starts, and second in strikeouts.

The ERA (2.27) for the Philadelphia Phillies during the 1950 World Series. Luckily for New York fans, the Yankees staff gave up only three earned runs during the four game series for a rather salty 0.73 ERA—and a four game sweep of the Phillies.

The number of homeruns (228) allowed by Whitey Ford. His total is the highest in franchise history, but Ford has also started the most games, pitched the most innings, won the most games, thrown the most shutouts, and struck out the most batters in franchise history.

The ERA (2.29) for Mariano Rivera from 1995-2006. The future HOF closer gave up only 224 earned runs in 881 innings of work, and as he entered play in 2007 his ERA was the second best in franchise history.

The number of World Series at bats (230) for Mickey Mantle. He played 65 post-season games, and picked up 59 hits. Mantle holds World Series records with 18 homeruns, 42 runs, and 40 RBI. He also won seven World Series titles.

The number of hits (231) for Earle Combs in 1927. He led the league with the second highest total in franchise history. Combs batted a career high .356, but he only placed sixth in the race for the league batting title.

The number of times on base (232) for Tom Tresh in 1965. His total was the best on the team, and seventh best in the league. Tresh also was third in the league with 61 extra-base hits, including a team leading 26 homeruns.

The number of stolen bases (233) for Roy White. He stole a career high 31 bases in 1976, and his career total is the fifth highest in franchise history.

The ERA (2.34) for Mariano Rivera in 2001. He led the league with 50 saves. Rivera pitched 80 innings, but gave up only 61 hits and 21 earned runs, and earned the Rolaids Relief Award.

The number of walks (2.35) per nine innings for Orlando Hernandez in 2000. His ratio was the best on the club, but he was only 12-13 for his first losing record during three seasons in the Bronx. Hernandez struck out 141 batters in 195 innings, but he gave up only 51 walks.

The number of games (236) Whitey Ford won. His total is a franchise record. Ford won a career high 25 games in 1961, and ten times he posted 15 or more wins in a season. He also won ten World Series games, and six World Series titles.

The number of innings (237) for Red Ruffing in 1931. He was 39-96 for his career after beginning 1930, his sixth season in Boston, 0-3. Ruffing came to the Yankees in a mid-season trade, and was 15-5 the rest of the way. He won 16 more games in 1931, and he led the club in starts and complete games. Ruffing went on to post a 231-124 record for New York, and ended his career 273-225. He was also 7-2 during World Series games for the Yankees, and he won six World Series titles.

238 The number of hits (238) for Don Mattingly in 1986. His total is the franchise record. Mattingly batted a career high .352, but was second in both the batting title race and league MVP balloting.

239 The number of strikeouts (239) for pitcher Jack Chesbro in 1904. His total was second in the league, but it is also the second highest total in franchise history.

240 The number of walks (2.40) per nine innings for Pat Dobson in 1974. He walked 75 batters during his team high 281 innings for the best ratio on the club. Dobson and teammate Doc Medich led the club in wins after posting identical 19-15 records.

241 The ERA (2.41) as a member of the Yankees for Sparky Lyle. He gave up only 200 earned runs in 745 innings for the third best ERA in franchise history. Lyle won the 1977 CYA after posting a 13-5 record with 26 saves.

242 The number of homeruns (242) for the Yankees in 2004. The club set a franchise record for most homeruns in a season. Alex Rodriguez and Gary Sheffield led the club with 36 homeruns each, Hideki Matsui hit 31, and nine different players hit at least 12 big flies on the season.

243 The number of times on base (243) for Wade Boggs in 1993. His total led the team, and Boggs also led the team with 169 hits. Boggs got on base 4,445 times in his career, one of the top 20 totals in baseball history.

244 The batting average (.244) for Jake Powell in 1939. He was a seldom used infielder who played only 31 games and batted 86 times on the season. Powell hit one homerun with nine RBI. He spent five years in New York and never played more than 97 games in a season, but on a club that boasted HOF legends Bill Dickey, Lou Gehrig, Tony Lazzeri, and Joe DiMaggio, it was Powell who posted a .455 batting average in the 1936 World Series. He also added a homerun and five RBI in that series, and by the time 1939 came around, he had already won three consecutive World Series titles with the club.

245 The ERA (2.45) for Dave Righetti in 1986. He was 8-8 in 74 games out of the bullpen. Righetti struck out 83 batters in 106 innings, but gave up only 88 hits. He also saved a career high 46 games and won the Rolaids Relief Award.

246 The number of hits (246) allowed by Shane Rawley in 1983. He gave up the most hits, walks, and runs on the club. Rawley made 33 starts and logged an impressive 238 innings though, and he posted a respectable 14-14 record.

247 The ERA (2.47) for Whitey Ford in 1956. He was 19-6, and he led the league in both ERA and winning percentage. Ford was also among the top five league leaders with 18 complete games and a 1.20 WHIP.

248 The number of stolen bases (248) as a member of the Highlanders for Hal Chase. He stole at least 20 bases eight consecutive seasons from 1905-12, including a career high 40 in 1910. Chase never led the league in steals, but his total in New York is the fourth highest in franchise history.

249 The number of stolen bases (249) for Derek Jeter from 1996-2006. Jeter stole 14 bases as a rookie in 1996, and seven times he stole 20 or more bases. Jeter is among the top 15 in steals for all active players in 2007, but his career total is the second highest in franchise history.

250 The number of homeruns (250) as a member of the Yankees for Graig Nettles. His total is the seventh highest in franchise history. Nettles hit a career high 37 homeruns in 1977, and he hit 20 or more in seven consecutive seasons from 1973-79.

251 The number of stolen bases (251) as a member of the Yankees for Willie Randolph. His total is the third highest in franchise history. Randolph stole a career high 37 bases in 1975, and from 1978-80 he posted three consecutive seasons of 30 or more steals.

The strikeouts to walk ratio (2.52) as a member of the Yankees for Jimmy Key. He struck out 400 batters in 604 innings, but gave up only 159 walks for the ninth best ratio in franchise history. Key played only three seasons and made 94 starts for the Yankees, and he posted a 48-23 record.

The number of innings (253) for Spud Chandler in 1943. His total led the club, and he also won MVP honors after posting a 20-4 record. Chandler gave his best performance though in the post-season. He tossed two complete game victories against the Cardinals as the Yankees won the 1943 World Series.

The ERA (2.54) as a member of the Yankees for Russ Ford. His ERA is the fourth best in franchise history. Ford got off to a good start, as he posted a 26-6 record as a rookie in 1910. He won 73 games in four seasons in New York, but played only two additional seasons of baseball before his career ended.

The batting average (.255) for Joe Pepitone in 1966. He was the star of an offense that struggled all season. Pepitone led the team with a .463 slugging percentage, 31 homeruns, 85 runs, and 83 RBI.

The ERA (2.56) for Herb Pennock in 1928. He led the club with the second best ERA in the league. Pennock tossed 18 complete games and won 17, and he also led the club with five shutouts.

The ERA (2.57) for the Highlanders in 1904. It was only the fifth best team ERA in the league that season, but it is the best team ERA in franchise history. New York won 92 games for the highest total during the Highlanders era of the franchise.

The ERA (2.58) as a member of the Highlanders for Jack Chesbro. His ERA is the fifth best in franchise history. Chesbro pitched in New York from 1903-09, and he posted a 3.00 ERA or less six times.

The number of World Series at bats (259) for Yogi Berra. He won 14 pennants from 1947-63, and his 75 World Series games are the most in history. Berra also owns the records for most World Series at bats, hits, and titles. He won ten titles as a player, and he added two more as a coach.

260 The strikeouts to walk ratio (2.60) for Ron Guidry in 1983. He was 21-9, and he tossed 21 complete games. Guidry struck out 156 batters in 250 innings, but gave up only 60 walks for the best ratio on the team, and the fourth best ratio in the league.

261 The number of complete games (261) as a member of the Yankees for Red Ruffing. His total is a franchise record. Ruffing set a career high with 25 complete games in 1936, and he completed 18 or more games in ten consecutive seasons from 1931-40.

262 The World Series batting average (.262) for Tony Lazzeri. He hit only .192 as the Cardinals beat the Yankees in the 1926 World Series—but he won five pennants with the club, and five championships, from 1927-37. Lazzeri did not lose in the post-season again until 1938, when as a member of the Cubs he lost to his former team, the Yankees.

263 The batting average (.263) for Johnny Mize in 1952. He is among the top 100 in baseball history for average and homeruns, but he spent ten seasons in the N.L. and never won a pennant. Mize came to the Yankees mid-season in 1949, as the club was battling Boston down the stretch for the pennant. In 1952, Mize was at the end of his career and his numbers were down. He hit only four homeruns to go with his .263 average, but he came to life in the 1952 World Series against the Dodgers. Mize batted .400 and hit three homeruns as the Yankees won the series—but for the HOF slugger who could not win a pennant in the N.L., it was not his first title. The Yankees also won that 1949 showdown with the Red Sox, and the victory against the Dodgers gave him four consecutive World Series titles. Mize retired after winning a fifth consecutive title in 1953.

264 The number of total bases (264) for Joe Gordon in 1942. He hit only 18 homeruns, but he batted a career high .322 with 103 RBI, and won the MVP. Gordon is one of the best power-hitting second basemen in history with 253 homeruns.

The number of games (265) started as a member of the Yankees for Fritz Peterson. His total is the tenth highest in franchise history. Peterson started a career high 37 games in 1969 and 1970, and he posted a 109-106 record during his tenure with the club. He is an anomaly though, in that he spent nine seasons in the Bronx but never made it to the post-season.

The number of total bases (266) for Don Mattingly in 1992. He batted only .288, but led the team in total bases and average. Mattingly also led the club with 188 hits and 54 extra-base hits.

The number of hits (267) allowed by Mel Stottlemyre in 1969. His total led the team, but he also amassed a staggering 303 innings, also the highest on the team. Stottlemyre only gave up 1.20 base runners per inning, and with a 20-14 record, he led the club in wins for the fifth consecutive season.

The World Series batting average (.268) for Tino Martinez. He won five pennants from 1996-2001, and won four World Series titles. He also hit one of the most dramatic homeruns in World Series history. Martinez blasted a two-run shot, with two outs in the bottom of the ninth inning, to tie up game four of the 2001 World Series against the Arizona Diamondbacks. The bat used by Martinez to hit that shot can be seen on display at the Hall of Fame.

The strikeouts to walk ratio (2.69) as a member of the Yankees for Fritz Peterson. He posted league leading ratios in 1969 and 1970, and his career ratio for the Yankees is the sixth best in franchise history. Peterson struck out 893 batters in nine seasons, but gave up only 332 walks.

The number of total bases (270) for Steve Sax in 1991. He batted .304 and led the team with 198 hits. Sax also led the team in total bases, a feat rarely accomplished by someone who is not a power hitter—and Sax was definitely not a power threat, although he did lead the team with 50 extra-base hits, and set a career high with ten homeruns.

The World Series batting average (.271) for Joe DiMaggio. He began his career with four consecutive World Series titles from 1936-39. New York lost the pennant in 1940, but won another title in 1941. St. Louis beat the Yankees in the 1942 World Series, but it was the only time DiMaggio lost in the post-season. He missed 1943-45 completely because of his military service during World War II. DiMaggio returned in 1946, and won another title in 1947. He began his career with four straight titles, and he won three straight from 1949-51 to close out his career. All total, DiMaggio won ten pennants and nine World Series titles, and yet he only played 13 seasons.

The ERA (2.72) as a member of the Yankees for Al Orth. His ERA is the sixth best in franchise history. Orth won a career high 27 games in 1906. Jack Chesbro and Carl Mays are the only other pitchers to win as many games in a season for New York.

The ERA (2.73) as a member of the Yankees for Tiny Bonham. His ERA is the seventh best in franchise history. Bonham was 9-3 with a 1.90 ERA as a rookie in 1940, but his best record came in 1942 when he was 21-5.

The ERA (2.74) as a member of the Yankees for Hank Borowy. His ERA is the ninth best in franchise history, and his career best 2.52 ERA came as a rookie in 1942. Borowy posted totals of 15, 14, and 17 wins respectively from 1942-44. He won 21 games in 1945, but only ten were for the Yankees, as he was traded mid-season to the Cubs.

The ERA (2.75) for Whitey Ford. He was 9-1 as a rookie in 1950, but he spent the next two years serving in the military during the Korean War. Ford returned in 1953, and posted an 18-6 record. His ERA is among the top 100 in baseball history, but it is the tenth best in franchise history.

The number of games (276) started as a member of the Yankees for Waite Hoyt. His total is the seventh highest in franchise history. Hoyt was traded from the Red Sox to the Yankees after 1920, and he started a career high 32 games in 1921. He completed a career high 23 games in 1927, and won a career high 23 games in 1928. Hoyt was 157-98 for the Yankees, and won three World Series titles.

277 The strikeouts to walk ratio (2.77) as a member of the Yankees for Goose Gossage. His ratio is the fifth best in franchise history. Gossage was 42-28 with 151 saves during six seasons in the Bronx. He tossed 533 innings and struck out 512 batters, but gave up only 185 walks.

278 The ERA (2.78) for Ron Guidry in 1979. It was the second consecutive season that he led the league in ERA. Guidry was 18-8, and he also led the club with 15 complete games and 201 strikeouts.

279 The batting average (.279) for Tom Tresh in 1965. He led the Yankees in hitting, and his team high 26 homeruns ranked fifth among league leaders. Tresh also led the Yankees in on-base percentage, slugging percentage, runs, hits, total bases, and RBI.

280 The ERA (2.80) for the Yankees during the 1949 World Series. Brooklyn won the N.L. pennant with the highest scoring offense in the league, but the Dodgers managed only two hits against Allie Reynolds in game one of the World Series. Yankees pitchers dominated the entire series, giving up only 34 hits and 14 earned runs in 45 innings, and the Yankees won the series in five games.

281 The strikeouts to walk ratio (2.81) for Ron Guidry. His ratio is the fourth best in franchise history. Guidry struck out 1,778 batters in 2,392 innings, but gave up only 633 walks.

282 The ERA (2.82) for David Cone in 1997. He led the club with the third best ERA in the league. Cone was 12-6, and he was also third in the league with 222 strikeouts.

283 The batting average (.283) for Don Mattingly in 1983. He was a rookie, and he came to bat 279 times in 91 games. Mattingly picked up 79 hits, and drove home 32 runs. One year later, Mattingly hit .343 and won his only career batting title.

284 The number of times on base (284) for Jason Giambi in 2003. He only batted .250, but he led the team with a .412 on-base percentage and a .527 slugging percentage. Giambi belted 41 homeruns and 25 doubles, but the reason he got on base more than anybody on the team was his league leading 129 walks.

285 The number of total bases (285) for Yogi Berra in 1954. He batted .307 with 125 RBI, and was among the top ten league leaders in ten statistically significant categories, including total bases. Berra won his second career MVP.

286 The World Series ERA (2.86) for Lefty Gomez. He won five pennants during 13 seasons with the Yankees. Gomez tossed a complete game against the Cubs in the 1932 Worlds Series for his first post-season win. His final post-season win came against the Cubs in the 1938 World Series. All total, Gomez posted a 6-0 record, and gave up only 16 earned runs in 50 innings during World Series games. Gomez won all five World Series he played in.

287 The number of homeruns (287) for Bernie Williams. His total is the sixth highest in franchise history. Bernie hit a career high 30 homeruns in 2000, and he hit 20 or more seven times. He also retired as the leading homerun hitter in the post-season with 22.

288 The ERA (2.88) for Andy Pettitte in 1997. He was 18-4 and his ERA was nearly a full point lower than it was in 1996. Pettitte was fourth among league leaders in wins, winning percentage, and ERA. He placed fifth in CYA balloting.

289 The number of stolen bases (289) for the Highlanders in 1910. Rookie outfielder Bert Daniels led the club with a career high 41 steals. Hal Chase was right behind him with 40, and in total the club boasted ten players in double-digits. The Highlanders not only led the league in steals, they also set a franchise record.

290 The ERA (2.90) for Fritz Peterson in 1970. He was 20-11, and he led the club in wins and ERA. Peterson was only fifth among

league leaders for wins, and his ERA was only fourth best, but he earned his only career All-Star appearance.

291 The batting average (.291) for Don Mattingly in 1993. He only played 134 games, but got 154 hits. Mattingly was slowed by back trouble in his career, but he played 14 seasons in the Bronx and retired as the ninth leading hitter in franchise history.

292 The batting average (.292) for Wade Boggs in 1997. He was limited to only 103 hits in 103 games during his final season in the Bronx. Boggs batted just 353 times, but scored 55 runs and posted a .373 on-base percentage.

293 The World Series ERA (2.93) for Ralph Terry. He was MVP of the 1962 World Series after posting two wins and a 1.80 ERA against the Giants. Terry was 0-3 with a 4.29 ERA in four other trips to the World Series.

294 The batting average (.294) for Frank Baker in 1921. The HOF third baseman won three World Series titles with the Philadelphia Athletics before joining the Yankees in 1916. Baker was in his second to last season in 1921. By then his experience and leadership were as important as his offensive production, but combined, they helped the club claim the first pennant in franchise history.

295 The number of times on base (295) for Derek Jeter in 2006. His total led the league, but his .343 average was second in the batting title race. Jeter's 214 hits were third among league leaders, and he was second in MVP balloting.

296 The number of at bats (296) for Leo Durocher in 1928. His HOF status is the result of his managerial record, but he got his start as a middle infielder for New York in 1928. He batted .270, and played in 102 games. Durocher was 0 for 2 in the 1928 World Series, but he won his first title playing for the Yankees.

297 The ERA (2.97) for Bob Turley in 1958. Turley, who once struck out 22 batters in a 16 inning minor league game, led the Yankees with 168 strikeouts, 19 complete games, and a 21-7 record. He won CYA honors, and then he picked up two wins and a save in the World Series, got a title, and earned series MVP honors.

298 The batting average (.298) for Mickey Mantle. His 2,415 hits are among the top 100 totals in baseball history. Mantle batted .353 in 1956 for his only batting title, and he batted a career high .365 in 1957. Mantle's career average is among the top 15 in franchise history.

299 The number of times on base (299) for Phil Rizzuto in 1950. His total was the highest on the team. Rizzuto also set a career high with a team leading .418 on-base percentage.

300 The batting average (.300) for Reggie Jackson in 1980. It was a career high average, but he did not sacrifice any power to get it. Jackson led the club with 41 homeruns and 111 RBI, and placed second in league MVP balloting.

Paul O'Neill

"You play the game to win the game, and not to worry about what's on the back of the baseball card at the end of the year."

— *Paul O'Neill*

Chapter Four

O'Neill

George Steinbrenner once called him a warrior, and more recently, Mariano Rivera referred to him as a clutch player who knew how to win. Pretty high accolades, especially considering the sources—but then, Paul O'Neill really was that kind of player. The list of guys who hit more homeruns is pretty long. He won a batting title, and his career average is better than most, but again, there is a long list of guys who got more hits. If you could measure heart, though, or desire, or some intangible ability to get the job done when it counted the most, then O'Neill is your guy.

He was born in Columbus, Ohio, and he grew up a die-hard Reds fan. O'Neill realized his childhood dream when the Reds selected him in the fourth-round of the 1981 amateur draft. He came out of Brookhaven High School in Columbus, Ohio, as the 93rd pick overall. He was drafted ahead of some great talent: Mark McGwire, Fred McGriff, and Roger Clemens. Some great players were drafted ahead of O'Neill: David Cone, Tony Gwynn, John Elway, and Joe Carter. Tony Gwynn and John Elway are both in the Hall of Fame—one in Cooperstown, the other in Canton. Joe Carter hit one of the most dramatic homeruns in World Series history, and David Cone is one of only 17 pitchers to throw a perfect game. Of course, there are many ways to measure greatness. One such way is to consider the success of a player's team—and Paul O'Neill won five rings.

Good timing as much as anything else can be a critical factor in getting a ring for a player. But much longer than the list of guys who hit more homeruns and got more base hits than O'Neill is the list of guys who never got a ring—and it is a list stocked with talent: Ted Williams, Ernie Banks, Ryne Sandberg, and Barry Bonds, just to get started. It seems reasonable to assume then that talent and timing are not always enough, but what is it exactly that elevates some players to post-season immortality?

It could be attitude is a large part of it.

O'Neill famously said, "If you're a Yankee fan, or if you're not a Yankee fan, you have to admit—we're winners." He wasn't being arrogant, he was stating a fact. David Cone is the only other player chosen in the 1981 draft to win five rings. Cone and O'Neill won four of them as teammates wearing pinstripes.

O'Neill got a cup of coffee with the Reds in 1985, and again in 1986. He became a regular in 1988, and he was exactly the kind of player you need on a championship team. He demanded success, both from himself and from his teammates. O'Neill was often criticized for wearing his emotions so openly, but no one could question his desire to win—and in 1990, Cincinnati won the World Series.

He was only getting started in terms of post-season play.

It is true that a lot of players posted better career numbers in a lot of categories, but try finding guys who can match this kind of success in today's era—O'Neill made the post-season eight times in only 14 full seasons in the majors. He won six pennants, and five rings. His clubs won 16 of 19 post-season series he played in, and swept the World Series three times. O'Neill hit 11 post-season homeruns, and he tied a record by getting nine hits in only five games during the 2000 World Series against the New York Mets. He won four titles from 1996-2000 with the Yankees, and he played the final game of the 1999 World Series against the Atlanta Braves just hours after his dad died.

It was for all these reasons, and more, that Yankees fans came to love Paul O'Neill.

The fans in the Bronx are notorious for making their displeasure known to players, but few players have ever experienced such appreciation as did O'Neill when he played the final home game of his career during game five of the 2001 World Series. The entire stadium stood, chanted his name, and cheered for the retiring outfielder as he stood in right field in the top of the ninth inning. He came off the field after the third out, tipped his cap, and the crowd, still standing, and knowing they were witnessing a modern legend in his final moments, grew louder still.

He really was that kind of player.

The number of times on base (301) for Alex Rodriguez in 2005. His total was the best in the league. Rodriguez batted .321, and was second in the batting title race. Throw in his 48 homeruns and 130 RBI, and A-Rod won his second career MVP.

The batting average (.302) for Wade Boggs in 1993. He led the club with 169 hits during his first season in the Bronx. Boggs also led the club with a .378 on-base percentage, and was the only player for the Yankees to make the All-Star team.

The batting average (.303) for Don Baylor in 1983. He led the club in batting, and the former MVP for the California Angels also hit 21 homeruns with 85 RBI, and won his first career Silver Slugger award.

The number of total bases (304) for Bernie Williams in 2000. He got 73 extra-base hits for a career high, and he led the club in total bases. Williams also posted a .566 slugging percentage, just shy of his career high .575 percentage from 1998.

The batting average (.305) as a member of the Yankees for Ben Chapman. He was an All-Star outfielder who played seven seasons with the club from 1930-36, and his career average with the Yankees is the tenth highest in franchise history.

The batting average (.306) for Gil McDougald in 1951. He hit 14 homeruns and scored 72 runs on his way to ROY honors. McDougald also hit a homerun and drove in seven runs as the Yankees beat the Giants in the 1951 World Series.

The batting average (.307) for Don Mattingly. His average is the ninth highest in franchise history. Mattingly batted .352 in 1986 for a career high, and he hit .300 or better seven times in 13 seasons in the Bronx.

The number of total bases (308) for Alex Rodriguez in 2004. His total led the team and was among the top ten league leaders. It was his first season in the Bronx, and Rodriguez tied teammate Gary Sheffield for the team lead with 36 homeruns.

The batting average (.309) for the Yankees in 1930. Lou Gehrig led the club with a .379 average, but he was only one of six starters to hit .300 or better for the season. The offense led the league in hitting, and set a franchise record for team average.

The number of hits (310) allowed by Carl Mays in 1920. His total is the tenth highest in franchise history, but he was on the mound for 312 innings. Mays pitched 26 complete games, and his 26-11 record gave him the third highest win total in franchise history.

The batting average (.311) as a Yankee for Bob Meusel. His average is the eighth highest in franchise history. Meusel hit a career high .337 in 1927, but that was the only time he placed among the top ten in the batting title race. His career high 190 hits in 1921 were among the top ten league leaders though, as were his 33 homeruns and 138 RBI in 1925.

The batting average (.312) for Mickey Rivers in 1976. He led the club with the seventh highest average in the league. Rivers got 184 hits and scored 95 runs, but only played 137 games. He also led the team with 43 steals, and placed third in league MVP balloting.

313 The batting average (.313) for Bill Dickey. He is tied with Wade Boggs for the sixth highest average in franchise history. Dickey only placed among the top ten league leaders in batting three times, and yet his average is one of the top 100 in baseball history.

314 The number of hits (314) allowed by Jack Chesbro in 1906. His total is tied for the eighth highest in franchise history with George Pipgras, who gave up 314 hits in 1928. Chesbro tossed 325 innings though, and posted a 23-17 record after appearing in a league leading 49 games.

315 The batting average (.315) for Joe DiMaggio in 1947. His average was only seventh in the league, but he was second in the league with a .522 slugging percentage and a .913 OPS. DiMaggio was also among the top ten league leaders in runs, hits, total bases, doubles, triples, homeruns, and RBI—and he won his third MVP.

316 The number of batters (316) Mariano Rivera faced in 2004. He was 4-2, and pitched in a career high 74 games. Rivera also converted 53 saves, and in 78 innings he gave up only 65 hits and 17 earned runs. He only placed third in CYA balloting, but won his third Rolaids Relief Award.

317 The batting average (.317) for Derek Jeter from 1995-2006. Six times he placed among the top five in the batting title race, and Jeter began play in 2007 with the fifth highest average in franchise history.

318 The batting average (.318) for Thurman Munson in 1975. His average led the club, as did his career high 190 hits. Munson also surpassed 100 RBI for the first time, a feat he repeated in 1976 and 1977.

319 The number of games (319) started for Lefty Gomez. His total is the fifth highest in franchise history. Gomez started a career high 34 games in 1937, and posted a 21-11 record with a career high 25 complete games. He also started 26 or more games for nine consecutive seasons from 1931-39.

The number of at bats (320) for Bernie Williams in 1991. He only batted .238 in 85 games as a rookie. Of course, Bernie went on to bat .297 for his career, and his 7,869 at bats are the third highest total in franchise history, trailing only Mickey Mantle and Lou Gehrig.

The batting average (.321) for Alex Rodriguez in 2005. He won league MVP honors during his second season in the Bronx, after leading the club in a host of categories: OPS, batting, slugging percentage, runs, total bases, homeruns, times on base, extra-base hits, and RBI.

The batting average (.322) for Dave Winfield in 1988. He led the club and was fourth in the league in batting during his last full season in the Bronx. Winfield also led the club in on-base percentage, slugging percentage, RBI, and total bases.

The number of games (323) started for Ron Guidry. His total is the fourth highest in franchise history. Guidry started a career high 35 games during his 1978 CYA season, and six times he made 30 or more starts in a season.

The batting average (.324) for Bill Dickey in 1929. He was a 22-year-old rookie playing alongside legends Lou Gehrig, Tony Lazzeri, Earle Combs, and Babe Ruth. Dickey held his own as he got 145 hits and 65 RBI in 130 games.

The batting average (.325) for Earle Combs and Joe DiMaggio. Both players share the third highest average in franchise history. Combs spent 12 seasons with the club, and picked up 1,866 hits. DiMaggio won back-to-back batting titles in 1939 and 1940, and got 2,214 hits in only 13 seasons.

The number of stolen bases (326) for Rickey Henderson. He posted totals of 80, 87, 41, and 93 during four seasons from 1985-88. Henderson was traded to Oakland during mid-season 1989, but stole 25 bases during his final 65 games in the Bronx. He only played 596 games for the Yankees, but he is the franchise leader for steals.

The number of doubles (327) for Tony Lazzeri. He hit 20 or more doubles 11 times from 1926-37, and his total is the tenth highest in franchise history.

The number of times on base (328) for Lou Gehrig and Babe Ruth in 1931. They led the league, and share the ninth highest total in franchise history. Ruth got 199 hits, 128 walks, and was hit by a pitch once. Gehrig got 211 hits, and drew 117 walks.

The number of times on base (329) for Babe Ruth in 1927. Only four players in history have led their league in times on base in eight different seasons: Stan Musial, Ted Williams, Wade Boggs, and Babe Ruth. Pete Rose is the only player in history to do so nine times. Lou Gehrig led the league in times on base in 1927 with 330, only one more than his teammate Babe Ruth—and if the Babe could have reached one more time that season, he would have shared the lead with Gehrig, and he would share the record with Rose.

The number of times on base (330) for Lou Gehrig in 1927. It was the first time Gehrig led the league in times on base, and his total is the seventh highest in franchise history. Gehrig reached base 4,274 times in his career, one of the top 30 totals in baseball history.

The number of times on base (331) for Babe Ruth in 1926 and Lou Gehrig in 1937. Both players led the league, and share the fifth highest total in franchise history. It was the sixth time in eight seasons Ruth posted a league leading total, and for Gehrig, it was the sixth time overall that he led the league.

The number of hits (332) allowed by Carl Mays in 1921. His total is the fifth highest in franchise history, but he did not have a bad season. Mays pitched 336 innings, and posted a 27-9 record.

The number of hits (333) allowed by Harry Howell in 1901. His total is the fourth highest in franchise history. Howell pitched for the Highlanders during the inaugural season for the franchise. He pitched 32 complete games, but was only 14-21.

334 The batting average (.334) for Lou Gehrig in 1933. He was third in the batting title race, and his 198 hits were fifth most in the league. Gehrig led the Yankees though in batting, hits, runs, and RBI—just another monster year for the HOF legend.

335 The on-base percentage (.335) for Tony Kubek in 1957. He was a 20-year-old rookie who hit three homeruns in 127 games as the Yankees shortstop. Kubek hit two homeruns in only 28 at bats during the 1957 World Series against the Atlanta Braves. He also won ROY honors on the season.

336 The ERA (3.36) for Waite Hoyt in 1928. He was 23-7, and he led the club in winning percentage. Hoyt added two more wins against the St. Louis Cardinals during the 1928 World Series. He tossed complete game gems in games one and four to clinch his third title with the Yankees.

337 The batting average (.337) for Bob Meusel in 1927. His average was a career high, and his 103 RBI made him the fourth member of the club to surpass the century mark that season. Meusel batted .309 during 11 big league seasons, and won three World Series titles.

338 The number of doubles (338) as a member of the Yankees for Bob Meusel. His total is the ninth highest in franchise history. Meusel hit a career high 47 doubles in 1927, tying him with Lou Gehrig for the fifth highest season total in franchise history. He also posted 40 or more doubles five times in ten seasons.

339 The batting average (.339) for Derek Jeter in 2000. He led the club, but was fifth in the league in batting. Jeter was fourth in the league with 201 hits, and he also won his fourth World Series title.

340 The batting average (.340) for legend Lou Gehrig. His average is the second highest in franchise history. Gehrig won the 1934 batting title with a .363 average, and he batted .370 or higher three times.

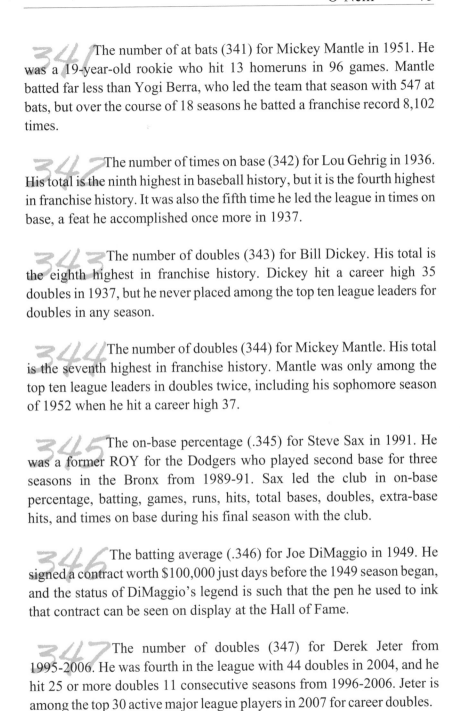

The number of at bats (341) for Mickey Mantle in 1951. He was a 19-year-old rookie who hit 13 homeruns in 96 games. Mantle batted far less than Yogi Berra, who led the team that season with 547 at bats, but over the course of 18 seasons he batted a franchise record 8,102 times.

The number of times on base (342) for Lou Gehrig in 1936. His total is the ninth highest in baseball history, but it is the fourth highest in franchise history. It was also the fifth time he led the league in times on base, a feat he accomplished once more in 1937.

The number of doubles (343) for Bill Dickey. His total is the eighth highest in franchise history. Dickey hit a career high 35 doubles in 1937, but he never placed among the top ten league leaders for doubles in any season.

The number of doubles (344) for Mickey Mantle. His total is the seventh highest in franchise history. Mantle was only among the top ten league leaders in doubles twice, including his sophomore season of 1952 when he hit a career high 37.

The on-base percentage (.345) for Steve Sax in 1991. He was a former ROY for the Dodgers who played second base for three seasons in the Bronx from 1989-91. Sax led the club in on-base percentage, batting, games, runs, hits, total bases, doubles, extra-base hits, and times on base during his final season with the club.

The batting average (.346) for Joe DiMaggio in 1949. He signed a contract worth $100,000 just days before the 1949 season began, and the status of DiMaggio's legend is such that the pen he used to ink that contract can be seen on display at the Hall of Fame.

The number of doubles (347) for Derek Jeter from 1995-2006. He was fourth in the league with 44 doubles in 2004, and he hit 25 or more doubles 11 consecutive seasons from 1996-2006. Jeter is among the top 30 active major league players in 2007 for career doubles.

The number of games (348) finished as a member of the Yankees for Sparky Lyle. He closed out 56 games during his first season in the Bronx in 1972, and posted a 9-5 record with a career high 35 saves. Lyle closed out 45 or more games five times from 1972-78, and his total is the third highest in franchise history.

The batting average (.349) as a member of the Yankees for Babe Ruth. He played 15 seasons for New York, and got 2,518 hits in 2,084 games. Ruth is the franchise leader for average, on-base percentage, slugging percentage, and homeruns.

The on-base percentage (.350) for Mickey Rivers in 1977. He led the club in hits and average, but was fourth in the league batting title race. Rivers batted .326 with a career high 12 homeruns.

The ERA (3.51) for Roger Clemens in 2001. He posted a career best .870 winning percentage on the strength of a 20-3 record. Clemens made 33 starts and tossed 220 innings. He gave up just 205 hits and struck out 213 batters, and earned his sixth CYA.

The batting average (.352) for Don Mattingly in 1986. He set career highs with 238 hits and 53 doubles. His average was also a career high, but he was second in the race for the batting title behind Wade Boggs of the Boston Red Sox. Mattingly was also second in MVP balloting behind Red Sox ace Roger Clemens, and New York came in second behind Boston in the race for the division title as well.

The number of times on base (353) for Babe Ruth in 1921. He led the league and set a franchise record, but it only lasted two years. Ruth got on base a major league record 379 times in 1923.

The batting average (.354) for Tony Lazzeri in 1929. His average and 193 hits both set career highs. Lazzeri also tied a career high with 18 homeruns, and he was among the top ten league leaders in average, on-base percentage, slugging percentage, OPS, hits, total bases, RBI, and extra-base hits.

355 The on-base percentage (.355) for the Yankees in 1953. The club got on base more often and scored more runs than any other team in the league. Gene Woodling was the team leader with a .306 average and a .429 on-base percentage. Yogi Berra led the team with 27 homeruns and 108 RBI. In the 1953 World Series against the Brooklyn Dodgers, Woodling reached base at a .462 clip, and Berra posted a .538 on-base percentage as the Yankees won the title in six games.

356 The number of games (356) started for Mel Stottlemyre. His total is the third highest in franchise history. Stottlemyre made 35 or more starts in nine consecutive seasons from 1965-74, including a career high 39 games in 1969. He posted a 164-139 record, and he is sixth in franchise history for wins.

357 The batting average (.357) for Joe DiMaggio in 1941. He inspired a nation that season by hitting in 56 consecutive games. Ted Williams won the batting title with a .406 average, but DiMaggio picked up his second career MVP award.

358 The number of homeruns (358) for Yogi Berra. His total is the fifth highest in franchise history. Berra hit 20 or more homeruns in ten consecutive seasons from 1949-58, and he is among the top 75 homerun hitters in baseball history.

359 The World Series on-base percentage (.359) for Yogi Berra. He posted a .348 on-base percentage in the regular season during his career, and won 14 pennants in 17 seasons from 1947-63. Berra's best post-season effort came in 1953 against the Brooklyn Dodgers, when he reached base at a .538 clip and won his sixth title in seven years.

360 The on-base percentage (.360) for Dave Winfield in 1981. Ten out of 14 teams in the league scored more runs than did the Yankees offense that season. If not for Winfield, it would have been worse. He led the club in 11 different categories, including on-base percentage, slugging percentage, hits, total bases, doubles, and RBI. Winfield and a strong pitching staff led the Yankees to the pennant.

The number of homeruns (361) for Joe DiMaggio. His total is the fourth highest in franchise history. DiMaggio hit a career high 46 homeruns in 1937, and seven times he hit 30 or more in a season. He also ranks among the top 75 homerun hitters in baseball history.

The batting average (.362) for Bill Dickey in 1936. His career high average led the team, but was only the third best in the league. Dickey did set a record though for the highest average in history by a catcher. Mike Piazza tied him with a .362 average in 1997, and both players now share the record.

The ERA (3.63) for the Yankees in 1956. It was the second best ERA in the league, led by Whitey Ford, who posted a league leading 2.47 ERA on the season. Ford also won 19 games, and Johnny Kucks won 18. The pitching was even better against the Dodgers during the 1956 World Series. Don Larsen tossed a perfect game, and the club posted a 2.48 ERA as they won the title in seven games.

The on-base percentage (.364) for Tommy Henrich during the 1947 World Series. He batted .323 in the series against the Brooklyn Dodgers, and picked up ten hits in seven games. Henrich also had a homerun and five RBI, and won his third World Series title.

The at bats per strikeout ratio (36.5) for Everett Scott in 1924. He struck out only 15 times in 548 at bats for the ninth best ratio in franchise history. Scott is also one of the toughest 100 batters to strike out in baseball history.

The number of total bases (366) for Roger Maris in 1961. He set a career high with 81 extra-base hits, and of course he also hit a record 61 homeruns. Maris led the league in total bases, extra-base hits, homeruns, and RBI, and won his second consecutive MVP.

The number of games (367) for pitcher Lefty Gomez. His total is the tenth highest in franchise history. Gomez made 319 starts and posted a 189-101 record, and he also posted a 6-0 record during World Series games.

The number of games (368) for pitcher Ron Guidry. His total is the ninth highest in franchise history. Guidry made 323 starts, and his 26 shutouts are tied for the sixth highest total in club history. He posted a 170-91 record for the Yankees.

The at bats per strikeout ratio (36.9) for Earle Combs in 1932. His ratio is the eighth best in franchise history. Combs batted .321, and struck out only 16 times in 591 at bats. He is also one of the toughest 100 batters to strike out in baseball history.

The on-base percentage (.370) for Derek Jeter in 1996. His strong play contributed to the Yankees claiming both a division title and the first World Series title of the Joe Torre managerial era. Jeter was only 22 years old, but he batted .314 and scored 104 runs on his way to winning ROY honors.

The on-base percentage (.371) for Roger Maris in 1960. He batted .282, and led the league with a .581 slugging percentage. Maris also led the league with 64 extra-base hits, and he won his first career MVP.

The batting average (.372) for Babe Ruth in 1926. He led the club with the tenth highest average in franchise history, but placed second in the league, a feat he managed to accomplish three times in his career. Ruth also hit 47 homeruns with 150 RBI.

The batting average (.373) for Lou Gehrig in 1927 and Babe Ruth in 1931. Gehrig picked up 175 RBI and won league MVP honors. Ruth picked up 163 RBI, but only placed fifth in league MVP balloting. Both players share the eighth highest average in franchise history.

The batting average (.374) for Lou Gehrig in 1928. His average is the seventh highest in franchise history, but he only placed third among league leaders. Gehrig also led the league with a .467 on-base percentage, but what he did in the 1928 World Series was just ridiculous. He batted .545 with four homeruns and nine RBI, and the Yankees swept the Cardinals.

The World Series on-base percentage (.375) for Derek Jeter from 1996-2003. He won six pennants and played in 32 games during the World Series. Jeter batted .302, scored 27 runs, and won four rings.

The batting average (.376) for Babe Ruth in 1920. He led the club with the sixth highest average in franchise history, but only placed fourth in the race for the league batting title.

The number of at bats (377) for Mickey Mantle in 1962. He batted .321 with 30 homeruns in only 123 games. Mantle won his third career MVP, and he also led the Yankees to a World Series title for the seventh time.

The batting average (.378) for Babe Ruth in 1921 and 1924. His average is the fourth highest in franchise history. Ruth only placed third in the race for the league batting title in 1921, but three years later the same average won him his only career batting title.

The batting average (.379) for Lou Gehrig in 1930. He got a career high 220 hits, and his average is the third highest in franchise history. Gehrig did not win the batting title though, as Al Simmons hit .381 for the Philadelphia Athletics.

The number of total bases (380) for Babe Ruth in 1928. He led the league in total bases, but he did so with only 173 hits. Of course, 54 of his hits left the yard. It was the sixth and final time Ruth led the league in total bases.

The batting average (.381) for Joe DiMaggio in 1939. He won the batting title with the second highest average in franchise history. DiMaggio picked up 176 hits and 126 RBI in only 120 games, and also won the MVP.

The on-base percentage (.382) for Reggie Jackson in 1979. He also batted .297 as he posted the fourth highest on-base percentage of his career. Jackson led the club in both categories, as well as homeruns, slugging percentage, total bases, extra-base hits, and RBI.

The number of games (383) as a member of the Yankees for pitcher Johnny Murphy. His total is among the top ten in franchise history. Murphy made only 40 starts for the club, but posted a 93-53 record. He also won six pennants from 1932-46, and he won all six World Series he played in.

The on-base percentage (.384) for Don Bollweg in 1953. He signed with the Cardinals in 1942, but it was 1950 before he made his big league debut. Bollweg got only 11 at bats that season. He only batted nine times in 1951, and then he was traded to the Yankees for Billy Johnson. Bollweg did not make the club in 1952, but in 1953 he played in 70 games and batted .297 with six homeruns. The Yankees also won the pennant in 1953, and Bollweg got two at bats in the World Series. He struck out both times, and never played again in the post-season, but the Yankees won the series. Bollweg was traded again in the off-season, and by 1955 his career was over—but he did get to play for the Yankees, and he won a World Series title.

The on-base percentage (.385) for Mickey Mantle in 1968. He was in his final season and he batted only .237, but he drew 106 walks and led the club in on-base percentage, despite the fact that it was the lowest number of his career.

The number of times (386) the Highlanders made an error in 1912. It is the highest total in franchise history, and the club was so bad that the outfield made 63 errors.

The ERA (3.87) for Andy Pettitte in 1996. He led the league in wins with a 21-8 record, but placed second in CYA balloting. Pettitte also won two more games in the post-season, and he got his first ring.

The at bats per strikeout ratio (38.8) for Frank Baker in 1918. His ratio was only the fourth best in the league, but it is the seventh best in franchise history. Baker, who is a HOF third baseman, struck out only 13 times in 504 at bats.

389 The number of doubles (389) for Joe DiMaggio. His total is the fifth highest in franchise history. DiMaggio hit a career high 44 doubles as a rookie in 1936, and though he never led the league in doubles, he was among the top ten league leaders five times.

390 The on-base percentage (.390) for Mickey Mantle in 1959. He only batted .285, but he drew 93 walks for the highest on-base percentage on the team, and the sixth highest percentage in the league.

391 The number of total bases (391) for Babe Ruth in 1924. He batted .378 with 46 homeruns, and he led the league with the tenth highest number of total bases in franchise history. Ruth, Gehrig, and DiMaggio are the only names next to the top ten totals on that list.

392 The on-base percentage (.392) for Roy White in 1969. He batted .290 and led the club in both on-base percentage and average. White, who spent 15 seasons playing outfield for the Yankees, also made his first All-Star team in 1969.

393 The batting average (.393) for Babe Ruth in 1923. His average set the franchise record, but it was second in the league behind Harry Heilmann of the Detroit Tigers. Heilmann batted .403, and kept Ruth from winning the Triple Crown.

394 The number of earned runs (394) allowed by the Highlanders in 1904. The club posted a 92-59 record and gave up the lowest number of earned runs in franchise history, but placed second in the standings behind the Red Sox. The starting rotation of Jack Chesbro, Jack Powell, Al Orth, and Clark Griffith all posted a 3.00 ERA or better on the season.

395 The on-base percentage (.395) for Bernie Williams in 2001. He batted .307 and led the team in on-base percentage. Williams also scored 102 runs, surpassing the century mark for the sixth consecutive season.

396 The on-base percentage (.396) as a member of the Yankees for Wade Boggs. He spent only five seasons in the Bronx, but his on-base percentage is the tenth highest in franchise history. Boggs reached base at a .433 clip in 1994 for his highest mark with the club.

397 The on-base percentage (.397) for Earle Combs. His percentage is among the top 75 in baseball history, but it is the ninth highest in franchise history. Combs was among the top ten league leaders for on-base percentage five times, including his career high .424 mark in 1930.

398 The on-base percentage (.398) for Joe DiMaggio. His percentage is the eighth highest in franchise history, and though he never led the league in any one season, DiMaggio was among the top ten league leaders six times. DiMaggio reached base at a career high .459 clip in 1949, but he was limited to only 76 games because of injuries, and he did not qualify for official league rankings that season.

399 The number of total bases (399) for Babe Ruth in 1923. He led the league with the ninth highest total in franchise history. Ruth was fourth in the league with a career high 205 hits, but he also led the league with 99 extra-base hits.

400 The on-base percentage (.400) for George Selkirk. He batted .306 and set a career high when he reached base at a .452 clip in 1939. Selkirk batted .290 during nine seasons as an All-Star outfielder for the Yankees, and his on-base percentage is the seventh highest in franchise history.

Bernie Williams

"Don't be afraid to take risks. Make the most
of your journey—make it fun and exciting."

— Bernie Williams

Chapter Five

Bernie

Chuck Cary was a left-handed pitcher who played three seasons in the Bronx. His numbers were not great, as he posted an 11-24 record during his tenure with the club, but it is quite likely that Cary will one day soon become a footnote to part of the storied history that is Yankees baseball. Cary, who was released by the club in 1991, wore jersey number 51 for the Yankees.

New York was the first franchise to retire a number in honor of a player.

Lou Gehrig was the first player to receive the honor when his number four jersey was retired in 1939. Babe Ruth was the second player to receive the honor when the club retired his number three jersey in 1948, and Ron Guidry became the most recent when his number 49 jersey was retired in 2003. New York has retired 17 different jersey numbers, by far the most among major league teams. It is one of the most sought after, coveted, and exclusive clubs that a major league player can belong to.

Currently, no member of the Yankees wears the number 51 jersey, and it is likely that no one will ever wear it again unless it happens to be for Old-Timers Day at Yankee Stadium. Cary will see his number 51 jersey retired by the Yankees. Of course, he will be the footnote, known as the player who last wore the number 51 before the legendary Bernie Williams made his presence known on the greatest stage in professional sports.

Bernie is one of only seven players who spent at least 16 seasons playing for the Yankees, and few players who were privileged to suit it up in pinstripes did so with as much class. Many who know Bernie use the term flow to describe him, and it is a good choice—because whether they are referring to his Gold Glove ability in the outfield, his pure, sweet swing from either side of the plate, his track and field ability that gained him international recognition as a teenager, his intellectual prowess and commitment to charity work that earned him an honorary doctorate degree, or his post-baseball career as a classical guitarist and professional musician, Bernie makes everything he does look easy.

He was born in San Juan, Puerto Rico, and he grew up in Vega Alta.

His ancestry can be traced back to the slave trade that brought untold numbers of Africans to the Caribbean many centuries ago—and perhaps one reason he is successful in every endeavor is because of his keen awareness of who he is, and of what is truly important in life. Bernie signed as an amateur free agent with the New York Yankees on September 13, 1985—the same day he turned 17 years old—but baseball was not his only option. Music, academics, and track and field were all options, and he performed all of them exceptionally well. Bernie chose baseball, but those who know him best will laugh and tell you that Bernie would be a household name no matter what path he chose as a teenager. He really is that talented, but perhaps more important still is that Bernie has always been in complete control of who he is.

Bernie made his debut in the Bronx as a 22-year-old rookie in 1991.

He hit only .238, but what people noticed most was his quiet demeanor. Here was a switch-hitting outfielder with good speed and all the right tools, but what he lacked was the arrogant, self-righteous attitude carried by so many young players today who feel a sense of entitlement when it comes to being a star athlete. Bernie often played his guitar in the corner of the clubhouse, content with who he was as a player and a person—and yet, he really was driven to be the best in everything he did. He never wore his emotions openly for others to see. There was no need for that, because by the time Bernie became the everyday center fielder in 1993 his actions on the field spoke clearly enough about who he was.

His numbers on the field improved steadily each season from 1991-95, but it was during the 1995 division series against the Seattle Mariners that fans caught a glimpse of the Bernie Williams who became a Yankee legend. Bernie hit .429 in the five game series. He got nine hits, including two doubles and two homeruns, and picked up five RBI. Seattle won the series, but Bernie and the Yankees put baseball on notice that the swagger was back for the Bronx Bombers.

New York won the division title in 1996. Bernie hit .467 against the Texas Rangers during his second career playoff series. He also hit three more homeruns and picked up five more RBI, and this time the Yankees advanced to the league championship series against the Baltimore Orioles. Bernie hit a walk-off homerun in extra-innings to win game one against the Orioles, and he won MVP honors after batting .474 in the series. He hit six homeruns during the 1996 post-season—including one in the World Series against the Atlanta Braves—and the Yankees claimed their first World Series title since 1978.

Bernie became a superstar in a city that could easily have changed him.

He held on to his music though, his roots, and his family—and his success did not change him. He remains a fan favorite as much for who he is as for what he accomplished:

- Four World Series titles
- Twelve consecutive post-season appearances
- Five-time All-Star
- 1996 League Championship Series MVP
- Four-time Gold Glove recipient
- 1998 American League Batting Champion
- Eight consecutive .300 seasons from 1995-2002
- Retired with a post-season record 22 homeruns, 82 runs, and 80 RBI
- Only player in history to hit a homerun from both sides of the plate in a playoff game—and he did it twice

- Franchise switch-hitting record 204 hits in 2002
- Second in franchise history in singles and doubles
- Third in franchise history in at bats
- Sixth in franchise history in runs

Bernie quietly left the game after the 2006 season—and so far no one has put on his number 51 jersey. Good thing, too, as no one could wear it with as much respect, poise, professionalism, or flow as did Bernie.

The strikeouts to walk ratio (4.01) as a member of the Yankees for David Wells. His career ratio is the second best in franchise history. Wells played four seasons during two tours of duty with the club, and he posted a 68-28 record in 123 starts. He tossed 851 innings and struck out 557 batters, but he gave up only 139 walks.

The strikeouts to walk ratio (4.02) for Jimmy Key in 1993. His season ratio is the ninth best in franchise history. Key made 34 starts during his first season in the Bronx, and posted an 18-6 record. He struck out 173 batters in 236 innings, but gave up only 43 walks.

The number of total bases (403) for Lou Gehrig in 1936. Hal Trosky led the league with 405 total bases for the Cleveland Indians, but Gehrig's total is the eighth highest in franchise history. Gehrig also hit 49 homeruns, and won the MVP.

The winning percentage (.404) for manager Bucky Dent. He was at the helm for parts of two seasons from 1989-90, but is best known for his on the field exploits that caused countless Red Sox fans to seek therapy following the 1978 season. Dent sent Boston packing with a dramatic homerun during a one game playoff that earned the Yankees a spot in the post-season. Dodgers' fans remember him as well because he went on to earn MVP honors in the World Series against Los Angeles that same season. Unfortunately, his managerial career did not go as well. He lasted only 89 games and posted a 36-53 record.

405 The on-base percentage (.405) for Jorge Posada in 2003. He batted .281 with a career high 101 RBI. Posada also hit a career high 30 homeruns and won his fourth consecutive Silver Slugger award.

406 The slugging percentage (.406) for the Yankees in 1992. The club was third in the league in slugging. Bernie Williams, in his second season, posted an identical .406 slugging percentage as his stock in the organization began to go up. Kevin Mass, in his second to last season, also posted an identical .406 slugging percentage as his stock continued to decline. The most powerful member of the Yankees line-up was Danny Tartabull, who led the team with a .489 slugging percentage and 25 homeruns.

407 The at bats per strikeout ratio (40.7) for Bill Dickey in 1935. His ratio led the league, and is the sixth best in franchise history. Dickey, who is one of the toughest men to strike out in baseball history, went down on strikes only 11 times in 448 at bats.

408 The on-base percentage (.408) for Bernie Williams in 1997. His percentage led the team and was seventh among league leaders. Bernie also batted .328 to lead the team and place fourth in the batting title race. He also posted 107 runs and 100 RBI, in only 129 games.

409 The batting average (.409) for Derek Jeter during the 2000 World Series. Jeter batted 9 for 22 against the Mets and scored six runs during the five game series. He also hit two homeruns—including one on the first pitch of game three—won his fourth ring, and earned series MVP honors. Jeter was a guest on the *Late Show with David Letterman* following the series, and when asked about getting his fourth ring at the age of 26, he said, "One of the things playing with the Yankees is you've got all the legends that come in all the time. Yogi Berra always seems to find his way to my locker and remind me he's got ten rings—so we've got a ways to go."

410 The on-base percentage (.410) as a member of the Yankees for Charlie Keller. He was an All-Star outfielder who posted a career best .447 on-base percentage as a rookie in 1939. Keller never led the league in on-base percentage, but his career mark is one of the top 40 in baseball history, and it is the fifth best in franchise history.

411 The on-base percentage (.411) for Paul O'Neill in 1996. His percentage was tenth in the league, but it was the best on the team. O'Neill batted .302, and he also led the team by getting on base 271 times. He got on base six more times in the league championship series against the Orioles for a .429 on-base percentage, and though he struggled at the plate against the Braves during the 1996 World Series, O'Neill went on to win the first of four rings as a member of the Yankees.

412 The number of hits (412) allowed by Joe McGinnity in 1901. He made 43 starts during the inaugural season for the franchise. McGinnity pitched 382 innings and posted a 26-20 record, and more than a century later his hits total remains the franchise record. Only 13 times has a Yankee pitcher allowed as many as 300 hits in a single season—but the last time anyone on the staff gave up that many hits in a season was George Pipgras in 1928. The highest total allowed during the 1960s was 267, by Mel Stottlemyre in 1969; the highest total allowed during the 1970s was 282, by Pat Dobson in 1974; and the highest total allowed during the 1980s was 270, by Tommy John in 1980. David Wells gave up 242 hits in 2003—the most hits allowed by a Yankee pitcher since the turn of the new century.

413 The number of saves (413) for Mariano Rivera from 1995-2006. He set a franchise record with 50 saves in 2001, and then set the record again with 53 saves in 2004. Rivera holds eight of the top ten saves totals in franchise history. He also leads Dave Righetti, who is second in franchise history, by more than 200 saves.

414 The slugging percentage (.414) for Roy White in 1968. He led the team in slugging, and batted .267 during his first season as a full-time starter. White also led the club with 44 extra-base hits, and came up one shy of the team leading 18 homeruns hit by Mickey Mantle.

The on-base percentage (.415) as a member of the Yankees for Jason Giambi from 2002-06. He led the league with a .440 on-base percentage in 2005, and was among the top six league leaders four times in his first five seasons in the Bronx. Giambi closed out 2007 ranked fourth in franchise history for career on-base percentage.

The at bats per strikeout ratio (41.6) for Joe DiMaggio in 1941. His ratio was second in the league, but it is the fifth best ratio in franchise history. DiMaggio hit safely in 56 consecutive games and earned MVP honors that season, and he only struck out 13 times in 541 at bats.

The number of total bases (417) for Babe Ruth in 1927. His total is the fifth highest in franchise history, but was not even the highest on the team in 1927. Lou Gehrig posted 447 total bases that same season for the second highest total in franchise history.

The number of total bases (418) for Joe DiMaggio in 1937. He recorded 96 extra-base hits to set a career high, but trailed fellow HOF member Hank Greenberg of the Detroit Tigers, who posted 103 extra-base hits. DiMaggio picked up 15 more hits than did Greenberg though, and so he led the league with the fourth highest number of total bases in franchise history.

The number of total bases (419) for Lou Gehrig in 1930. He led the league with the third highest total in franchise history. Gehrig batted a career high .379, and hit 41 homeruns.

The number of games (420) as a member of the Yankees for pitcher Sparky Lyle. He was 57-40 out of the bullpen during seven seasons in the Bronx from 1972-78. Lyle also saved 141 games, and he is among the top ten in franchise history for games pitched.

The on-base percentage (.421) for Mickey Mantle. His percentage is among the top 20 in baseball history, but he trails only Babe Ruth and Lou Gehrig in the franchise record book. Mantle posted a career high .512 on-base percentage during his 1957 MVP campaign, and he led the league three times.

The World Series slugging percentage (.422) for Joe DiMaggio. He hit at least one homerun in seven different trips to the World Series. DiMaggio picked up 14 extra-base hits in 51 World Series games. He also scored 27 runs, drove home 30, and won nine World Series titles.

The number of strikeouts (4.23) per nine innings for Andy Hawkins in 1989. He only struck out 98 batters in 208 innings on the mound, but his ratio was the best on the team. Hawkins also led the club in ERA, wins, innings, strikeouts, starts, complete games, and shutouts.

The number of doubles (424) as a member of the Yankees for Babe Ruth. His total is the fourth highest in franchise history. Ruth hit a career high 45 doubles in 1923, and though he never led the league in doubles during any one season, his 506 career doubles place him among the top 40 in baseball history.

The slugging percentage (.425) for the Yankees in 1985. The club was third in the league in slugging. Mike Pagliarulo established himself as the starting third baseman on the strength of 19 homeruns and a .442 slugging percentage. Don Baylor was one of four Yankees with 23 or more homeruns. Rickey Henderson and Dave Winfield posted homerun totals of 24 and 26 respectively, but it was Don Mattingly who was the offensive star that season. Mattingly batted .324 with a .567 slugging percentage, and he led the team in 18 different offensive categories.

The number of games (426) as a member of the Yankees for pitcher Red Ruffing. His total is the fifth highest in franchise history, and only fellow HOF pitcher Whitey Ford tossed more innings for the club. Ruffing made 391 starts for the Yankees, and posted a 231-124 record with 261 complete games.

The on-base percentage (.427) for Willie Randolph in 1980. His percentage led the team and was second in the league. Randolph also led the team by reaching base 272 times in only 138 games. He reached base 3,491 times in his career, one of the top 100 totals in baseball history.

428 The number of at bats (428) for Scott Brosius in 2001. He won a fourth consecutive pennant during his final major league season. Brosius batted .287 with a .446 slugging percentage in 2001, and he won game five of the World Series with a walk-off homerun. But unfortunately, he struggled to a .167 average in the series, and the Yankees lost a heartbreaking game seven to the Arizona Diamondbacks.

429 The batting average (.429) for Yogi Berra during the 1953 World Series. It was the highest average of any of his 14 post-seasons, as he got nine hits in six games against the Brooklyn Dodgers. Yogi must have broken the hearts of a lot of Dodgers fans during his career, as 1953 was the fourth time he won a World Series against Brooklyn—and he did it yet again in 1956.

430 The slugging percentage (.430) for Derek Jeter in 1996. He was a 22-year-old rookie who hit .314 with 41 extra-base hits. Jeter won ROY honors, and he also got his first ring.

431 The number of strikeouts (431) for the Yankees pitching staff in 1927. It was the lowest total in franchise history. Waite Hoyt struck out only 86 batters in 256 innings, but led the team. Only two other pitchers struck out as many as 75 batters, but thanks to one of the most dominant offenses in baseball history, the club won the World Series anyway.

432 The slugging percentage (.432) for Alfonso Soriano in 2001. He was a rookie who batted .268 with 55 extra-base hits. Soriano hit 18 homeruns, stole 43 bases, and placed third in ROY balloting.

433 The ERA (4.33) for Jon Lieber in 2004. He posted the best ERA among starting pitchers on the team, he was second in innings, and his 14-10 record tied him with Javier Vazquez for the most wins on the team.

434 The slugging percentage (.434) for Mickey Mantle in 1967. He led the club in slugging despite batting only .245 in his second to last season. Mantle also drew 107 walks, demonstrating the amount of respect opposing pitchers still held for his abilities.

The on-base percentage (.435) for Jason Giambi in 2002. His percentage led the team and was third best in the league. Giambi batted .314, and blasted a team leading 41 homeruns and 122 RBI during his first season in the Bronx.

The slugging percentage (.436) for the Yankees in 1997. The club was fifth in the league in slugging, but scored 891 runs for the second highest total in the league. Tino Martinez led the team with a career high 44 homeruns and 141 RBI. Martinez also set a career high with his team leading .577 slugging percentage, and he earned a Silver Slugger award for his performance.

The slugging percentage (.437) for the Yankees in 1926. Guys like Ruth, Gehrig, and Lazzeri made it pretty unfair at times as the club posted the highest slugging percentage and scored the most runs in the league. New York won the pennant with a 91-63 record on the strength of their sluggers.

The number of games (438) started for Whitey Ford. He started a career high 39 games in 1961 when he earned CYA honors with a 25-4 record. Ford made at least 30 starts eight times for the club, and his career total is the highest in franchise history.

The slugging percentage (.439) for Phil Rizzuto in 1950. He only hit 38 homeruns in 13 seasons, but Rizzuto hit a career high seven homeruns in 1950. Rizzuto also set a career high in slugging that season, and won his only career MVP.

The on-base percentage (.440) for Jason Giambi in 2005. His percentage was the best in the league. Giambi batted only .271, but he drew a team leading 108 walks in only 139 games.

The slugging percentage (.441) for Tom Tresh in 1962. He won ROY honors after he batted .286 with 20 homeruns. Tresh also hit a homerun against the San Francisco Giants during the 1962 World Series, and he won a ring.

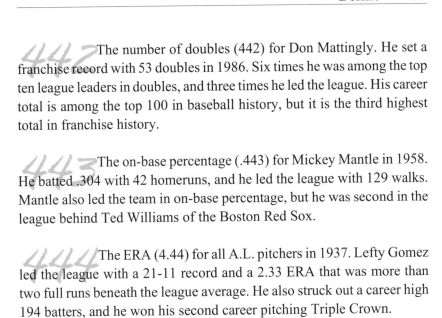

The number of doubles (442) for Don Mattingly. He set a franchise record with 53 doubles in 1986. Six times he was among the top ten league leaders in doubles, and three times he led the league. His career total is among the top 100 in baseball history, but it is the third highest total in franchise history.

The on-base percentage (.443) for Mickey Mantle in 1958. He batted .304 with 42 homeruns, and he led the league with 129 walks. Mantle also led the team in on-base percentage, but he was second in the league behind Ted Williams of the Boston Red Sox.

The ERA (4.44) for all A.L. pitchers in 1937. Lefty Gomez led the league with a 21-11 record and a 2.33 ERA that was more than two full runs beneath the league average. He also struck out a career high 194 batters, and he won his second career pitching Triple Crown.

The winning percentage (.445) for manager Johnny Keane during parts of two seasons in New York. He led the Cardinals to victory against the Yankees in the 1964 World Series, and then left St. Louis to take the helm in New York in 1965. He did not fare as well in pinstripes. Keane led the club to an 81-101 record before he was let go in 1966.

The number of at bats (446) for Elston Howard in 1961. He set career highs when he batted .348 and posted a .549 slugging percentage. Howard led the club in batting, but because he did not have enough at bats to qualify for the batting title, Mickey Mantle, who hit .317, is credited with being the Yankees leading hitter that season.

The on-base percentage (.447) for Lou Gehrig. His percentage is the fifth highest in baseball history, but it is the second highest in franchise history. Gehrig led the league in on-base percentage five times, and was among the top five league leaders 11 times. He posted a career best .478 on-base percentage during his 1936 MVP season.

The strikeouts to walk ratio (4.48) for Scott Sanderson in 1991. His ratio was second in the league, but it is the eighth best in franchise history. Sanderson posted a 16-10 record during his first season in the Bronx. He struck out 130 batters in 208 innings, but gave up only 29 walks.

449 The number of doubles (449) for Bernie Williams. He hit a career high 38 doubles in 2001. Williams was among the top ten league leaders in doubles only twice in his career, but his total is still among the top 100 in baseball history, and it is the second highest in franchise history.

450 The batting average (.450) for Reggie Jackson during the 1977 World Series. He batted 9 for 20 against the Dodgers. Jackson also hit five homeruns, won his third ring, and was named series MVP for the second time. He hit three of those homeruns during game six of the series—and his performance was so impressive that Steve Garvey, the star first baseman for the Dodgers, later said, "I must admit, when he hit his third homerun, and I was sure nobody was looking, I applauded in my glove."

451 The number of walks (451) allowed by the Yankees in 1970. It was the lowest total in the league, and it led to the club posting a 3.24 ERA that was the third best in the league. Fritz Peterson led the club with a 20-11 record and a 2.90 ERA. New York was 93-69 overall, but Baltimore boasted three pitchers who each won 20 or more games, and the Yankees came in a distant 15 games back of the division champion Orioles.

452 The World Series slugging percentage (.452) for Yogi Berra. He hit ten doubles and 12 homeruns during 75 games played in the World Series. Berra was at his best against the Brooklyn Dodgers during the 1956 World Series. He batted .360, but he hit two doubles and three homeruns for a .800 slugging percentage. Berra also had ten RBI that series, and won his seventh World Series title.

453 The number of at bats (453) for Thurman Munson in 1970. He was a 23-year-old catcher who batted .302 and hit six homeruns. Munson also scored 59 runs, picked up 53 RBI, and earned ROY honors.

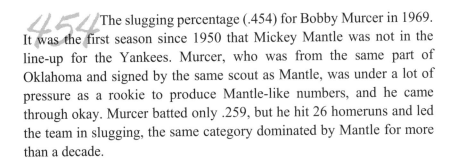

The slugging percentage (.454) for Bobby Murcer in 1969. It was the first season since 1950 that Mickey Mantle was not in the line-up for the Yankees. Murcer, who was from the same part of Oklahoma and signed by the same scout as Mantle, was under a lot of pressure as a rookie to produce Mantle-like numbers, and he came through okay. Murcer batted only .259, but he hit 26 homeruns and led the team in slugging, the same category dominated by Mantle for more than a decade.

The slugging percentage (.455) for Mel Hall in 1991. He led the team in slugging after hitting a career high 19 homeruns. Hall batted .285, and he also led the club with 80 RBI.

The number of games (456) as a member of the Yankees for pitcher Mike Stanton. He appeared in 64 or more games in six consecutive seasons from 1997-2002, and his total is the fourth highest in franchise history. Stanton posted a 31-14 record in the Bronx, and he also won three World Series titles with the club.

The number of total bases (457) for Babe Ruth in 1921. His total is a major league record. Ruth batted .378 and got 119 extra-base hits. He hit 59 homeruns, but he also hit a career high 16 triples on his way to a staggering .846 slugging percentage.

The slugging percentage (.458) for Bucky Dent during the 1978 World Series. He only posted a .321 slugging percentage during his career, and hit just 40 homeruns in 12 major league seasons. Dent got just one extra-base hit during the 1978 World Series, a double, but he did go 10 for 24 at the plate and hit .417 in the series. He also scored three runs and picked up seven RBI. Dent won series MVP honors, and got his second career ring.

The number of runs (459) for the Highlanders in 1908. It was the lowest total in the league, and it is also the lowest total in franchise history. Charlie Hemphill led the club with only 62 runs.

The number of at bats (460) for Bobby Richardson in 1960. He only hit .252, but his bat came to life in the post-season.

Richardson batted 11 for 30 against the Pirates in the World Series. He hit a grand slam, picked up 12 RBI, and won series MVP honors—but unfortunately, the Yankees lost the series in seven games, making Richardson the only player in history from a losing team to be named series MVP.

The number of assists (461) at second base for Tony Lazzeri in 1926. He was playing for Salt Lake City of the Pacific Coast League in 1925, but the next season he was a 22-year-old rookie who took over for Aaron Ward to play second base for the Yankees. Lazzeri made an immediate impact both on offense and defense, and playing alongside the likes of Ruth, Gehrig, and Combs, he placed tenth in league MVP balloting.

The batting average (.462) for Reggie Jackson during the 1978 league championship series. The Royals held Jackson to a .125 average during the 1977 league championship series, but he made up for that in a big way when the two clubs met again in 1978. Jackson batted 6 for 13 and hit two homeruns. He also scored six runs and picked up five RBI as he powered the Yankees to the pennant. Jackson hit two more homeruns against the Dodgers in the World Series, picked up eight RBI, and won his fourth career ring.

The slugging percentage (.463) for Joe Pepitone in 1966. He hit a career high 31 homeruns and led the club in slugging. Pepitone was also among the top ten league leaders for homeruns, total bases, extra-base hits, and runs.

The on-base percentage (.464) for Mickey Mantle in 1956. He batted .353 for the only batting title of his career. Mantle also led the league with 52 homeruns and 130 RBI, earning him both the Triple Crown and MVP. Legendary manager Casey Stengel, when asked about Mantle's performance, said, "He should lead the league in everything. With his combination of speed and power he should win the Triple Batting Crown every year. In fact, he should do anything he wants to do."

The on-base percentage (.465) for Lou Gehrig in 1934. He led the league in on-base percentage, a feat he accomplished five times in his career, but of greater significance is the fact that Gehrig also won the Triple Crown. Gehrig batted .363, hit 49 homeruns, and picked up 165 RBI.

466 The on-base percentage (.466) for Lou Gehrig in 1935. It was the second of four consecutive seasons from 1934-37 that Gehrig led the league in on-base percentage. Gehrig reached base at a .447 clip during his career, the fifth highest percentage in baseball history.

467 The slugging percentage (.467) for Bob Meusel in 1928. He hit only 11 homeruns, and his slugging percentage was below his career average, but Meusel did not have a bad year. He produced 45 doubles and 113 RBI while playing alongside HOF members Babe Ruth, Lou Gehrig, Tony Lazzeri, and Earle Combs. Meusel also hit a homerun during game one of the 1928 World Series as the Yankees swept the Cardinals.

468 The slugging percentage (.468) for Tim Raines in 1996. He was a dominant player in the N.L. during the 1980s, but in 17 seasons he never made it to the World Series. Raines came to the Bronx for his 18th big league season to fill a part-time role and provide veteran leadership. He responded just as the club knew he would, hitting nine homeruns and stealing ten bases in only 59 games—and courtesy of the Yankees, he got to play deep into October and won the only ring of his career.

469 The winning percentage (.469) for the Yankees in 1992. Buck Showalter guided the club to a 76-86 record during his first year as manager. Mr. Steinbrenner could not have been more displeased, as it was the fourth consecutive losing season, and the sixth consecutive season the club placed no better than fourth in the division. The next season though, the Yankees came in second with an 88-74 record, and through 2007 the club has not posted a losing record since 1992. In 1994, the club was 70-43 and held a 6.5 game lead in the standings when the season came to a halt because of the labor dispute. In 1995, Showalter led the club to the post-season for the first time since 1981, beginning a streak of 13 consecutive playoff appearances—and counting—through 2007.

470 The slugging percentage (.470) for Paul O'Neill. He surpassed the .500 mark in slugging during five of his first six seasons in the Bronx, a feat he did not accomplish once during six seasons in Cincinnati. O'Neill won the batting title in 1994 when he hit .359, but he also belted 21 homeruns in only 103 games for a career high .603 slugging percentage.

471 The batting average (.471) for Scott Brosius during the 1998 World Series. He was 8 for 17 against the Padres and hit two homeruns during his first World Series. Brosius posted a .824 slugging percentage in the series—and he also fielded the final out of the series, setting off the first of three consecutive season-ending celebrations in New York, claiming the first of three consecutive rings, and for 1998, earning World Series MVP honors. He later said, "I think it's every player's dream to get to the World Series and feel like you've played a part of the team getting there and the team winning."

472 The slugging percentage (.472) for Jorge Posada from 1997-2006. His entire career has been with the Yankees organization and he is one of the premier catchers in baseball. Posada hit 198 homeruns during his first decade in the Bronx, including a career high 30 in 2003 when he posted a .518 slugging percentage.

473 The slugging percentage (.473) for Roy White in 1970. He led the team in slugging and rejuvenated a Yankees offense that scored the fourth highest number of runs in the league. White also led the club in on-base percentage, runs, hits, total bases, and RBI.

474 The on-base percentage (.474) for Lou Gehrig in 1927. He was third in the league behind teammate Babe Ruth and Harry Heilmann of the Detroit Tigers. Gehrig also batted .373 with 175 RBI for the most legendary offensive unit in baseball history, and earned league MVP honors for his part.

475 The number of plate appearances (475) for Bernie Williams in 1994. He came to bat more often than any player on the club during the strike-shortened season. Bernie used them well, as he also led the club with 29 doubles and 80 runs in only 108 games.

476 The on-base percentage (.476) for Babe Ruth during the 1921 World Series. Ruth won three World Series titles for Boston before coming to New York, but of course he was a pitcher then, and he batted only 11 times in the post-season for the Red Sox. Ruth led the Yankees to the first pennant in franchise history in 1921, and he batted .312 with five walks against the Giants in the World Series. Ruth also scored three runs and picked up four RBI, but it was not enough, and for the first time in his career Ruth played for a losing team in the World Series.

477 The World Series on-base percentage (.477) for Lou Gehrig. He batted .361, and he walked 26 times in 34 games. Gehrig also hit ten homeruns on the grandest stage in all of sports—and he won seven pennants, and six World Series titles.

478 The on-base percentage (.478) for Lou Gehrig in 1936. It was the third consecutive season he led the league in on-base percentage. Gehrig also batted .354 with 49 homeruns, and won his second career MVP.

479 The winning percentage (.479) for the Yankees during games decided by only one run in 1988. New York was 85-76 on the season, but only 23-25 during close ballgames that came down to a single run. It gets worse, though, because the Yankees also struggled against the Boston Red Sox, posting a losing 4-9 record against their most hated division rival—and when the season ended, the difference between fifth place and first place for the division title was only 3.5 games, but it was the Yankees in fifth and the Red Sox in first.

480 The ERA (4.80) for Andy Hawkins in 1989. He did not post an impressive ERA, but he was clearly the best starter on a team that lacked good pitching. Hawkins posted a 15-15 record to lead the club in both wins and losses, but he was also the only starter on the club to not have a losing record.

481 The number of at bats (481) for Jorge Posada in 2003. He made great use of them, as he batted .281 with 30 homeruns and 101 RBI. Posada made his fourth consecutive All-Star team, and placed third in league MVP balloting.

The number of earned runs (482) allowed by the Yankees in 1952. Allie Reynolds ran off a 20-8 record in 29 starts, and he led the team with an impressive 2.06 ERA. Vic Raschi started 31 games and was equally impressive with a 16-6 record and a team best .727 winning percentage. All total, the team posted a league best 3.14 ERA, and won another World Series title.

The number of earned runs (483) allowed by the Yankees in 1953. It was the second consecutive season the club gave up the fewest earned runs in the league. Ed Lopat posted a 16-4 record, and led the team with a 2.42 ERA and a .800 winning percentage. Whitey Ford led the club with 18 wins during his sophomore season. All total, the team posted a league best ERA, and yet again, they won a World Series title.

The on-base percentage (.484) as a member of the Yankees for Babe Ruth. His percentage is a franchise record. Ruth led the league in on-base percentage ten times, and his career on-base percentage is the second highest in baseball history. Only Ted Williams, who led the league a record 12 times, got on base more often than Ruth.

The slugging percentage (.485) for Hideki Matsui from 2003-06. He played ten seasons for the Yomiuri Giants in his native Japan, and came to the Big Apple after hitting a career high 50 homeruns in 2002. Matsui quickly earned the respect of fans and teammates alike because of his work ethic and dedication to the organization. Plus, he posted some impressive numbers as well. Matsui hit 70 homeruns during 2003-05, and posted 100 RBI or more each season before an injury slowed him down in 2006.

The on-base percentage (.486) for Mickey Mantle in 1962. He led the league in on-base and slugging percentage after batting .321 with 30 homeruns. Mantle also drew 122 walks, and tied Babe Ruth for the tenth highest on-base percentage in franchise history. Only three names can be found next to the top 20 on-base percentages in franchise history: Ruth, Lou Gehrig, and Mantle.

The slugging percentage (.487) for Thurman Munson in 1973. He batted .301 and set a career high with 53 extra-base hits as he led the club in slugging. Munson also hit 20 homeruns, and made the first of six consecutive All-Star teams.

The strikeouts to walk ratio (4.88) for Mike Mussina in 2003. His ratio was the third best in the league, but it is the sixth best in franchise history. Mussina led the club with 195 strikeouts in 214 innings, but gave up only 40 walks.

The on-base percentage (.489) for Babe Ruth in 1932. It was the last time he led the league in on-base percentage, and he did so with the ninth highest mark in franchise history. Ruth batted .341, and hit 41 homeruns in only 133 games.

The slugging percentage (.490) for Reggie Jackson. He played 21 seasons in the majors, but he spent five of his most productive years in the Bronx. Jackson hit 144 homeruns and posted a .526 slugging percentage in only 653 games for New York. He also won two rings with the Yankees.

The strikeouts to walk ratio (4.91) for Mike Mussina in 2006. His ratio was the third best in the league, but it is the fifth best in franchise history. Mussina was 15-7 and struck out 172 batters in 197 innings, but he gave up only 35 walks.

The number of earned runs (492) allowed by the Yankees in 1955. Whitey Ford led the league in wins and earned *The Sporting News* A.L. Pitcher of the Year award when he posted an 18-7 record. Tommy Byrne posted a 16-5 record and led the league in winning percentage. All total, the club posted a league best 3.23 ERA, good enough for a 96-58 record and the pennant.

The on-base percentage (.493) for Babe Ruth in 1930. His percentage led the league and is the eighth highest in franchise history. Ruth batted .359, and drew 136 walks. He also hit 49 homeruns and led the league in slugging percentage.

The number of earned runs (494) allowed by the Yankees in 1963. It was the second lowest total in the league behind the Chicago

White Sox. The Yankees also posted the second best ERA in the league behind the White Sox. The clubs were also one and two in the standings at the end of the season, but where it counts the most, it was the Yankees that came out on top by 10.5 games.

495   The on-base percentage (.495) for Babe Ruth in 1931. He led the league with the seventh highest on-base percentage in franchise history. Ruth batted .373 and hit 46 homeruns, and it was the ninth time he led the league in both on-base and slugging percentage in the same season.

496   The post-season slugging percentage (.496) for Thurman Munson. New York fans love Thurman Munson for many reasons, but one of them is the way he raised his game when it counted the most. He batted .357 during six post-season series, and batted .373 during three trips to the World Series. Munson got 46 hits, including nine doubles and three homeruns, during 30 post-season games. He posted a .529 slugging percentage in the 1976 World Series, and a .520 slugging percentage in the 1977 World Series. Munson consistently demonstrated why he was the team captain as he led the club to victory in five out of the six post-season series he played in.

497   The number of strikeouts (4.97) per nine innings for Ralph Terry in 1960. His ratio was the ninth best in the league, but it was the best on the team. Terry was also the team leader in strikeouts, despite the fact that he struck out only 92 batters in 166 innings.

498   The at bats per strikeout ratio (49.8) for Yogi Berra in 1950. He led the league with the fourth best ratio in franchise history. Berra batted .328 with 28 homeruns, but he only struck out 12 times in 597 at bats.

499   The number of at bats (499) for Bernie Williams in 1998. He led the club with a .339 average, .422 on-base percentage, and a .575 slugging percentage. Bernie also hit 26 homeruns and scored 101 runs, and he did so in only 128 games.

500 The number of times (500) Derek Jeter made an out in 1997. He batted .291 and led the club with 190 hits during his sophomore season. Jeter also led the club in outs. His total was the fourth highest in the league, and it is the tenth highest total in franchise history.

Joe Torre's New York Yankees Managerial Record

Year	Games	Wins	Losses	WP	Finish
1996	162	92	70	.568	WS
1997	162	96	66	.593	WC
1998	162	114	48	.704	WS
1999	162	98	64	.605	WS
2000	161	87	74	.540	WS
2001	161	95	65	.594	AL
2002	161	103	58	.640	DIV
2003	163	101	61	.623	AL
2004	162	101	61	.623	DIV
2005	162	95	67	.586	DIV
2006	162	97	65	.599	DIV
2007	162	94	68	.580	WC
Total	1,942	1,173	767	.605	

"Competing at the highest level is not about winning. It's about preparation, courage, understanding and nurturing your people, and heart—winning is the result."

— *Joe Torre*

Chapter Six

Torre

ong time major league infielder and manager Jimmie Dykes once said of Ernie Banks, "Without him, the Cubs would finish in Albuquerque." It was a famous line, often repeated, and probably truer than many Cubs fans would care to admit. The Cubs lost, and they lost a lot—despite the presence of Banks, who hit more homeruns than any other shortstop in baseball history. Banks played for Chicago from 1953-71, but the Cubs posted a winning record only once during his first 14 seasons, and only six times during his career. Chicago never made the post-season with Banks, and only came close twice—in 1969, when they lost the division to the Mets by eight games, and in 1970, when they lost the division to the Pirates by five games. Banks is a Hall of Fame legend who played 2,528 games in his career, but because of the futility of the teams he played for he also has the distinction of having played the most games in history without making an appearance in the post-season.

Banks is on top of that list, but he is not alone, and he is in good company.

Hall of Fame shortstop Luke Appling, who played 20 seasons on Chicago's south side for the White Sox, is second with 2,422 games and no post-season. Mickey Vernon won two batting titles and tried his luck with five different clubs, but none of his 2,409 games came in the playoffs. Buddy Bell is next. He played primarily for Cleveland and Texas from 1972-89, and so he never really had a chance at all. Ron Santo was a teammate of Ernie Banks who hit 342 homeruns of his own—but every one of them came during the regular season. The man sixth on that list is well-known to Yankee fans. His name is Joe Torre.

Joe Torre made his major league debut for the Milwaukee Braves on September 25, 1960. He suited it up that day in the same clubhouse as teammates and Hall of Fame legends Hank Aaron, Eddie Mathews, and Warren Spahn—not to mention his older brother, Frank Torre.

He was a 19-year-old catcher who only three years earlier saw Frank hit two homeruns as the Braves beat the Yankees in the 1957 World Series, but now he was a major league ball player in his own right. The Braves trailed the Pittsburgh Pirates 2-0 in the bottom of the eighth inning when Torre came into the game as a pinch-hitter for pitcher Warren Spahn. Torre grounded a solid single through the middle of the infield against Pirates starter Harvey Haddix, and ignited a two run rally that tied the game. Eddie Mathews hit a homerun in the tenth to win the game 4-2.

It was a successful debut for Torre, but he only got one other at bat that season and he struck out. Joe and Frank never got to play in a game together either—at least not as teammates, though they did play against each other several times when Frank was with the Phillies.

Torre made the club for good in 1961 and placed second in Rookie of the Year balloting behind Chicago Cubs Hall of Fame outfielder Billy Williams. He hit ten homeruns and played 113 games that season. Torre made his first All-Star team in 1963 as he began to post some big numbers on offense. His playing resume is impressive:

- Hit the first homerun at Atlanta's Fulton County Stadium
- Was behind the plate for Warren Spahn's 300th career win
- Hit 36 homeruns in 1966 to set a franchise record for Braves catchers that stood until 2003

- 1965 Gold Glove recipient
- Nine-time All-Star
- In 1964 he became the first N.L. catcher in a decade to bat .300 with 20 homeruns and 100 RBI—and he did it again in 1966
- Won 1971 MVP honors as the third baseman for the St. Louis Cardinals—and he became the first N.L. player since Stan Musial in 1948 to lead the league in at least four significant offensive categories when he batted .363 with 230 hits, 137 RBI, and 352 total bases
- He became the first player-manager in major league baseball since Solly Hemus in 1959 when he took over as skipper for the Mets in 1977
- He batted .297 with 252 homeruns and 1,185 RBI in his career

Torre was not just an average player—he was good enough that the St. Louis Cardinals traded Hall of Fame first baseman Orlando Cepeda straight-up to get him from the Braves in 1969, only two seasons after Cepeda was league MVP—but he played for some very average teams. The Braves were fourth in the league when Torre was a rookie in 1961, and they never placed higher than fifth from 1962-68. St. Louis won their second consecutive pennant in 1968, brought Torre over from Atlanta, but then fell to fourth during the first season of division play in 1969.

Torre came close with the Cardinals in 1971.

St. Louis spent 25 days in first place during the first half of the season, but a seven game losing streak beginning on June 8 knocked the club out of the lead for good. The Cardinals posted a 90-72 record, but lost the division to the Pirates by seven games.

He came even closer in 1973.

St. Louis spent 44 days in first place and held a five game lead on August 5—but they lost eight games in a row beginning August 6. The Cardinals closed out the season with an 81-81 record, and the Mets won the division after posting only 82 wins. Torre never got any closer to playing in the post-season. He played 18 years and 2,209 games of major league baseball, but every one of them came during the regular season.

Joe Torre once said, "I played and managed in more than 4,000 big league games before I ever got to a World Series. But all that experience without a championship helped me prepare for what I needed to do when I came to the Yankees. When I first accepted the job at the end of 1995, my brother Frank said I was crazy. Others were writing about how I wasn't capable of doing this. All I knew was that George Steinbrenner was the guy who was going to give me the tools. Then it was up to me. I wasn't afraid of the challenge."

Of course, all he did once he joined the Yankees was punch his ticket to the Hall of Fame.

Torre managed all three national league teams he played for—the Braves, Cardinals, and Mets—and he won a division title in Atlanta for his first taste of the post-season in 1982, but it was not until he became the first native New Yorker to manage in the Bronx that Torre won a pennant and a chance to celebrate in October. It took 39 years and more than 4,000 games for Joe to win the title his brother Frank won back in 1957, but it was worth the wait. Of course, his managerial record in New York is even more impressive than his playing career. Torre made one trip to the post-season during 15 years managing in the national league, but he was perfect during 12 seasons in the Bronx from 1996-2007. He is the only manager in franchise history to lead the club to the post-season 12 consecutive times, during which he won six pennants and four World Series titles, and he has also won more games in the post-season than any manager in baseball history—including a record 14 consecutive World Series games beginning in 1996, and continuing from 1998-2000.

You could say perseverance is the lesson to learn from Joe Torre, but he might say it a bit differently: "I love players with heart, not necessarily emotion, but those who deep down are driven by something more than mind and body."

Sounds a lot like the kind of player Joe was, and the kind of manager he still is.

501 The slugging percentage (.501) for Tino Martinez in 2001. He led the Yankees with 34 homeruns and 113 RBI. Martinez was a first-round draft pick for the Mariners, but his best numbers came in the Bronx. He had 100 RBI only once in six seasons in Seattle, but 2001 was the fifth time in six seasons he hit that mark for New York.

502 The slugging percentage (.502) as a member of the Yankees for Alfonso Soriano. He hit 98 homeruns for the club from 1999-2003, and his slugging percentage is the tenth highest in franchise history.

503 The number of strikeouts (5.03) per nine innings for Pat Dobson in 1974. His ratio was the best on the team as he struck out 157 batters in 281 innings. Dobson led the club in wins with a 19-15 record, and he also led the club in innings, winning percentage, and ERA.

504 The slugging percentage (.504) for Paul O'Neill in 1993. He batted .311 and led the club in batting and slugging during his first season in the Bronx. O'Neill also began a streak of nine consecutive seasons during which he hit at least 18 homeruns. Prior to O'Neill, the last member of the Yankees to do so was Mickey Mantle.

505 The strikeouts to walk ratio (5.05) for David Wells in 2003. He was a 40-year-old veteran in his final season in the Bronx when he posted the second best ratio in the league, and the fourth best ratio in franchise history. Wells struck out only 101 batters in 213 innings, but he gave up only 20 walks.

506 The number of strikeouts (506) for the Yankees pitching staff in 1923. It was the first season for Yankee Stadium, and Babe Ruth hit as many or more homeruns (41) than did the entire rosters of the Tigers (41), Senators (26), and the Red Sox (34); but it was the pitching that led the club to a pennant-winning 98-54 record. Yankees pitchers struck out the highest total in the league, led the league with 101 complete games, and posted a league best 3.62 ERA.

507 The number of runs (507) allowed by the Yankees in 1942. Tiny Bonham led the club with a 21-5 record and a 2.27 ERA. The club gave up the fewest runs in the league and won the pennant on the strength of the pitching staff, and set a franchise record for fewest runs given up in a season.

508 The slugging percentage (.508) for Charlie Keller in 1940. He was a 23-year-old slugger who batted .286 and scored 102 runs in only 138 games. Keller got 21 big flies out of his 54 extra-base hits, and made his first career All-Star team. Keller, who went on to make five All-Star appearances and win three World Series titles during his tenure with the club, was so tough that Lefty Gomez supposedly said, "Keller didn't look like he'd been scouted, he looked like he'd been trapped." Keller hit one long ball during All-Star play—and got five more during World Series play.

509 The number of times (509) Roy White made an out in 1973. He batted 639 times, but posted only a .246 average. It was the only time in his career that White led the league in outs, but his total is also the eighth highest in franchise history.

510 The strikeouts to walk ratio (5.10) for Mike Mussina in 2001. His ratio was the second best in the league, and it is the third best in franchise history. Mussina made 34 starts and posted a 17-11 record. He struck out 214 batters, but gave up only 42 walks. In his first season pitching in the Bronx, Moose also gave the club a lot of innings—posting a team high 228 frames on the mound. Unfortunately, as the starter for the Yankees during game one of the 2001 World Series, he lasted only three innings against Arizona and got lit up for five runs. Mussina signed with the Yankees as a free agent prior to 2001 because he wanted to win a championship—but despite making the post-season seven consecutive years with the club, he will begin play in 2008 still in search of his first ring.

511 The number of at bats (511) for Jorge Posada in 2002. He batted just .268, but 61 of his 137 hits went for extra-bases and he earned his third consecutive Silver Slugger award.

512 The on-base percentage (.512) for Mickey Mantle in 1957. He batted .365 and won his second consecutive MVP award. Mantle also drew 146 walks, and his on-base percentage tied Babe Ruth for the fifth highest in franchise history.

The on-base percentage (.513) for Babe Ruth in 1924. He led the league with the fourth highest percentage in franchise history. Ruth also led the league in slugging, and he batted .378 to win his only career batting title.

The slugging percentage (.514) for Mickey Mantle in 1959. He led the club in slugging, but was third in the league for the second consecutive season. Mantle led the league in slugging four times, placed second five times, and placed outside of the top three only once. His .557 career slugging percentage is among the top 30 in baseball history.

The slugging percentage (.515) as a member of the Yankees for Roger Maris. His percentage is the ninth highest in franchise history. Maris posted a career high .620 slugging percentage during his record breaking 1961 campaign, but was only fourth among league leaders. He trailed teammate Mickey Mantle, Norm Cash of the Tigers, and Jim Gentile of the Orioles. Maris led the league in slugging only once, when he posted a .581 percentage in 1960.

The on-base percentage (.516) for Babe Ruth in 1926. He led the league with the third highest percentage in franchise history. Ruth batted .372 and drew 144 walks, and it was the third time in four seasons he led the league in both on-base and slugging percentage.

The number of at bats (517) for Mickey Mantle in 1955. He used them well as he led the league in on-base and slugging percentage. Mantle batted .306 and scored 121 runs, and he also led the league with 73 extra-base hits.

The slugging percentage (.518) as a member of the Yankees for Charlie Keller. His percentage is the eighth best in franchise history. Keller posted a career high .580 slugging percentage when he hit 33 homeruns in 1941. He was among the top ten league leaders for slugging four times, and his career mark is among the top 60 in baseball history.

519 The number of at bats (519) for Rick Cerone in 1980. It was his first season as catcher for the Yankees, and he set career highs in almost every statistically significant category: hits, average, runs, doubles, triples, homeruns, and RBI. He placed seventh in league MVP balloting, but he did not make the All-Star team.

520 The slugging percentage (.520) for Tino Martinez during the 2000 league championship series. Martinez posted a .591 slugging percentage against the Yankees during the division round of the playoffs in 1995, and led the Mariners to their first post-season series victory in franchise history. Martinez turned the tables on his former club when the Yankees met the Mariners again in 2000. Tino batted .320 and scored five runs in the six game series, and three of his eight hits went for extra-bases.

521 The number of strikeouts (5.21) per nine innings for Catfish Hunter in 1976. Catfish won 88 games and three World Series titles for Oakland during a four year stretch from 1971-74, and then cashed in on his success by signing a lucrative free agent contract to play for the Yankees in 1975. To say expectations were high is an understatement. The club missed out on the post-season during the first year of his contract, despite 23 wins from Hunter. He won only 17 games in 1976, but his strikeouts per nine innings ratio was the eighth best in the league and he led the club to their first pennant since 1964. Hunter and the Yankees went on to claim three consecutive pennants and two World Series titles from 1976-78.

522 The number of games (522) as a member of the Yankees for pitcher Dave Righetti. His total is the second highest in franchise history. Righetti made 89 starts for the club, but the rest of his games came in relief. He tossed 1,136 innings and posted a 74-61 record. Righetti is also second in franchise history with 224 saves.

523 The number of times (523) Bobby Richardson made an out in 1961. He led the league with the sixth highest total in franchise history, but he also batted .391 in the World Series and won his second career title.

The slugging percentage (.524) for Bill Skowron in 1955. He was a 24-year-old part-time first baseman who batted .319 with 12 homeruns in only 288 at bats. Skowron also made his post-season debut in 1955. He batted .333 against the Dodgers in the World Series, and he hit two doubles and a homerun for a .750 slugging percentage.

The slugging percentage (.525) for Mickey Mantle in 1954. He batted .300, and his 56 extra-base hits tied teammate Yogi Berra for the team lead. Mantle also led the team with the third highest slugging percentage in the league.

The slugging percentage (.526) as a member of the Yankees for Reggie Jackson. His slugging percentage is the seventh highest in franchise history. Jackson placed among the top seven league leaders for slugging percentage four times in five seasons playing in the Bronx.

The number of times (527) Bobby Richardson made an out in 1965. He led the league with the fifth highest total in franchise history. Richardson led the league in outs four times in five seasons from 1961-65, and all four totals rank among the top six in franchise history, but he also recorded more at bats than any other player in the league from 1961-65.

The slugging percentage (.528) for Elston Howard in 1963. He led the club with the third highest slugging percentage in the league. Howard batted .287 with a career high 28 homeruns, and earned league MVP honors.

The number of times (529) Bobby Richardson made an out in 1962. He led the league with the fourth highest total in franchise history, but he also placed second in league MVP balloting after setting career highs with a .302 average and 209 hits.

The number of times (530) Frankie Crosetti made an out in 1939. He led the league in outs for the third consecutive season, and his total is the third highest in franchise history. Crosetti, who was an All-Star infielder, struggled all season as he posted a .233 average in 656 at bats.

531 The number of runs (531) allowed by the Yankees in 1968. The club posted a 2.79 ERA, but that was only the fifth best number in the league. Mel Stottlemyre led the club in wins for the fourth consecutive season when he posted a 21-12 record. Stan Bahnsen won ROY honors after he pitched 267 innings with a 2.05 ERA. New York only won 83 games though, and came in fifth in the standings.

532 The number of hits (532) for Alex Rodriguez from 2004-06. In 471 games, Rodriguez hit 119 homeruns. He batted .299 and scored 349 runs, including a league leading 124 runs in 2005 when he earned MVP honors. Rodriguez did even better during the 2007 season—he batted .314 and led the league with 54 homeruns and 156 RBI as he won his second MVP as a member of the Yankees, and third overall. Rodriguez, when asked about the significance of his third MVP, said, "This one is a lot more satisfying—for me it has been a magical season, with my teammates and the fans, certainly a season I'll never forget."

533 The on-base percentage (.533) for Babe Ruth in 1920. He led the league with the second highest percentage in franchise history. Ruth batted .376, and he also hit 54 homeruns and drew 150 walks. It was the first time Ruth led the league in on-base percentage, a feat he accomplished ten times total before he hung up his spikes.

534 The number of doubles (534) for Lou Gehrig. His total is among the top 30 in baseball history, but it is the franchise record. Gehrig hit a career high and league leading 52 doubles in 1927, and then led the league again with 47 doubles in 1928.

535 The slugging percentage (.535) for Jason Giambi from 2002-06. He hit 41 homeruns in each of his first two seasons wearing pinstripes, and he posted slugging percentages of .527 or better in four of his first five seasons with the club. Giambi began play in 2007 with the sixth highest slugging percentage in franchise history.

536 The number of homeruns (536) for Mickey Mantle. He played his entire career in the Bronx and won four homerun titles. Mantle is one of the top 15 homerun hitters in baseball history, but he is second behind only Babe Ruth in franchise history. On May 14, 1967, Mantle hit career homerun number 500. He became the first switch-hitter in history to achieve that feat, and the bat he used to hit that homerun is on display at the Hall of Fame.

537 The winning percentage (.537) for manager Lou Piniella from 1986-88. He posted a 90-72 record as a rookie manager in 1986, but that was only good enough for a second place finish behind the hated Red Sox. Piniella posted a similar 89-73 record during his sophomore season, but the club slipped to fourth in the standings. The club continued to go the wrong way in 1988. Piniella and the Yankees were 45-48 and in fifth place when The Boss gave him the hook. Piniella won the 1990 World Series during his first year as manager of the Cincinnati Reds.

538 The slugging percentage (.538) for David Justice during the 2000 league championship series. Justice was a mid-season pick-up who had 21 homeruns in 68 games for the Indians at the time of the trade. He came through for the Yankees as well, batting .305 with 20 homeruns in only 78 games. Justice then hit two doubles and two homeruns, and picked up eight RBI against the Mariners as he earned MVP honors for the league championship series. He got his second career ring when the Yankees beat the Mets in the Subway Series.

539 The winning percentage (.539) for manager Ralph Houk from 1961-73. Houk is a World War II veteran who fought in the Battle of the Bulge and earned a Purple Heart. His toughness was as clear on the diamond as it was on the field of battle, as he spent parts of eight seasons trying to get playing time as the third-string catcher behind Yogi Berra. He only came to bat 158 times in his career and never hit a major league homerun. Houk did bat twice during World Series play, and he got one hit—but most importantly, he won two World Series titles as a player. Later he became a successful manager, and he guided the club to a 944-806 record during his tenure. Houk also won two World Series titles as manager, leading the club to back-to-back championships in 1961 and 1962.

540 The winning percentage (.540) for the Yankees in 2000. The club posted an 87-74 record for skipper Joe Torre, and though it may not sound too impressive, it was enough for a division title; and the club also won the pennant, and yet another World Series title.

The number of at bats (541) for Yogi Berra in 1955. He only batted .272, but he hit 27 homeruns and led the club with 108 RBI. Berra also earned his third career MVP.

The number of times (542) Horace Clarke made an out in 1970. Clarke batted only .251 during a league leading 686 at bats, and he also led the league and set a franchise record for outs.

The slugging percentage (.543) for Bobby Murcer in 1971. His career high slugging percentage led the team and was second highest in the league. Murcer also batted a career high .331, and he led the club with 25 homeruns.

The slugging percentage (.544) for Reggie Jackson in 1979. His slugging percentage led the club and was fifth in the league. Jackson also led the Yankees in all of the Triple Crown categories: batting, homeruns, and RBI.

The on-base percentage (.545) for Babe Ruth in 1923. His percentage led the league and set a franchise record. Ruth batted .393, and he also set a franchise record with 170 walks.

The number of strikeouts (546) as a member of the Yankees for Tino Martinez. He played 1,054 games and got 392 extra-base hits during his tenure in the Bronx, but unlike most modern sluggers, Martinez never struck out 100 times in a season.

The number of runs (547) allowed by the Yankees in 1963. Jim Bouton led the team with a 2.53 ERA in only his second major league season, and Whitey Ford led the league in wins for the third time when he posted a 24-7 record. The club posted a 3.07 ERA for the second best number in the league, and easily won a fourth consecutive pennant with a 104-57 record.

548 The number of games (548) for Bobby Brown. He made his debut in 1946 as a 21-year-old infielder who was the youngest player on the team. Brown batted .279 and scored only 233 runs during his career, and though he is relatively unknown in terms of Yankees history, his playing record is quite significant. Of the thousands upon thousands of us who grew up dreaming of playing home games at Yankee Stadium, only 80 players lucky enough to realize their dream went on to play more games in pinstripes than did Brown. He played eight seasons in the Bronx, batted .439 during four trips to the World Series, and won four titles.

549 The slugging percentage (.549) for Alex Rodriguez from 2004-06. He won MVP honors in 2005 when he hit 48 homeruns and posted a .610 slugging percentage. Rodriguez began play in 2007 with the fifth highest slugging percentage in franchise history.

550 The slugging percentage (.550) for Reggie Jackson in 1977. He led the club during his first season in the Bronx with the third highest slugging percentage in the league. Jackson batted .286, and he also led the club and was third in the league with 73 extra-base hits.

551 The ERA (5.51) for Mariano Rivera in 1995. He was a 25-year-old rookie who struggled during ten starts and nine relief appearances. Rivera gave up 71 hits in 67 innings, but he also gave up 41 earned runs. Rivera began his journey to Cooperstown when manager Joe Torre moved him to the bullpen in 1996. He posted a 2.09 ERA in 61 games, and then from 1997-2006 he posted a 2.00 ERA or less seven times.

552 The slugging percentage (.552) for Derek Jeter in 1999. He led the Yankees in slugging after 70 of his league leading 219 hits went for extra-bases. Jeter placed second among league leaders in the batting title race, triples, and runs. He was also third in on-base percentage, fourth in total bases, and fifth in OPS, but he only placed sixth in league MVP balloting.

553 The winning percentage (.553) as a member of the Yankees for pitcher Luis Tiant. He was a long-time member of the rival Red Sox, and many fans forget he played two seasons in the Bronx near the end of his career. Tiant won 229 games in 19 seasons, but he was 21-17 during 55 starts for the Yankees.

554 The number of batters (554) Sparky Lyle faced in 1977. He pitched in a career high 72 games and logged 137 innings. Lyle posted a 13-5 record with 26 saves, and earned his only career CYA.

555 The ERA (5.55) for Lefty Gomez in 1930. He was a 21-year-old rookie who pitched in 15 games. Gomez posted a 2-5 record and gave up 37 earned runs in only 60 innings. The HOF legend got on track in 1931 though. Gomez posted a 21-9 record with a 2.67 ERA during his sophomore season.

556 The on-base percentage (.556) for Babe Ruth during the 1923 World Series. He batted .368 and hit three homeruns, but Ruth also drew eight walks and reached base 15 times during six games, as the Yankees won the first title in franchise history.

557 The slugging percentage (.557) for Mickey Mantle. He led the league in slugging four times, including a career high .705 slugging percentage during his 1956 Triple Crown season. Mantle is among the top 25 in baseball history for slugging, but he is fourth in franchise history.

558 The slugging percentage (.558) for Jason Giambi in 2006. He led the club with 37 homeruns and was among the top seven league leaders for homeruns and slugging. Giambi also drove home 113 runs, surpassing the century mark for the seventh time in nine seasons.

559 The slugging percentage (.559) for Don Mattingly in 1987. He batted .327 during 141 games, and he led the club with 70 extra-base hits. Mattingly also led the club in slugging with the seventh highest percentage in the league.

560 The slugging percentage (.560) for Dave Winfield in 1982. He led the team with the second highest slugging percentage in the league. Winfield was third in the league with 37 homeruns, and he was among the top ten league leaders in seven different categories.

561 The number of at bats (561) as a member of the Yankees for Cecil Fielder. He batted .260 and hit 26 homeruns during parts of two seasons. Fielder also batted .391 during the 1996 World Series, and won his only career ring as a member of the club.

562 The strikeouts to walk ratio (5.62) for David Wells in 1998. He led the league with the second best ratio in franchise history. Wells was 18-4 and struck out 163 batters in 214 innings, but he gave up only 29 walks

563 The number of at bats (563) for Bernie Williams in 1995. He made good use of his team leading total, as he also led the club in runs, hits, total bases, triples, walks, times on base, and extra-base hits.

564 The number of at bats (564) for Willie Randolph in 1984. He batted .287, and struck out only 42 times in 142 games. Randolph scored 86 runs, and led the club with 86 walks.

565 The winning percentage (.565) for manager Yogi Berra during parts of three seasons at the helm. Berra was a rookie manager when he led the club to the pennant in 1964, but he did not manage the next season. His second stint with the club did not begin until two decades later. Berra led the club to an 87-75 record and a third place finish in 1984, but he was fired by owner George Steinbrenner in 1985 after the club began the season 6-10. Berra posted an overall 192-148 record in the Bronx.

566 The slugging percentage (.566) for Bernie Williams in 2000. He led the club in slugging, and he also posted a team high 73 extra-base hits. Bernie also set career highs when he led the club with 30 homeruns and 121 RBI, and he won his fourth ring that post-season.

567 The strikeouts to walk ratio (5.67) for Jon Lieber in 2004. He set a franchise record with the second best ratio in the league. Lieber struck out 102 batters in 176 innings, but he gave up only 18 walks.

568 The winning percentage (.568) for the Yankees in 1996. Joe Torre led the club to a 92-70 record during his first season managing in the Bronx. It was good enough to win the division by four games over the Baltimore Orioles. The Yankees went on to beat the Texas Rangers in the division series, the Wild Card Orioles in the league championship series, and the Atlanta Braves in the World Series.

569 The number of runs (569) allowed by the Yankees in 1955. It was the second lowest total in the league. Bob Turley led the club with 210 strikeouts and Whitey Ford led the club with a 2.63 ERA. The Yankees posted a 3.23 ERA overall for the best number in the league, and the result was a 96-58 record and another pennant.

570 The number of at bats (570) for Roger Peckinpaugh in 1914. He was a 23-year-old shortstop who batted just .223 with three homeruns in 157 games; but, that season he also earned the distinction of being named the second team captain in franchise history, a title he held for seven years.

571 The World Series winning percentage (.571) for pitcher Bob Turley. He won five pennants and made eight starts in the Fall Classic, but he also appeared out of the bullpen seven times. Turley posted a 4-3 record with a 3.19 ERA, and won two titles. His best series came in 1958 against the Milwaukee Braves. Turley tossed a complete game shutout in game five, got the save in game six, and then he got another win with six innings of relief in game seven. His efforts earned him series MVP honors.

572 The number of strikeouts (5.72) per nine innings for Allie Reynolds in 1954. He led the club with the fifth best ratio in the league. Reynolds posted a 13-4 record in 18 starts, and he struck out 100 batters in 157 innings during the final season of his All-Star career.

573 The slugging percentage (.573) for team captain Don Mattingly in 1986. He led the league with a career high slugging percentage after posting 86 extra-base hits, also the best number in the league. Mattingly also led the league in doubles, hits, and total bases, but placed second behind Roger Clemens in MVP balloting.

574 The number of at bats (574) for Willie Randolph in 1979. He batted only .270, but he led the club with 33 steals and 98 runs. Randolph played 13 seasons in the Bronx, and his 6,303 at bats are the tenth highest total in franchise history.

575 The slugging percentage (.575) for Bernie Williams in 1998. He led the team with a career high slugging percentage after batting .339 with 26 homeruns in only 128 games. Bernie also scored 101 runs and picked up 61 extra-base hits, but he only placed seventh in league MVP balloting.

576 The number of RBI (576) for George Selkirk. He played nine seasons, but he only played in 846 games. Selkirk posted 107 RBI in 1936, and 101 RBI in 1939, but his career total is deceptively low. He actually posted 110 RBI per 162 games throughout his career.

577 The slugging percentage (.577) for Tino Martinez in 1997. He led the club and was sixth in the league with a career high slugging percentage. Martinez was second in the league with 44 homeruns and 141 RBI. He never won a homerun title, but he did win the Homerun Derby at the 1997 All-Star game. He hit five in round one, eight in round two, and then he defeated Larry Walker 3-1 in the final round to win the competition.

578 The number of runs (578) for the Yankees in 1919. The total was fourth highest among eight teams in the league, and the club placed third in the standings with an 80-59 record. The club bought Babe Ruth from the Red Sox in the off-season, and in 1920 the Yankees led the league with 948 runs and won the first pennant in franchise history.

579 The slugging percentage (.579) for Joe DiMaggio. He is among the top 15 for slugging in baseball history, but he is third in franchise history. DiMaggio led the league and set a career high when he posted a .673 slugging percentage with 46 homeruns in 1937. He also led the league in slugging in 1950.

580 The number of extra-base hits (580) for Derek Jeter from 1995-2006. He began 2007 in tenth place for most extra-base hits in franchise history, but he has since surpassed HOF legends Tony Lazzeri and Bill Dickey to move into eighth place, and he now has modern-day legend Don Mattingly in his sights for the seventh position.

581 The slugging percentage (.581) for Roger Maris in 1960. He hit 39 homeruns and led the league with 64 extra-base hits. Maris also led the league with 112 RBI, was second in the league with a .952 OPS, and won his first MVP.

582 The number of games (582) for Buck Showalter as manager from 1992-95. He led the club to a disappointing 76-86 record his first season, but improved to 88-74 in 1993. New York led the division at 70-43 when the labor dispute ended the 1994 season, but Showalter guided the club to the post-season for the first time since 1981 when he posted a 79-65 record and won the Wild Card in 1995. But Showalter left the Bronx to join the newly formed Arizona Diamondbacks, and so he was not around when the Yankees won the 1996 World Series. Showalter left Arizona after the 2000 season, and he missed out again as the Diamondbacks beat the Yankees to win the 2001 World Series.

583 The number of hits (5.83) allowed per nine innings for Russ Ford in 1910. He led the league with the second best ratio in franchise history. Ford pitched 299 innings as a 26-year-old rookie, but gave up only 194 hits.

584 The number of hits (5.84) allowed per nine innings for Al Downing in 1963. He led the league with the third best ratio in franchise history. Downing pitched 175 innings as a 22-year-old rookie, but gave up only 114 hits. Unfortunately, he got shelled during his only start of the 1963 World Series, and he never won a ring.

585 The slugging percentage (.585) for Joe DiMaggio in 1950. He was among the top six league leaders in slugging every season that he played from 1936-48, and he would have been again in 1949 except injuries kept him from getting enough at bats to qualify. DiMaggio came right back in 1950, and he led the league in slugging when he batted .301 with 32 homeruns in his second to last season.

586 The number of walks (586) as a member of the Yankees for Paul O'Neill. He batted .303 for the club, and posted an impressive .377 on-base percentage in nine seasons. O'Neill drew a career high 102 walks in 1996, the same season the Yankees won their first World Series title in 18 years.

587 The number of runs (587) allowed by the Yankees in 1969. The club posted a 3.23 ERA for the second best number in the league, but unfortunately, the offense scored the second lowest run total in the league, and the result was an 80-81 record.

588 The number of runs (588) allowed by the Yankees in 1975. Catfish Hunter led the league in wins with a 23-14 record during his first season in the Bronx. He also posted a 2.58 ERA and placed second in CYA balloting. Doc Medich and Rudy May won 14 and 16 games respectively for the club, and all total, the Yankees gave up the second lowest run total in the league. The offense struggled though, and the club missed the playoffs after posting an 83-77 record.

589 The number of strikeouts (5.89) per nine innings for Allie Reynolds in 1952. He led the club with the second best ratio in the league, but he also led the league with 160 strikeouts in 244 innings. Reynolds was 20-8 and placed second in league MVP balloting. He also struck out 18 batters in 20 innings against the Dodgers in the 1952 World Series, and won his fifth career title.

590 The number of at bats (590) for Roger Maris in 1961. He used them pretty well, seeing as he set career highs with 61 homeruns, 132 runs, and 142 RBI.

591 The winning percentage (.591) for manager Billy Martin during eight seasons in the Bronx. He got fired by George Steinbrenner five times, but his love for the Yankees kept bringing him back. Martin posted a 556-385 record during his tenure. He also won two pennants and one World Series title.

592 The slugging percentage (.592) for Mickey Mantle in 1958. He led the league with 42 homeruns and 307 total bases, but he tied former teammate Bob Cerv of the Kansas City Athletics for the second highest slugging percentage in the league. Rocky Colavito posted a .620 slugging percentage for the Cleveland Indians to lead the league.

593 The winning percentage (.593) for the Yankees in 1962. Ralph Houk managed the club to a 96-66 record and the pennant, and Mickey Mantle batted .321 and won MVP honors. Pitcher Ralph Terry came up big against the San Francisco Giants in the 1962 World Series. He tossed a complete game 1-0 shutout in game seven to win the title.

594 The number of walks (594) allowed by the Yankees in 1959. It was the second highest total in the league and the result was a 79-75 record and no post-season. Whitey Ford led the club with 89 walks, but he was also the team leader in wins, strikeouts, and innings.

595 The number of at bats (595) for Tino Martinez in 1996. He led the club in at bats, and made good use of them as he hit .292 and led the club with 117 RBI. Martinez also won his first ring when the Yankees defeated the Braves in the 1996 World Series.

596 The number of runs (596) as a member of the Yankees for Joe Gordon. He scored a career high 112 runs in 1940, but his best season was 1942 when he batted .322 and won league MVP honors. Gordon played exactly 1,000 games for the Yankees, and he batted .271 with exactly 1,000 base hits. He also won five pennants and four World Series titles.

597 The winning percentage (.597) for manager Miller Huggins during 12 seasons in New York. Huggins posted a 1,067-719 record from 1918-29. He won six pennants and three World Series titles.

598 The slugging percentage (.598) for Jason Giambi in 2002. He led the team with the fourth highest percentage in the league. Giambi batted .314 with 76 extra-base hits, and he also led the club with 41 homeruns during his first season in the Bronx.

599 The number of at bats (599) for Don Mattingly in 1988. He batted .311, and he led the club with 186 hits in only 144 games. It was also the fifth consecutive season he batted .300 or higher. Dwight Gooden, who at the time was the ace of the New York Mets, once said of Mattingly, "I'm glad I don't have to face that guy every day. He has that look that only a few hitters have. I don't know if it's his stance, his eyes, or what—but you can tell he means business."

600 The number of games (600) finished for Mariano Rivera from 1995-2006. He owns the franchise record by a large margin. Rivera began 2003 tied for second with Sparky Lyle, but by the end of that season he surpassed the record 379 games finished held by Dave Righetti, and he continues to add to his total.

Don Mattingly

"That's my game, not to be noticed. I'm not worried about the lights. I just want to keep doing my job and be consistent."

— Don Mattingly

Chapter Seven

Mattingly

*I*t is an honor to be named captain of any team, but to earn the title team captain of the New York Yankees a player must first prove themselves worthy under the most intense scrutiny the sporting world has to offer. Some players want to be in New York because of the bright lights of the media, some thrive under that kind of pressure, and others wilt—but on occasion, there are those who come to New York only because they are getting a chance to play baseball, and that is the only thing they care about.

Don Mattingly retired more than a decade ago, but his popularity among Yankee fans has only grown stronger since his playing days. He grew up in the heartland of America, in Evansville, Indiana, a long way from the bright lights of New York City, but when the All-American farm boy came to the city to play baseball he did not wilt beneath the intense pressure and scrutiny of the media or the city. Mattingly did not intentionally seek out the spotlight either, but instead he quietly went about the business of playing baseball the only way he knew how—in complete control of both his emotions and his actions. Mattingly once said, "The athlete I admire as much as anyone is Julius Erving. That's who I want to be like. I remember a few years ago watching a playoff game between Philadelphia and Portland, and there was a fight or something between Maurice Lucas and Darryl Dawkins and things were getting crazy on the court. Then the camera pans over and shows a picture of Dr. J. He was watching from the bench, totally composed and within himself."

He earned the nickname Donnie Baseball because he played the game exactly as he thought it should be played, totally composed and within himself.

Mattingly was a 24-year-old first baseman when he won the 1984 batting title.

In 1985, he earned Most Valuable Player honors and was named Major League Player of the Year. He also did something else extraordinary—he stood up to owner George Steinbrenner for his teammates after Mr. Steinbrenner suggested the Yankees should hold a workout on an off-day. Mattingly said the players could use a break, prompting Mr. Steinbrenner to tell the press, "He ought to get a real job, be a taxi driver or steelworker and find out what life and hard work are all about." The team got the day off though, and Mattingly quietly went back to work, dismantling every pitcher in the American League. The next spring, Mattingly said, "George wants to win, but I want to win as much as he does and I was always taught that we are all in this together—that the team was more important than any one player. There is not a franchise player in baseball. So when he goes off and says stuff about Dave Winfield being Mr. May or starts firing back at me about steelworkers and farmers just because I'm from Indiana, I don't agree with it." Then he quietly went back to work, and set the franchise record with 238 hits during the 1986 season.

Sports Illustrated did an article on Don Mattingly for their special 1986 baseball preview issue. In that article, E.M. Swift wrote "Composure—that's what Mattingly has. It is what any young player needs in order to thrive on Steinbrenner's Yankees, or to win a batting title, or to drive in runs during a pennant race." He took his composure and his success back to Indiana in the off-seasons, and he could be found frequently shooting free throws and listening to Bruce Springsteen in the restaurant he owned called Mattingly's 23, content to be away from the bright lights, but always intent on returning to the city for the sole purpose of playing the game to the best of his ability.

He was a fan favorite because he was authentic—that and he could flat hit.

Mattingly continued to etch his name into the franchise record book with a quiet consistency that was formally recognized in 1991 when owner George Steinbrenner named him as the tenth team captain in franchise history. He earned the title, but he never sought it out. He came to play, the right way, and the awards and accolades came later, on their own. His number 23 jersey was retired by the Yankees in 1997 and his plaque in Monument Park at Yankee Stadium reads, "A humble man of grace and dignity, a captain who led by example, proud of the pinstripe tradition and dedicated to the pursuit of excellence—a Yankee forever."

601 The number of at bats (601) for Alex Rodriguez in 2004. He batted .286 and hit 36 homeruns during his first season in the Bronx. Rodriguez also led the club with 308 total bases and 28 steals.

602 The winning percentage (.602) for the Yankees in 1985. Don Mattingly batted .324 to lead the club, and Ron Guidry led the league in wins when he posted a 22-6 record. George Steinbrenner fired Yogi Berra after a 6-10 start, and Billy Martin led the club to a 91-54 record the rest of the way. The club was 97-64 overall, but still came up two games short of the Blue Jays for the division title.

603 The slugging percentage (.603) for Paul O'Neill in 1994. He batted .359 and won the batting title after getting 132 hits in only 103 games. O'Neill also got 47 extra-base hits, and he led the club with the fourth highest slugging percentage in the league.

604 The number of runs (604) allowed by the Yankees in 1965. The team posted a 3.28 ERA, but it was only the fifth best in the league.

Mel Stottlemyre led the club and was second in the league in wins when he posted a 20-9 record, but overall the team struggled to a 77-85 record and a sixth place finish.

605 The winning percentage (.605) for the Yankees in 1999. The club was 98-64 and won the division by four games over the Red Sox. Boston won the Wild Card, but the Yankees beat the Red Sox in the league championship series to win the pennant, and then they beat the Braves in the World Series for the second time in four seasons.

606 The number of at bats (606) for Bobby Murcer in 1974. He led the club in at bats, and he also led the club with 166 hits and 225 times on base. Murcer made his fourth consecutive All-Star team, and he was also among the top seven RBI leaders for the fourth consecutive season.

607 The winning percentage (.607) for manager Joe Torre from 1996-2006. He posted a 1,079-699 record during his first 11 seasons in the Bronx. Torre also led the club to six pennants and four World Series titles.

608 The slugging percentage (.608) for Hideki Matsui during September and October of 2006. On May 12, 2006, Matsui broke his left wrist as he attempted to make a sliding catch against the Boston Red Sox. He was not expected to play the rest of the season, but Matsui, who had played every regular season game for the Yankees from 2003-05, made his return on September 12. He did so by going 4 for 4 with an RBI and a run scored. Matsui batted .412 with three homeruns during the Yankees' final 18 games.

609 The number of walks (609) allowed by the Yankees in 1960. It was the second highest total in the league, led by Bob Turley who gave up 87 walks. The Yankees overcame the obvious control issues though and posted a 3.52 ERA that tied Baltimore for the best in the league. On September 16, the Yankees and Orioles were also tied in the standings, but New York won 15 games in a row to close out the season with a pennant-winning 97-57 record.

The slugging percentage (.610) for Alex Rodriguez in 2005. He led the league in slugging for the second time in his career, but it was the sixth time from 1996-2005 that he surpassed the .600 mark in a season. Rodriguez also hit 48 homeruns to win his fourth homerun title, and he earned his second MVP.

The number of extra-base hits (611) for Tony Lazzeri. His total is the tenth highest in franchise history. Lazzeri hit a career high 18 homeruns four times, and he was among the top ten league leaders for extra-base hits three times in four seasons from 1926-29.

The number of hits (6.12) allowed per nine innings for Bob Turley in 1957. He led the league with the fourth best ratio in franchise history. Turley was 13-6, and he gave up only 120 hits in 176 innings.

The number of hits (6.13) allowed per nine innings for Bob Turley in 1955. It was the second consecutive season he posted a league best ratio, and he did it with the fifth best ratio in franchise history. Turley gave up only 168 hits in 246 innings.

The number of strikeouts (614) for pitcher Spud Chandler. He struck out a career high 138 batters in 1946, and though he was not known for high numbers of strikeouts, he was a consistent player who posted a 2.85 ERA and a .717 winning percentage in 11 seasons. Chandler also won MVP honors in 1943, and three World Series titles.

The number of hits (6.15) allowed per nine innings for Ron Guidry in 1978. He led the league with the sixth best ratio in franchise history. Guidry gave up only 187 hits in 273 innings, and won both CYA and Major League Player of the Year honors.

The number of at bats (616) for Thurman Munson in 1976. He batted .302 when he won ROY honors in 1970, and he batted .302 again in 1976 as he earned MVP honors.

The number of extra-base hits (617) for Bill Dickey. The HOF backstop was only among the league leaders in extra-base hits once, when he got a career high 66 in 1937, but his total is the ninth highest in franchise history.

The number of runs (618) allowed by the Yankees in 1922. The club posted a 3.39 ERA and gave up the fewest runs in the league. Joe Bush led the club with 26 wins, and overall the Yankees posted a 94-60 record and won their second consecutive pennant.

The number of at bats (619) for Lou Gehrig in 1931. He used his career high at bats total to pick up a franchise record 184 RBI. Gehrig is second behind Mickey Mantle for the most at bats in franchise history with 8,001.

The slugging percentage (.620) for Roger Maris in 1961. In addition to setting the homerun record, Maris also set career highs for hits, on-base percentage, slugging percentage, total bases, extra-base hits, and RBI. Maris also won the first of three career World Series titles.

The number of runs (621) allowed by the Yankees in 1967. The club posted a 3.24 ERA that was fourth best among A.L. teams. Mel Stottlemyre led the club in wins for the third consecutive season, and Al Downing led the club with a 2.63 ERA that was eighth best in the league. But the Yankees offense was the worst in the league, so despite some strong pitching, the club posted a disastrous 72-90 record.

The winning percentage (.622) for pitcher Catfish Hunter in 1975. He led the league in wins with a 23-14 record, and his winning percentage was the best on the team. Hunter was second in the league with a 2.58 ERA, and he was a true workhorse as he completed 30 starts and led the league with 328 innings.

The winning percentage (.623) for manager Casey Stengel during 12 seasons in the Bronx. Stengel managed the team to a 1,149-696 record, ten pennants, and seven World Series titles. The Yankees won five consecutive titles from 1949-53, Stengel's first five seasons with the club.

The number of plate appearances (624) for Gil McDougald in 1957. His total led the club, and he made the most of them as he put together his most productive season. McDougald batted .289 and got a career high 156 hits. He was among the top seven league leaders for on-base percentage and runs, and he led the league with 19 sacrifice bunts and nine triples. McDougald, who won ROY honors in 1951, placed fifth in league MVP balloting.

The batting average (.625) for Babe Ruth during the 1928 World Series. He batted 10 for 16 in a four game sweep of the Cardinals. Ruth hit three doubles and three homeruns, and scored nine runs. He also posted a 1.375 slugging percentage, and won his sixth World Series title.

The number of runs (626) as a member of the Yankees for Ben Chapman. He played seven seasons in the Bronx and his runs total is one of the top 35 in franchise history. Chapman, who scored a career high 120 runs in 1931, batted .305 during his tenure with the club. He was also on the club that beat the Chicago Cubs in the 1932 World Series.

The winning percentage (.627) for manager Joe McCarthy during 16 seasons in the Bronx. He posted a 1,460-867 record and won eight pennants. McCarthy led the club to seven World Series titles, including four in a row from 1936-39.

The number of at bats (628) for Bobby Cox. Originally signed by the Dodgers in 1959, Cox did not make his big league debut until nine years and three franchises later. He batted .225, and played only 220 games for the Yankees. Of course, Cox is better known as the longtime manager of the Atlanta Braves than he is for his brief major league career. He won the 1995 World Series as manager of the Braves, and he almost won a second title in 1996 against the Yankees. Atlanta won the first two games of the 1996 World Series before New York won four in a row to claim the title. New York beat Cox and the Braves again in the 1999 World Series, this time taking all four games.

The number of plate appearances (629) for Phil Rizzuto in 1951. His total led the club, and he also led the club in singles, times on base, and steals.

630 The winning percentage (.630) for the Yankees in 1956. The club was 97-57, and won the pennant by nine games over the Cleveland Indians. It was the seventh pennant for manager Casey Stengel. The Yankees went on to beat the Brooklyn Dodgers in the 1956 World Series, giving Stengel his sixth title.

631 The number of walks (631) allowed by Waite Hoyt as a member of the Yankees. His total is the tenth highest in franchise history, but he also tossed the seventh highest total of innings in franchise history. Hoyt won 157 games during ten seasons with the club.

632 The slugging percentage (.632) for Lou Gehrig. His slugging percentage is the third highest in baseball history, and it is the second highest in franchise history behind Babe Ruth. Gehrig only led the league in slugging percentage twice, but he placed second during a season Ruth led the league in slugging four times.

633 The number of walks (633) allowed by Ron Guidry. His total is the ninth highest in franchise history, but Guidry also pitched the sixth highest total of innings in franchise history. He never gave up more than 80 walks in a season, but he struck out 6.69 batters per nine innings for one of the top 100 ratios in baseball history.

634 The winning percentage (.634) for pitcher Mike Mussina from 2001-06. He spent ten seasons pitching for the Orioles before he came to New York. Mussina won 15 or more games four times during his first six seasons in the Bronx, and his record during that time was an impressive 92-53.

635 The number of walks (635) for the Yankees in 1927. The club drew the highest number of walks in the league. Babe Ruth led the league with 137, and Lou Gehrig was second in the league with 109. The Yankees posted a .381 on-base percentage as a team, and scored a major league leading 975 runs.

636 The winning percentage (.636) for the Yankees in 1951. The club posted a 98-56 record and won the pennant by five games over the Cleveland Indians. Ed Lopat led the team with a 21-9 record, and he also tossed two complete game victories against the New York Giants in the 1951 World Series. He gave up only one run in 18 innings, as the Yankees won a third consecutive title.

637 The number of at bats (637) for Joe DiMaggio in 1936. He was a 21-year-old rookie who was sixth in the league with 206 hits. DiMaggio led the league with 15 triples, and was among the top ten leaders in slugging, runs, total bases, doubles, homeruns, and RBI.

638 The number of plate appearances (638) for Mickey Mantle in 1955. His total led the team, and he made good use of them as he also led the club in batting, runs, on-base percentage, slugging percentage, hits, total bases, doubles, homeruns, extra-base hits, and times on base.

639 The number of at bats (639) for Roy White in 1973. He only batted .246, but he led the club with 88 runs and 16 steals. White played 15 seasons in the Bronx, and his 6,650 at bats are the ninth highest total in franchise history.

640 The number of hits (6.40) allowed per nine innings for Spec Shea in 1947. He was a 26-year-old rookie who led the league with the seventh best ratio in franchise history. Shea gave up only 127 hits in 178 innings, and posted a 14-5 record. Shea was also 2-0 during the 1947 World Series against the Brooklyn Dodgers. He gave up only ten hits in 15 innings as the Yankees won the series.

641 The number of at bats (641) for Roberto Kelly in 1990. His total led the club as he played all 162 games for the only time in his career. Kelly batted .285, and led the team in runs, hits, total bases, doubles, triples, extra-base hits, and times on base. He made four trips to the playoffs during 14 seasons, but none were with the Yankees, and he never won a ring. Kelly lost in the division series against the Yankees in 1998 and 1999 as a member of the Texas Rangers.

642 The number of plate appearances (642) for Willie Randolph in 1980. His total led the team, and he used them to work a league leading 119 walks. Randolph also led the club with a .427 on-base percentage and 99 runs.

The number of plate appearances (643) for Willie Randolph in 1982. His total led the club for the second time in three seasons, and he also led the club in runs, hits, walks, steals, and times on base.

The number of plate appearances (644) for Wade Boggs in 1993. His total led the club during his first season in the Bronx. Boggs batted .302 in 143 games, and posted a team leading .378 on-base percentage.

The winning percentage (.645) for the Yankees in 1923. Miller Huggins guided the club to a 98-52 record and a third consecutive pennant. It was the first season for Yankee Stadium, and the Yankees beat the Giants in the 1923 World Series for the first title in franchise history.

The number of hits (6.46) allowed per nine innings for Ray Caldwell in 1914. His ratio was the second best in the league, and it is the eighth best in franchise history. Caldwell was 17-9, and in 213 innings he gave up just 153 hits.

The slugging percentage (.647) for Lou Gehrig during the 1937 World Series. He got five hits and batted .294 against the New York Giants, but three of his hits went for extra-bases, including the tenth and final World Series homerun of his career. It was also the second consecutive season the Yankees beat the Giants in the World Series.

The number of at bats (648) for Earle Combs in 1927. He used his career high at bats total to also set career highs with 231 hits and a .356 average. Combs led the league in hits, and he also batted .313 against the Pirates during the 1927 World Series as he won the first of three career titles.

The number of strikeouts (6.49) per nine innings for Jack McDowell in 1995. His ratio was the best on the team, and his 157 strikeouts were the eighth highest total in the league. McDowell also led the club with a 15-10 record and a 3.93 ERA, but he opted to sign as a free agent with the Cleveland Indians in the off-season. The Indians won the pennant in 1995, but lost in the division series in 1996 while the Yankees went on to win the World Series. McDowell never got a ring.

650   The winning percentage (.650) for pitcher John Candelaria in 1988. He posted a 13-7 record for the most victories and the highest winning percentage on the team. Candelaria tossed 157 innings in 24 starts, but it was his only season in the Bronx.

651   The winning percentage (.651) for the Yankees in 1938. Jimmie Foxx won MVP honors for Boston, but the Red Sox were a distant second behind the Yankees in the standings. Joe McCarthy managed the club to a 99-53 record, and the Yankees swept the Chicago Cubs to win their third consecutive World Series title.

652   The number of at bats (652) for Steve Sax in 1991. He used his team leading number of at bats well, as he also led the club in hits, average, on-base percentage, runs, total bases, doubles, extra-base hits, and times on base.

653   The number of hits (6.53) allowed per nine innings for Bob Turley in 1958. He led the league with the ninth best ratio in franchise history. Turley gave up only 178 hits in 245 innings. He also posted a 21-7 record, and won the CYA.

654   The number of at bats (654) for Derek Jeter in 1997 and 2005. His total is the tenth highest in franchise history. Jeter used them well both times. He batted .291 and scored 116 runs in 1997. Jeter batted .309 and scored 122 runs in 2005.

655   The number of plate appearances (655) for Dave Winfield in 1987. His total led the club because he also played in a team high 156 games that season. Winfield only batted .275, but he was good enough to earn his 11th consecutive All-Star appearance.

656   The number of at bats (656) for Frank Crosetti in 1939. He led the club with the ninth highest total in franchise history. Crosetti only batted .233, but he surpassed 100 runs for the fourth consecutive season.

657 The winning percentage (.657) as a member of the Yankees for pitcher Ed Lopat. He posted a 113-59 record during eight seasons in the Bronx, and his winning percentage is the tenth best in franchise history. Lopat won a career high 21 games for the club in 1951, and he ranks among the top 15 in franchise history for career wins.

658 The number of times (658) the Yankees struck out in 1955. HOF legend Mickey Mantle led the club with 97 strikeouts, but he also led the club with 37 homeruns. Yogi Berra hit 27 homeruns, but he struck out only 20 times all season. Only three teams in the league posted fewer strikeouts, but no other team hit as many homeruns.

659 The number of homeruns (659) as a member of the Yankees for Babe Ruth. He hit 334 of his homeruns for the Yankees at home, and the locker that held his uniform at Yankee Stadium is on permanent display at the Hall of Fame.

660 The number of runs (660) allowed by the Yankees in 1985. The total was the third lowest in the league. Ron Guidry led the league with a 22-6 record, Phil Niekro was 46 years old but won 16 games, and Dave Righetti earned 29 saves on the season—but the two teams that gave up fewer runs, the Toronto Blue Jays and Kansas City Royals, made the post-season.

661 The number of plate appearances (661) for Thurman Munson in 1975. His total led the club, and he used them to bat .318 and surpass 100 RBI for the third consecutive season.

662 The number of at bats (662) for Bobby Richardson in 1961. He led the club with the eighth highest total in franchise history. Richardson batted only .261 during the regular season, but he batted .391 against the Cincinnati Reds during the 1961 World Series.

663 The winning percentage (.663) for pitcher Atley Donald. He was 65-33 in his career, and his winning percentage is the ninth highest in franchise history. Donald made his big league debut in 1938, appearing in two games and picking up one loss. He was 13-3 in 1939 though, and he led the league with a .813 winning percentage. Donald was 0-1 in his career during the post-season, but he was on the club that won the 1941 World Series.

664 The number of at bats (664) for Bobby Richardson in 1965. He led the club with the seventh highest total in franchise history. Richardson struggled at times that season, but he still managed 164 hits and scored 76 runs, and he made the All-Star team for the sixth time.

665 The slugging percentage (.665) for Mickey Mantle in 1957. He led the club with the second highest slugging percentage in the league. Mantle also batted .365 and won his second consecutive MVP award. Ted Williams was the only player in baseball to post a higher slugging percentage than Mantle, and the top seven major league leaders in slugging from 1957 are all legendary members of the HOF: Williams, Mantle, Willie Mays, Stan Musial, Hank Aaron, Duke Snider, and Ernie Banks.

666 The number of plate appearances (666) for Roy White in 1972. His total led the club, as did his .384 on-base percentage, but the club struggled and was never in contention. Baseball also struggled through a players' strike in 1972 that cancelled the first two weeks of the season. White played all 155 games on the Yankees' schedule, but his total was second behind Ed Brinkman, who played in all 156 games on the Tigers' schedule. The strike caused the difference in games, but though it had no real effect on White or the Yankees, it sure burned Boston. The Red Sox also played 155 games, but they lost the division to the Tigers by a half-game, and Boston was not given the chance to play an additional game because Detroit won the season series between the two clubs.

667 The winning percentage (.667) for the Yankees in 1936. The club won the pennant after posting a 102-51 record. The New York Giants won the N.L. pennant with a 92-62 record, but they were no match for the Yankees in the World Series, as manager Joe McCarthy won the first of four consecutive titles from 1936-39.

668 The number of plate appearances (668) for Bobby Richardson in 1963. He led the club with the fourth highest total in the league. Richardson used his total to lead the club in hits, singles, and steals.

669 The winning percentage (.669) as a member of the Yankees for pitcher Carl Mays. He was 5-11 in 1919 before the Red Sox traded him to the Yankees, but after the trade he posted a 9-3 record the rest of the season. Mays then posted a 26-11 record in 1920, and came back in 1921 with a 27-9 record. He is one of only seven players in franchise history to win 26 games in a season, but he is the only player to do it twice.

670 The number of walks (670) for Earle Combs. He only struck out 278 times in 12 seasons, giving him an impressive 2.41 walks per strikeout ratio during his career.

671 The slugging percentage (.671) for Joe DiMaggio in 1939. He led the club and was second in the league in slugging after getting 68 extra-base hits in only 462 at bats. DiMaggio also hit .381 to win the batting title, and won his first MVP.

672 The number of RBI (672) as a member of the Yankees for Bill Skowron. His total is among the top 25 in franchise history. Skowron batted .309 with a career high 91 RBI in 1960. He also won his seventh pennant and fourth World Series title with the club in 1962, but the Yankees traded him to the Dodgers in the off-season. Skowron won his fifth career title when the Dodgers beat the Yankees in the 1963 World Series.

673 The winning percentage (.673) for the Yankees in 1961. Ralph Houk guided the club to a 109-53 record during his first season managing in the Bronx. The Yankees won the pennant by eight games over the Tigers, and then beat the Cincinnati Reds in five games to win the World Series.

674 The number of runs (674) for the Yankees in 1991. Only two teams scored fewer runs, and the club gave up 103 more runs than it scored. It took only 24 homeruns for Matt Nokes and 80 RBI for Mel Hall to lead the team. Steve Sax batted .304, but his team leading 85 runs were not even among the top ten league leaders. It was a dismal season as the club posted a 71-91 record and a fifth place finish.

The number of earned runs (675) allowed by the Yankees in 1990. The offense scored only 603 runs and statistically was the worst in the league. The pitching wasn't much help either. Only two teams gave up more runs, earned or otherwise, and the club was dead last in the division with a 67-95 record.

The number of runs (676) for the Yankees in 1945. The total was the best in the league, but the club could do no better than an 81-71 record and a fourth place finish. Snuffy Stirnweiss led the club with 107 runs. It could be it's just too hard to win a pennant when the team leader for runs is a guy named Snuffy, but Stirnweiss was no joke. He also won the batting title in 1945, and during his career he won three World Series titles with the Yankees.

The number of at bats (677) for Don Mattingly in 1986. He led the club with the sixth highest total in franchise history, and he used them well as he set a franchise record with 238 hits.

The number of batters (678) Bob Turley faced in 1959. He faced 335 fewer batters than he did in 1958, when he posted a 21-7 record in 33 games and won CYA honors. Turley also pitched 33 games in 1959, but was not nearly as effective, and he posted an 8-11 record.

The number of at bats (679) for Bobby Richardson in 1964. It was the third consecutive season he led the league, and he did so with the fifth highest total in franchise history. Richardson also led the club with 181 hits.

The winning percentage (.680) for pitcher Randy Johnson in 2005. He posted a 17-8 record and led the club in victories and winning percentage during his first season in the Bronx. Johnson also led the club and was second in the league with 211 strikeouts.

The winning percentage (.681) for pitcher Roger Clemens from 1999-2003. Toronto traded Clemens to the Yankees for Homer

Bush, Graeme Lloyd, and David Wells. He was 27-18 during his first two seasons in the Bronx, but in 2001 he posted a 20-3 record for a career high .870 winning percentage. Clemens was 77-36 overall during his first tour of duty with the club, and he won two World Series titles.

682   The number of at bats (682) for Alfonso Soriano in 2003. He used them well, as he was among the top six league leaders in total bases, steals, homeruns, hits, and runs. It was also the second consecutive season that Soriano led the league in at bats, and he did so with the fourth highest total in franchise history.

683   The number of strikeouts (6.83) per nine innings for Rudy May in 1980. He led the club with the second best ratio in the league. May started only 17 of his 41 games, but he posted a 15-5 record and struck out 133 batters in 175 innings.

684   The number of extra-base hits (684) for Don Mattingly. His total is the seventh highest in franchise history. Mattingly led the league in extra-base hits in 1985 and 1986, and he was among the top five league leaders five times from 1984-89.

685   The number of runs (685) allowed by the Yankees in 1928. It was the second lowest total in the league behind the Philadelphia Athletics, but Philadelphia was second in the league behind the 894 runs the Yankees scored that season. Of course the most important numbers are the standings, and with a 101-53 record it was the Yankees that won the pennant over the second place Athletics.

686   The number of at bats (686) for Horace Clarke in 1970. It was the second consecutive season he led the league, and he did so with the third highest total in franchise history. Clarke batted only .251, but his 172 hits and 212 total bases were both the second highest totals of his career.

687   The slugging percentage (.687) for Mickey Mantle in 1961. Roger Maris broke the homerun record that season, but Mantle led the league in slugging. Mantle also led the club in average, on-base percentage, and OPS, and he tied Maris for the team lead in runs.

688 The number of runs (688) allowed by the Yankees in 1997. It was the first season for Mariano Rivera as closer, and he was second in the league with 43 saves. Andy Pettitte, David Wells, and David Cone gave Rivera plenty of chances as the club gave up the second lowest number of runs in the league and posted a 96-66 record to win the Wild Card.

689 The winning percentage (.689) as a member of the Yankees for pitcher Mike Stanton. He is fourth in franchise history with 456 games. Stanton posted a 31-14 record during his tenure in the Bronx, but he was primarily used as a set-up man for closer Mariano Rivera.

690 The winning percentage (.690) for pitcher Whitey Ford. He posted a 236-106 record for one of the top five winning percentages in baseball history. Ford led the league in winning percentage three times, and he was among the top five league leaders nine times.

691 The number of runs (691) allowed by the Yankees in 1950. It was the second lowest total in the league behind the Cleveland Indians. Ed Lopat was 18-8 and led the club with a 3.47 ERA, and Vic Raschi was second in the league in wins after posting a 21-8 record. The Indians posted the best team ERA in the league, but the Yankees won the pennant with a 98-56 record, and then gave up only five runs in a four game sweep of the Philadelphia Phillies in the 1950 World Series.

692 The number of at bats (692) for Bobby Richardson in 1962. He led the league with the second highest total in franchise history. Richardson also put together his best season on offense. He batted .302 and scored a career high 99 runs, and placed second in league MVP balloting.

693 The number of RBI (693) for the Yankees in 1978. The club scored 735 runs for the fourth highest total in the league, despite not having anyone surpass 100 RBI or score 100 runs on the season. Reggie Jackson led the club with 97 RBI, and Willie Randolph led the club with 87 runs. The key was pitching—New York gave up the fewest runs in the league and won the division, pennant, and the 1978 World Series.

694 The winning percentage (.694) during blowouts for the Yankees in 1964. Of the 36 games played by the Yankees that resulted in a margin of victory that was five runs or greater, New York posted a record of 25-11. The club was second in scoring and third in pitching among all teams in the league, and they won the pennant by a single game over the Chicago White Sox.

695 The winning percentage (.695) for the Yankees in 1932. New York was 107-47 for the highest number of victories under manager Joe McCarthy. The Yankees swept the Chicago Cubs in the 1932 World Series to give McCarthy his first title. He won seven during his tenure with the club.

696 The number of at bats (696) for Alfonso Soriano in 2002. He used them well, as he led the league with 209 hits and was fifth in the league with 39 homeruns. Soriano's at bat total also led the league and set a franchise record.

697 The number of runs (697) allowed by the Yankees in 2002. It was the fourth lowest total in the league. David Wells led the club in wins with a 19-7 record. Andy Pettitte and Roger Clemens each won 13 games, and Clemens led the club with 192 strikeouts. Mike Mussina won 18 games and led the club with 215 innings. The end result was a 103-58 record that was the best in baseball.

698 The number of runs (698) for the Yankees in 1989. Steve Sax led the club with 205 hits and 88 runs during his first season in the Bronx, but overall the offense was only tenth in the league out of 14 teams, and the result was a 74-87 record and a fifth place finish.

699 The number of plate appearances (699) for Horace Clarke in 1969. He led the club with the fifth highest total in the league, and he used them to put together his finest offensive season. Clark batted a career high .285 to lead the club, and he also led the club in runs, triples, steals, and times on base.

700 The winning percentage (.700) as a member of the Yankees for Monte Pearson. His percentage is the fourth highest in franchise history. Pearson was 19-7 during his first season in the Bronx in 1936, and he was third in the league with a .731 winning percentage. He posted a 63-27 record during five seasons with the club, and he never lost more than seven games in any one season. Pearson was also 4-0 with a 1.01 ERA in the post-season for the Yankees, and won four World Series titles.

Mariano Rivera

"Without question we're talking about the best reliever, in my opinion, in the history of baseball. This guy has become branded with the Yankee logo. People are going to remember this man for so long for what he's done."

— *Brian Cashman*

Chapter Eight

Rivera

The son of a Panamanian fisherman, it was a long and difficult journey to the Bronx for Mariano Rivera. Yankee scout Herb Raybourn first saw Rivera play in Panama, but hardly noticed because Rivera was a tall, lanky, 20-year-old shortstop at the time. It was after seeing Rivera come into a game and pitch that Raybourn took an interest, only to find out that Rivera, who was clocked in the mid-80s on the radar gun, had never pitched before. Raybourn saw something in Rivera though that could not be taught—a good arm—and he signed Rivera as an amateur free agent in 1990.

Rivera got off to a promising start, posting good numbers in Fort Lauderdale as he began his journey through the minors, but his future in baseball became very uncertain when arm troubles in 1992 led to Tommy John surgery. He spent much of 1992-93 in rehabilitation, but by 1994 he was again putting up good numbers in the minors, and then in 1995 he made his big league debut for the Yankees.

It was not a good debut.

Rivera got the start against Chuck Finley and the California Angels. Finley came into the game 0-4 on the season, but he tossed a two-hit shutout as the Angels won 10-0. Rivera got only ten outs, lasting into the fourth inning. He gave up eight hits and five earned runs as he picked up the loss. Signing Rivera to pitch was a gamble from the beginning, but now he was a 25-year-old rookie who carried extra baggage associated with Tommy John surgery.

He was up-and-down that season, shuffling between the big club and Columbus.

His numbers improved for the most part, but his ERA was too high, the velocity on his fastball was too low, and once again his future in baseball was uncertain. Rivera closed out the season 5-3, but the big number that troubled the organization was his 5.51 ERA, and so it was a small surprise that management kept Rivera on the post-season roster after the Yankees claimed the Wild Card.

Once in the post-season though, it was lights out.

Joe Torre once said of Rivera, "He loves the competition and he has always responded real well in the big games. I think when you talk about his career, the reason he will go to the Hall of Fame is all about the post-season. He has been second to none."

Rivera struck out eight batters but gave up only three hits during five-plus innings of relief against the Seattle Mariners in the division series. He picked up a win in three games, but he did not give up a single run—and just like that, his future in baseball became infinitely clearer.

Joe Torre used Rivera exclusively out of the bullpen as the set-up man for John Wetteland in 1996. Rivera was so dominant that he placed third in CYA balloting, something almost completely unheard of for middle relievers, and the Yankees were 70-3 when they carried a lead into the seventh inning. He went on to pitch 14-plus innings during the 1996 post-season, and he gave up only one earned run as the Yankees claimed the 1996 World Series over the Atlanta Braves.

He became the closer in 1997 and was second in the league with 43 saves. Since then he has become a permanent fixture in both franchise and major league baseball record books. Rivera has been so good at closing out games that Buster Olney wrote in *New York Magazine* that, "No other player can instill calm in his team's fans as reliably as Mariano

Rivera, the game's dominant closer and arguably the best relief pitcher of all time."

His teammates feel the same way. Roger Clemens said, "I call him the equalizer. I can't tell you how comforting it felt to have him come in when I left the game."

Derek Jeter offered this assessment of Rivera, "He is the most mentally tough person I have ever played with." Rivera is accustomed to receiving high accolades, but they are well-earned—just look at the numbers:

- Four World Series titles
- Only player in history to close out three World Series
- One of only two players to save three All-Star games
- Major league record for World Series saves
- American League record for career saves
- Franchise leader for saves, games finished, and games
- 1999 World Series Most Valuable Player
- 2003 American League Championship Series Most Valuable Player
- Major league record for lowest ERA in division series history
- One of only two players with 400 saves for one team
- Major league record 23 consecutive post-season saves
- Major league record 34 consecutive scoreless innings in the post-season
- Major league record for post-season saves
- Major league record for lowest post-season ERA

It was the Yankees general manager Brian Cashman who said fans would remember Rivera for a very long time, and manager Joe Torre who said his post-season numbers would carry Rivera all the way to Cooperstown—and the numbers suggest that time will prove them both to be correct.

The number of strikeouts (7.01) per nine innings for Dave Righetti in 1983. He struck out a team high 169 batters in 217 innings, and his ratio led the club and was the third best in the league. Righetti made 31 starts in his final season before becoming the Yankees closer, and he posted a 14-8 record.

The winning percentage (.702) for the Yankees in 1939. Joe McCarthy managed the Yankees to a 106-45 record and won the pennant by 17 games over the Boston Red Sox. New York swept Cincinnati in the 1939 World Series for their fourth consecutive title.

The number of runs (703) allowed by the Yankees in 1983. Ron Guidry was 21-9 and led the club in wins and ERA, and Goose Gossage was 13-5 with 22 saves out of the bullpen as the club posted a 91-71 record. Baltimore and Detroit were two of only four teams in the league to give up fewer runs than New York, and the Orioles and Tigers also placed first and second in the division ahead of the third place Yankees.

The winning percentage (.704) for the Yankees in 1998. Joe Torre managed the club to a franchise record 114 wins against just 48 losses. The Yankees then went 11-2 during the post-season and swept the San Diego Padres in the 1998 World Series. Counting from opening day through the final game of the post-season, the Yankees ran off an impressive 125-50 record, prompting owner George Steinbrenner to say, "There has never been a better team than this one. We created something truly special here." Joe Torre added, "The one thing I would love to have people think about is there is no one name that comes to mind, but the team itself."

The number of hits (7.05) allowed per nine innings for Mariano Rivera from 1995-2006. He gave up only 691 hits in 881 innings, and his ratio as he began play in 2007 was the second best in franchise history.

706 The winning percentage (.706) as a member of the Yankees for pitcher Vic Raschi. He posted a 120-50 record for the third best winning percentage in franchise history. Raschi won 21 games three consecutive seasons from 1949-51, and he was among the top six league leaders for wins five consecutive seasons from 1948-52. He also won six World Series titles during eight seasons in the Bronx.

707 The number of plate appearances (707) for Steve Sax in 1991. His total led the club during his last season playing in the Bronx. Sax used them to bat .304 and hit a career high ten homeruns. He also led the club in hits, on-base percentage, and runs.

708 The winning percentage (.708) as a member of the Yankees for pitcher David Wells. He signed with New York as a free agent prior to 1997 and posted a combined 34-14 record during his first two seasons in the Bronx. He was then traded to the Blue Jays for Roger Clemens after the 1998 season, but returned again as a free agent prior to 2002. Wells posted an identical 34-14 record during his next two year stint with the Yankees, and his winning percentage with the club is the second highest in franchise history.

709 The slugging percentage (.709) for Babe Ruth in 1928. He led the league with the tenth highest slugging percentage in franchise history. Ruth owns 12 of the top 25 slugging percentages in the franchise record book.

710 The number of batters (710) Jimmy Key faced in 1994. He led the league in wins with a 17-4 record, and he placed second in CYA balloting after only 61 batters reached base and scored an earned run against him. Key never posted a 20 win season, despite a solid 15 year career. His best chance was 1994, and though he led the club with 168 innings, he made only 25 starts because of the players' strike that cut the season short and cost Key an additional ten chances to get to 20 wins.

711 The slugging percentage (.711) as a member of the Yankees for Babe Ruth. He owns the franchise record and his overall .690 slugging percentage is a major league record—but for all the bravado he was known for throughout his career, even the immortal Ruth understood that individual achievements are subordinate to the overall success of the team. He once said, "The way a team plays as a whole determines its success. You may have the greatest bunch of individual stars in the world—but if they don't play together the club won't be worth a dime."

712 The number of strikeouts (712) for the Yankees pitching staff in 1960. It was the third lowest total in the league. Ralph Terry led the team with 92 strikeouts, but was not even close to being among the top ten league leaders. The rest of the numbers were good though, as the club led the league in ERA, shutouts, saves, and most importantly, wins.

713 The number of hits (7.13) allowed per nine innings for Dennis Rasmussen in 1986. He gave up only 160 hits in 202 innings, and he led the club with the second best ratio in the league. Rasmussen posted an 18-6 record for the second best winning percentage in the league as well. Roger Clemens, who won both the CYA and MVP for the Boston Red Sox in 1986, was the only pitcher better than Rasmussen in either category.

714 The winning percentage (.714) for the Yankees in 1927. Miller Huggins managed the club to a 110-44 record for the highest victory total during his tenure. The Yankees won the pennant by 19 games over the Philadelphia Athletics, and then the club swept the Pittsburgh Pirates to win the 1927 World Series.

715 The number of hits (7.15) allowed per nine innings for David Cone in 1997. He led the club with the third best ratio in the league. Cone was only 12-6, but his numbers were much better than his record indicates. He was also among the top ten league leaders in ERA, winning percentage, WHIP, strikeouts, strikeouts per nine innings, and strikeouts to walk ratio.

716 The number of runs (716) allowed by the Yankees in 2003. It was the fourth lowest total in the league, and the club posted the third best

ERA in the league. Jeff Weaver was the only starting pitcher with a losing record. Roger Clemens was 17-9, Andy Pettitte was 21-8, Mike Mussina was 17-8, and David Wells was 15-7. The club was 101-61 overall, and tied with the Atlanta Braves for the best record in baseball.

717 The number of strikeouts (717) for Elston Howard. His total is the tenth highest in franchise history. Howard struck out a career high 76 times in 1962, and he struck out more times than he walked during every season he played. Of course, he also hit five World Series homeruns, and he won four World Series titles.

718 The number of games (718) for pitcher Dave Righetti. His games total is among the top 75 in baseball history, and the 522 games he pitched for New York are the second highest total in franchise history. Righetti set a career high when he pitched in 74 games for the Yankees in 1985, and again in 1986.

719 The number of games (719) Miller Huggins lost as manager of the Yankees. He managed the club from 1918-29, and his only sub-.500 seasons were in 1918 and 1925. Huggins never lost more than 63 games during his other ten seasons, and he won six pennants and three World Series titles.

720 The number of games (720) for closer Mariano Rivera from 1995-2006. He made ten starts in 1995, but the rest of his games have been out of the bullpen. Rivera once joked about the success he has had playing the role of closer for the Yankees, saying, "I get the ball, I throw the ball—and then I take a shower." His numbers are no joke though, as he holds the franchise record for games, games finished, and saves.

721 The slugging percentage (.721) for Lou Gehrig in 1930. He led the league with 100 extra-base hits and his slugging percentage is the ninth highest in franchise history, but he was second in the league in slugging behind the .732 mark for teammate Babe Ruth.

722 The number of strikeouts (7.22) per nine innings as a member of the Yankees for Orlando Hernandez. His ratio is the ninth best in franchise history. Hernandez played for the Yankees from 1998-2004, and he struck out 703 batters in 876 innings. He did even better in the post-season. El Duque signed with the club as a free agent in 1998 after defecting from his native Cuba—just in time to win three consecutive World Series titles and four pennants during his first four years with the club. Hernandez won a fifth pennant and a fourth World Series title as a member of the White Sox in 2005, and collectively, during those five trips to the Fall Classic, he posted a 4-1 record, a 2.20 ERA, and he struck out 11.30 batters per nine innings on the mound.

723 The number of plate appearances (723) for Roy White in 1973. His total led the league, and he was the only player for the Yankees to play all 162 games. White only batted .246, but he also led the club and was among the top ten in the league with 88 runs.

724 The number of hits (7.24) allowed per nine innings as a member of the Yankees for Tommy Byrne. He set a franchise record when he gave up only 5.74 hits per nine innings in 1949, and his career ratio is the third best in franchise history. Byrne gave up only 799 hits in 993 innings for the Yankees, but though he played more than a decade he only posted double digits in wins three times.

725 The number of RBI (725) for the Yankees in 1984. The club was fourth in the league with 758 runs. Don Mattingly led the club with 110 RBI, and Dave Winfield also picked up 100 RBI, but with a record of 87-75 the Yankees placed only third in their division.

726 The number of hits (7.26) allowed per nine innings for Whitey Ford in 1954. He led the club with the second best ratio in the league. Ford posted a 16-8 record and made his first All-Star team. He gave up only 170 hits in 210 innings, and he also led the Yankees in complete games, innings, strikeouts, and ERA.

727 The number of hits (7.27) allowed per nine innings as a member of the Yankees for Bob Turley. He posted the best ratio in the league four times from 1954-58, and his career ratio is the fourth best in franchise history.

The number of extra-base hits (728) for Yogi Berra. His total is the sixth highest in franchise history. Yogi was among the top ten league leaders for extra-base hits seven times, and he is one of the top 75 homerun hitters in baseball history. Berra, who is as famous for his "Yogi-sms" as he is for his on the field exploits, famously replied to a reporter who asked about Yogi's thoughts on his success at the plate by saying, "How can you hit and think at the same time?"

The winning percentage (.729) during blowouts for the Yankees in 2002. New York was 35-13 in games decided by five runs or greater, and they scored 366 of their league best 897 runs during those contests. On May 9, the Yankees trailed the Red Sox by five games in the standings, but on June 19 the club scored a season high 20 runs in a blowout against the Colorado Rockies, and the lead for Boston was down to only a half game. New York spent 95 days in first place during 2002, and from June 27 through the rest of the season they never trailed in the standings again—winning the division by a final margin of 10.5 games over Boston.

The number of runs (730) for the Yankees in 1976. It was the second highest total in the league behind Minnesota, but the Twins lost their division to Kansas City, and the Yankees beat the Royals in the league championship series to claim yet another pennant.

The World Series slugging percentage (.731) for Lou Gehrig. He batted 119 times during seven trips to the World Series and picked up 21 extra-base hits. Gehrig batted .361 overall with ten homeruns, and he ranks among the top five leaders in post-season history for homeruns, triples, slugging percentage, total bases, walks, and RBI.

The slugging percentage (.732) for Babe Ruth in 1930. He led the league with the eighth highest slugging percentage in franchise history. Ruth batted .359, and he also led the league with 49 homeruns.

The slugging percentage (.733) for Babe Ruth during the 1932 World Series. It was during this series that the legendary Ruth famously called his homerun by pointing with his bat to the center field bleachers in Wrigley Field. Or maybe it never happened. One thing is for certain though, Ruth did hit two monster shots during game three of his final post-season series, and the Yankees swept the Cubs.

734 The number of runs (734) for the Yankees in 1979. Willie Randolph led the team with 98 runs. Reggie Jackson led the club with 29 homeruns and 89 RBI, but overall the club was only tenth in the league for both runs and total offense. Solid pitching carried the team to an 89-71 record, but the Yankees were out of the post-season race all season.

735 The number of plate appearances (735) for Phil Rizzuto in 1950. The HOF shortstop put his league leading total to good use. Rizzuto set career highs when he batted .324 with 125 runs, and he earned his only career MVP.

736 The OPS (.736) for Alfonso Soriano in 2001. OPS measures a player's ability to get on base and hit for power. Soriano was a 25-year-old rookie who batted just .268, and struggled at times to get on base. He posted an unremarkable .304 on-base percentage, but his .432 slugging percentage demonstrated his true potential. Soriano posted a .879 OPS during his sophomore season, and in 2006 he posted a .911 OPS for the Washington Nationals.

737 The slugging percentage (.737) for Babe Ruth in 1926. He led the league with the seventh highest total in franchise history. Ruth batted .372 with 83 extra-base hits, and he led the league with 365 total bases.

738 The number of runs (738) allowed by the Yankees in 1986. It was the first season for manager Lou Piniella, who guided the club to a 90-72 record despite giving up the eighth highest runs total in the league. Dennis Rasmussen was the most effective starter as he posted a career best 18-6 record. He led the club in eight different categories, to include wins, innings, and ERA. Dave Righetti was the best relief pitcher in the league and he saved a career high 46 games.

739 The slugging percentage (.739) for Babe Ruth in 1924. He led the league with the sixth highest slugging percentage in franchise history. Ruth also led the league with 46 homeruns and 92 extra-base hits, but he was not eligible for the MVP because the rules at the time prohibited past winners from being considered for the award. Ruth won his only career MVP in 1923.

The number of plate appearances (740) for Frankie Crosetti in 1936. Red Rolfe also made 740 plate appearances in 1937 and both players share the eighth highest total in franchise history. Crosetti scored a career high 137 runs in 1936, and Rolfe scored a career high 143 runs in 1937, but most importantly, as teammates Crosetti and Rolfe won back-to-back World Series titles in 1936 and 1937.

The number of plate appearances (741) for Alfonso Soriano in 2002. He used them well, as he led the league with 209 hits and won his first Silver Slugger award. Soriano also led the league in plate appearances with the seventh highest total in franchise history.

The number of plate appearances (742) for Don Mattingly in 1986. He led the league with the sixth highest total in franchise history. Mattingly batted .352, and set a franchise record with 238 hits.

The number of plate appearances (743) for Frankie Crosetti in 1939. He led the league with the fifth highest total in franchise history. Crosetti only batted .233, but he scored 109 runs, giving him four consecutive seasons surpassing the century mark.

The number of strikeouts (7.44) per nine innings as a member of the Yankees for Dave Righetti. His ratio is the seventh best in franchise history. Righetti struck out 940 batters during 1,136 innings for the Yankees, and he is second in franchise history for both games and saves.

The number of batters (745) Andy Pettitte faced in 1995. He was a 23-year-old rookie who made 26 starts and pitched 175 innings. Pettitte posted a 12-9 record, and among rookie pitchers that season he received the most votes in ROY balloting—but overall, he only placed third. Twins outfielder Marty Cordova, who hit 24 homeruns, won the award. The next season though, Pettitte was second in CYA balloting and won his first career ring—something Cordova never got a chance to play for during his career (he retired in 2003, and his rookie homerun total was a career high).

746 The number of runs (746) allowed by the Yankees in 1992. Only two of the 14 teams in the league gave up more runs that season. Melido Perez, Scott Sanderson, Scott Kamieniecki, and Tim Leary all posted sub-.500 records as the core of the starting rotation, and the club struggled to a fourth place finish in the division.

747 The number of RBI (747) for the Yankees in 1954. The club was second in the league in hits, doubles, triples, homeruns, and walks, but no other team scored as many runs. Yogi Berra picked up 125 RBI and the MVP, and Mickey Mantle hit 27 homeruns and led the league with 129 runs. The Cleveland Indians were the second highest scoring team in the league, but unfortunately they still won the pennant by eight games over the Yankees.

748 The number of plate appearances (748) for Derek Jeter in 1997. He led the league with the fourth highest total in franchise history. Jeter was only 23 years old, but he led the club with 190 hits and 116 runs.

749 The number of strikeouts (7.49) per nine innings as a member of the Yankees for Al Downing. He led the league with an 8.76 ratio as a 22-year-old rookie in 1963, and his career ratio is the sixth best in franchise history. Downing tossed 1,235 innings for the Yankees, and he is among the top ten in franchise history with 1,028 career strikeouts.

750 The winning percentage (.750) for pitcher Bob Turley in 1958. His percentage led the club but was second in the league behind Dick Hyde of the Washington Senators. Turley tossed 19 complete games and six shutouts. He also won his only CYA when he posted a 21-6 record.

751 The number of batters (751) Ralph Terry faced in 1961. He only started 27 games but posted a 16-3 record for the second best winning percentage in the league. Only 66 batters reached base and scored an earned run against Terry, and he was also second in the league with a 1.08 WHIP.

The number of plate appearances (752) for Derek Jeter in 2005. He led the league with the third highest total in franchise history, and he used them to get a team leading 202 hits. Jeter was also second in the league behind teammate Alex Rodriguez with 122 runs.

The number of earned runs (753) allowed by the Yankees in 2000. It is the highest total in franchise history, and incredibly, Roger Clemens, Orlando Hernandez, David Cone, and Mariano Rivera were all on the staff. The Yankees' 87-74 record was good enough to win the division though, and the club went on to win the World Series.

The number of plate appearances (754) for Bobby Richardson in 1962. He led the league with the second highest total in franchise history. Richardson set a career high with 281 total bases and he made the All-Star team for the fourth time. He made eight All-Star teams total, but 1962 was the only time he scored a run during the All-Star game. Richardson also scored three runs during the 1962 World Series, and won his third title.

The number of strikeouts (755) for the Yankees in 1956. It was the third highest total in the league, led by Mickey Mantle who struck out 99 times. The high totals were not a problem though for New York or for Mantle, as the Yankees outscored and hit more homeruns than every other team in the league, and Mantle won the Triple Crown.

The number of batters (756) Dwight Gooden faced in 1996. He made 29 starts and won 11 games, but his 5.01 ERA soared well above the career mark for a player who was once one of the game's most dominating aces. Gooden recaptured some of his previous magic though on May 14 against the Seattle Mariners. He faced the minimum 27 batters in a complete game shutout, and pitched the only no-hitter of his career.

The number of plate appearances (757) for Frankie Crosetti in 1938. He led the league and set a franchise record, but more importantly, he made 19 additional plate appearances against the

Chicago Cubs in the 1938 World Series. Crosetti batted only .250 against the Cubs, but all of his hits went for extra-bases, including his only career World Series homerun. He also won his fourth career title.

758 The number of runs (758) for the Yankees in 1984. It was the fourth highest total in the league, led by 23-year-old first baseman Don Mattingly who had his breakout season on offense. He hit .343 to win the batting title and he led the club with 110 RBI. Mattingly barely led the club in batting though, as teammate Dave Winfield hit .340 and scored a team high 106 runs.

759 The number of batters (759) Don Larsen faced in 1956. He gave up 133 hits in 179 innings and 96 walks, and his 1.28 WHIP was ninth in the league. Larsen also posted a career best 11-5 record, but he fared even better in the 1956 World Series when he tossed a perfect game against the Brooklyn Dodgers and earned the hardware for series MVP.

760 The number of walks (760) as a member of the Yankees for Charlie Keller. His total is the tenth highest in franchise history. Keller led the league with 106 walks in 1940, and again in 1943, but his career high 114 walks in 1942 was not even close to the 145 times Ted Williams walked for the Boston Red Sox.

761 The number of walks (761) allowed by Bob Turley as a member of the Yankees. His total is the eighth highest in franchise history. Control was always an issue for Turley, who gave up 177 walks in 1955 for the second highest season total in franchise history. Turley also led the league with 128 walks during his 1958 CYA season.

762 The number of hits (7.62) allowed per nine innings for Dave Righetti in 1982. He led the club with the third best ratio in the league. Righetti gave up only 155 hits in 183 innings, and he also led the club with 163 strikeouts.

763 The number of walks (763) allowed by Tommy Byrne as a member of the Yankees. His total is the seventh highest in franchise

history, but Byrne also owns the franchise record for a single season after walking 179 batters in 1949.

764 The slugging percentage (.764) for Babe Ruth in 1923. He led the league with the fifth highest slugging percentage in franchise history. Ruth also batted a career high .393, and led the club to the first World Series title in franchise history.

765 The slugging percentage (.765) for Lou Gehrig in 1927. He posted the fourth highest slugging percentage in franchise history, and the seventh highest in baseball history, but he was second on the club that season behind Babe Ruth. Gehrig blasted 117 extra-base hits in 1927 for the second highest total in baseball history, trailing only the 1921 total of 119 extra-base hits for Ruth.

766 The number of walks (766) for the Yankees in 1932. It was the highest total in the league, and it also set a franchise record. Babe Ruth walked 130 times and led the league for the third consecutive season, and Lou Gehrig, Tony Lazzeri, and Earle Combs were all among the top ten league leaders.

767 The number of runs (767) allowed by the Yankees in 2006. It was the sixth highest total in the league, and the struggles of Randy Johnson and Jaret Wright were constant headlines. Johnson won 17 games, but posted a career worst 5.00 ERA. Wright signed a lucrative free agent deal with the Yankees after the 2004 season, but won only five games in 2005, and won only 11 games with a 4.49 ERA in 2006. Still, the club posted a 97-65 record and won the division title after scoring a major league leading 930 runs.

768 The number of batters (768) Roger Clemens faced in 2002. He was well back of the league leading 1,008 batters faced by Devil Rays pitcher Tanyon Sturtze, and in fact, Clemens was not even near the top ten league leaders. Clemens did post 192 strikeouts in only 180 innings though, and his strikeout total was the second highest in the league.

769 The winning percentage (.769) for pitcher Bob Grim in 1954. He was a 24-year-old rookie who posted a 20-6 record and led the

club in winning percentage. Grim also led the league in victories for the only time in his career, and he earned ROY honors.

770 The number of hits (7.70) allowed per nine innings for Hideki Irabu in 1998. He led the club with the third best ratio in the league, an impressive feat considering the other members of the starting rotation were Andy Pettitte, David Cone, Orlando Hernandez, and David Wells. Irabu gave up only 148 hits in 173 innings, and he posted a 13-9 record.

771 The number of hits (7.71) allowed per nine innings as a member of the Yankees for Tom Sturdivant. His ratio is the eighth best in franchise history. Sturdivant spent five seasons pitching in the Bronx. He posted only a 36-25 record, but he gave up just 449 hits in 524 innings.

772 The slugging percentage (.772) for Babe Ruth in 1927. He led the league with the third highest slugging percentage in franchise history, and of course he hit a record 60 homeruns, but despite his prodigious numbers he was not even close to winning the Triple Crown. Ruth batted .356, but placed only seventh in the batting title race, and was only third on the team behind Lou Gehrig and Earle Combs. He also posted 164 RBI, but again trailed his teammate Lou Gehrig by 11.

773 The number of hits (7.73) allowed per nine innings for Ron Guidry in 1979. He led the club with the third best ratio in the league. Guidry faced 946 batters in 236 innings, but he gave up only 203 hits. He posted an 18-8 record and placed third in CYA balloting.

774 The winning percentage (.774) for pitcher Whitey Ford in 1963. He was 24-7 and led the league in winning percentage for the third time. Ford was third in MVP balloting, but he was named *The Sporting News* A.L. Pitcher of the Year for the third time. It takes a special kind of player to earn that kind of hardware, but Ford fit the bill perfectly. His longtime teammate, Mickey Mantle, once said about him, "I don't care what the situation was, or how high the stakes were, the bases could be loaded and the pennant riding on every pitch, it never bothered him. He pitched his game—cool, crafty, nerves of steel."

775 The OPS (.775) for Derek Jeter in 1997. His sophomore season was just as solid as his ROY campaign in 1996, as he posted a .370 on-base percentage and a .405 slugging percentage. Jeter got 48 extra-base hits, and was fourth in the league with 116 runs.

776 The number of strikeouts (7.76) per nine innings for Bob Turley in 1957. He struck out 152 batters in 176 innings for the best ratio in baseball. Turley only gave up 120 hits, and his ratio of hits per nine innings was also the best in baseball. He only made 23 starts, but posted a 13-6 record.

777 The number of strikeouts (7.77) per nine innings as a member of the Yankees for Mike Mussina. His ratio was the fifth best in franchise history as play began in 2007. Mussina pitched 1,200 innings for the Yankees from 2001-06, and struck out 1,037 batters.

778 The winning percentage (.778) for pitcher Bob Wickman in 1993. He posted a 14-4 record despite a 4.63 ERA that was well above the league average, and he led the club with the second highest winning percentage in the league.

779 The number of chances (779) for Yogi Berra in 1952. The HOF catcher gave up only five passed balls, and made just six errors. The Gold Glove award was not a part of the hardware available in 1952, but that season represented one of the best defensive efforts of Yogi's career. He posted a .992 fielding percentage during 140 games, well above the .985 league average for catchers that season.

780 The number of batters (780) Bump Hadley faced in 1936. He made only 17 starts, but he pitched in 31 games and posted a 14-4 record during his first season in the Bronx. Hadley was already a ten-year veteran when he came to New York, but he had never played in the post-season prior to starting game three of the 1936 World Series against the New York Giants. He tossed eight strong innings to earn a 2-1 victory, and the club went on to win the series in seven games.

781 The OPS (.781) for Elliott Maddox in 1974. He led the club with a career high OPS, and he placed eighth in league MVP balloting.

Maddox batted .303, and though he only hit three homeruns all season, he also led the club in on-base percentage, walks, doubles, and runs.

782 The number of RBI (782) for the Yankees in 1961. Pitching against the Yankees in 1961 was about as much fun as pitching against the Yankees in 1927. Six players on the club hit 20 or more homeruns. Mickey Mantle batted .317 with 128 RBI, but was only second on the club behind the league leading 142 RBI for MVP Roger Maris.

783 The OPS (.783) for Mickey Mantle in 1968. He was a 36-year-old outfielder in his final season when he posted the lowest OPS of his career. Mantle's career numbers were so good though that his 1968 OPS still led the Yankees and was the ninth highest in the league.

784 The number of strikeouts (7.84) per nine innings for Mike Mussina in 2006. His ratio was the best on the club, a feat all the more impressive when you consider one of his teammates was Randy Johnson. Mussina struck out 172 batters in only 197 innings, and he also led the club in ERA.

785 The number of hits (7.85) allowed per nine innings for Whitey Ford. His ratio is one of the top 100 in baseball history, but it is the ninth best in franchise history. Ford gave up only 2,766 hits in 3,170 innings for the club, and seven times his ratio was among the top ten league leaders.

786 The winning percentage (.786) for pitcher Ron Guidry in 1985. He was 22-6, and he led the league in both wins and winning percentage, but placed second in CYA balloting. Guidry is among the top 30 in baseball history with a .651 career winning percentage.

787 The number of hits (7.87) allowed per nine innings as a member of the Yankees for Hank Borowy. His ratio is the tenth best in franchise history. Borowy only played four seasons in the Bronx, but he posted a 56-30 record and gave up only 683 hits in 780 innings.

788 The number of runs (788) for the Yankees in 1987. It was only the seventh highest total in the league. Willie Randolph led the club with a .411 on-base percentage and 96 runs, and Don Mattingly scored 93 runs and led the club with 115 RBI. Mike Pagliarulo was at his best when he hit a team leading 32 homeruns, but all total, the club managed only an 89-73 record and a fourth place finish.

The number of RBI (789) for the Yankees in 1934. Lou Gehrig led the league for the fifth and final time when he picked up 165 RBI. Gehrig also posted RBI totals of 151, 152, and 159 during seasons he placed second, second, and third in the league.

The number of walks (790) for Joe DiMaggio. His total is the ninth highest in franchise history, but DiMaggio never walked more than 80 times in a season. He still posted a .398 on-base percentage that ranks among the top 65 in baseball history, and the fact that he walked so few times makes it even more impressive.

The number of extra-base hits (791) for Bernie Williams. His total is among the top 100 in baseball history, but it is the fifth highest in franchise history. Bernie never led the league in extra-base hits, but his consistent play has him right between Joe DiMaggio and Yogi Berra in the franchise record book for his career total.

The number of walks (792) for Frankie Crosetti. He walked a career high 106 times in 1938, just one behind team leader Lou Gehrig, but Crosetti is better known for his HBP total. Crosetti led the league in getting hit by a pitch eight times. Derek Jeter is the only player in franchise history with more HBP.

The number of RBI (793) for the Yankees in 1985. The club scored the most runs in the league, led by the 145 RBI for MVP Don Mattingly. He also batted .324 and hit 35 homeruns, but his most impressive total was his strikeouts—Mattingly struck out only 41 times in 727 plate appearances.

The number of runs (794) for the Yankees in 1947. It was the highest total in the league, led by Tommy Henrich who scored 109 runs. The Yankees also gave up the lowest run total in the league. Allie

Reynolds won 19 games, Joe Page won 14 games and saved 17, and the Yankees posted a 97-57 record on their way to another World Series title.

The number of hits (7.95) allowed per nine innings for Mike Mussina in 2001. He gave up only 202 hits in 228 innings for the best ratio on the team. Mussina also led the club in shutouts, complete games, and ERA. He was 17-11, and was second on the team with 214 strikeouts. Mussina only placed fifth in CYA balloting though, and he has never won the award. Teammate Roger Clemens won the 2001 CYA with a 20-3 record.

The number of strikeouts (796) for the Yankees pitching staff in 1958. Bob Turley struck out a team high 168 batters and won 21 games to earn CYA honors, and the club total was the second highest in the league. Detroit struck out 797 batters for the highest total, but the Yankees gave up the fewest hits, pitched the most shutouts, posted the best ERA, and won the most games. Detroit came in 15 games back in the standings.

The number of hits (7.97) allowed per nine innings for Melido Perez in 1994. His older brother Pascual briefly pitched for the Yankees from 1990-91, but it was Melido who had the most success in the Bronx when he led the club with the ninth best ratio in the league in 1994. Perez tossed 151 innings, but gave up only 134 hits.

The number of runs (798) for the Yankees in 1951. It was the second highest total in the league, led by HOF catcher Yogi Berra. He was the team leader in average, slugging, homeruns, runs, and RBI. Berra won his first MVP, and the Yankees won the World Series after posting a 98-56 record during the regular season.

The number of strikeouts (799) for Frankie Crosetti. He struck out a career high 105 times in 1937, and his career total is the seventh highest in franchise history. Crosetti also walked 792 times during 17 seasons in the Bronx for the eighth highest total in franchise history.

800 The number of hits (8.00) allowed per nine innings for Steve Kline in 1972. He was 24 years old and in his third season when he gave up 210 hits in 236 innings for the best ratio on the club. Kline also won a career high 16 games—and he was among the top ten league leaders in five statistically significant categories—but he won only nine more games the rest of his career.

Ron Guidry

"I feel fortunate, not only to have lived my dream of playing baseball, but to have done it with the only team I ever wanted to play for."

— Ron Guidry

Chapter Nine

Guidry

Phil Rizzuto first called him Louisiana Lightning during his record-setting performance against the California Angels on June 17, 1978. Ron Guidry was a 27-year-old southpaw in his second full season pitching in the Bronx when he struck out a franchise record 18 batters during a four-hit shutout. His record improved to 11-0 after his dominating performance, and now three decades later people still call him Louisiana Lightning.

Rizzuto, the Hall of Fame shortstop-turned-broadcaster for the Yankees, got to make the call for plenty of great games that season—especially for Guidry, who began 13-0 and did not lose his first game until July 7. Statistically, Guidry put together one of the most mind-boggling seasons in modern baseball, leading the league in several categories:

- 1.74 ERA
- 25 wins
- .893 winning percentage
- .946 WHIP
- 6.15 hits per nine innings
- 9 shutouts

Of course the number from 1978 that haunts Boston Red Sox fans is 14, because that is how many games the Red Sox led the Yankees by at the end of the day on July 19. On July 20, Guidry struck out eight batters against the Minnesota Twins and tossed another four-hit shutout to cut the Red Sox lead to 13. On July 25, Guidry struck out eight more batters and tossed a six-hit shutout, this time against the Kansas City Royals, and now the deficit was down to 9.5 games. On August 10, Guidry struck out nine batters against the Milwaukee Brewers and tossed a three-hit shutout to cut the Red Sox lead down to 7.5 games. By the time the Red Sox and Yankees met for a four game series beginning on September 7, the Yankees were only four games back in the standings. On September 9, after Guidry tossed a two-hit shutout and struck out five, the Yankees were only one game back. The next day, New York completed the four game sweep and the two clubs were tied for the division lead with only two weeks left in the season.

The collapse of the 1978 Red Sox is one of the most horrific in sports history, which is exactly why Yankee fans enjoy reliving it so much. Boston and New York closed out the season with identical 99-63 records, but it was Guidry, along with Bucky Dent and a friendly breeze at Fenway, who closed out Boston in a one game playoff on October 2. Dent hit a three-run homerun as Guidry and the Yankees beat Boston 5-4 to claim the division. The win gave Guidry a 25-3 record and capped off one of the greatest seasons in baseball history, let alone franchise history. The only thing that could make the season a little sweeter was to also win in the post-season—and of course the Yankees did just that. They took the league championship series over the Royals, and claimed the 1978 World Series over the Los Angeles Dodgers.

Guidry did much more than post one spectacular season in pinstripes though, as his career achievements indicate:

- Two World Series titles
- Three-time 20 game winner
- Four-time All-Star
- 1978 Cy Young Award recipient
- 1978 *The Sporting News* Pitcher of the Year
- 1978 Major League Player of the Year
- Led the American League in wins in 1978 and 1985
- Led the American League in ERA in 1978 and 1979
- Franchise record 248 strikeouts in 1978
- Franchise record nine shutouts in 1978
- Five-time Gold Glove recipient
- 1984 Major League Roberto Clemente Award recipient
- Team co-captain from 1986-89
- Top ten in franchise history for games, innings, wins, winning percentage, strikeouts, and shutouts

On August 23, 2003, the New York Yankees recognized the many contributions of Guidry to the franchise by retiring his number 49 jersey and declaring it to be Ron Guidry Day at Yankee Stadium. A plaque for Guidry was added to Monument Park with the inscription: "A dominating pitcher and a respected leader of the pitching staff for three American League Pennants and two World Championships—a true Yankee."

801 The number of hits (8.01) allowed per nine innings for Al Downing in 1966. He gave up only 178 hits in 200 innings for the best ratio on the club. Downing made 30 starts, but he was only 10-11 despite a solid 3.56 ERA. None of the Yankees pitchers got much run support that season and the result was an overall 70-89 record. It was so bad that Mel Stottlemyre posted a 3.80 ERA and led the club with 12 wins, but he also lost 20 games.

802 The number of batters (802) Tommy John faced in 1987. It was the highest total on the club for the 44-year-old pitcher who began his career in 1963. John posted a 13-6 record for his highest victory total since 1982, and he led the team with 187 innings. Not too bad at all, especially considering he played 15 years after undergoing ulnar collateral ligament reconstruction on his pitching elbow in 1974—a surgery from which the odds of recovery at the time were estimated to be 1 in 100. John, who relied on hitting locations and changing speeds for his success, often would joke about the surgery that now bears his name by saying, "When they operated, I told them to put in a Koufax fastball. They did—but it was Mrs. Koufax's."

803 The OPS (.803) as a member of the Yankees for Wade Boggs. The HOF third baseman played five seasons in the Bronx, but his most productive was 1994. Boggs was fifth in the league when he batted .342, and his .922 OPS was the highest during his tenure with the club.

804 The number of runs (804) for the Yankees in 2001. Derek Jeter scored 110 runs to lead the team and Bernie Williams scored 102. Tino Martinez led the club with 34 homeruns and 113 RBI, but the club was only fifth in the league in scoring. Of course the Yankees only gave up 713 runs for the third lowest total in the league. The result was a 95-65 record and yet another pennant.

805 The number of hits (8.05) allowed per nine innings for Mike Mussina in 2003. He led the club with the sixth best ratio in the league. Mussina gave up only 192 hits in 214 innings, and he was also among the top ten league leaders in wins, innings, strikeouts, WHIP, and ERA.

806 The number of games (806) Ralph Houk lost as manager of the Yankees. He won three consecutive pennants and two World Series titles from 1961-63, his first three seasons at the helm. Houk left the dugout to be general manager from 1964-65, but returned to managing in 1966. He won 944 games during 11 seasons, but he never made it back to the post-season during his final eight seasons in the Bronx, the five years he spent in Detroit, or the five years he spent in Boston.

807 The number of games (807) for Clark Griffith as manager from 1903-08. John McGraw was the first manager in franchise history, but it was Griffith who took over as player-manager during the Highlanders third season in the league. His best record came in 1904 when the club was 92-59, but the club came in second in the pennant race. Griffith was 419-370 overall in six seasons, but never came any closer to winning the pennant.

808 The number of hits (8.08) allowed per nine innings for Catfish Hunter in 1976. He was on the mound for 298 innings, but he gave up only 268 hits for the best ratio on the team. Hunter gave up only 7.72 hits per nine innings during his career for one of the top 60 ratios in baseball history.

809 The number of walks (809) allowed by Mel Stottlemyre. His total is the sixth highest in franchise history. Of course he also ranks sixth in franchise history with 164 wins, and he led the club in wins for five consecutive seasons from 1965-69. Stottlemyre was a 22-year-old rookie when he pitched for the club in the 1964 World Series against the St. Louis Cardinals. He did well, posting a 1-1 record and a 3.15 ERA during three starts—but the Yankees lost, and he never got to play in the post-season again. No worries though, because Stottlemyre reemerged on the baseball scene in New York as a highly successful pitching coach, first with the Mets, where his tutelage of a young pitching staff led to victory in the 1986 World Series, and then with the Yankees, where in a decade of coaching with Joe Torre the club won four World Series titles.

810 The number of hits (8.10) allowed per nine innings for Roger Clemens in 2000. He led the club with the fourth best ratio in the league. Clemens was on the mound for 204 innings, but he gave up only 184 hits and posted a 13-8 record. His career 7.66 ratio of hits per nine innings is one of the top 50 in baseball history.

811 The OPS (.811) for Dave Winfield in 1986. He only batted .262, but 60 of his 148 hits went for extra-bases. Winfield posted a .349 on-base percentage, and with his .462 slugging percentage he surpassed 100 RBI for the fifth consecutive season.

The winning percentage (.812) for pitchers Russ Ford in 1910, Atley Donald in 1939, and Jim Coates in 1960. It is the ninth best winning percentage in franchise history. Ford was 26-6 in 1910, but he was only second in the league in wins. Donald made only 20 starts in 1939, but he set a career high for wins with a 13-3 record. Coates made only 18 starts in 1960, but he made 17 relief appearances and also set a career high for wins with an identical 13-3 record.

The OPS (.813) for Elston Howard in 1955. He was a 26-year-old rookie who got a hit in his first big league at bat, and had no trouble getting on base the rest of the season. Howard batted .290, and posted a .336 on-base percentage. He also posted a .477 slugging percentage after 25 of his 81 hits went for extra-bases.

The number of runs (814) allowed by the Yankees in 2000. It was the fourth best total in the league, but the team ERA was only the sixth best in the league after the pitching fell completely apart in September. New York led Boston by nine games on September 13, but the Yankees lost 15 out of their final 18 games. The Yankees gave up 11 or more runs seven times during those 15 losses, they gave up 15 or more runs three times, and they gave up 11 or more runs in three consecutive games during the final week of the season. Boston closed to 2.5 games, but fell short. Then in the World Series, the much maligned pitching staff for the Yankees won all three games decided by a single run, and took the title from the Mets in five games.

The OPS (.815) for Jesse Barfield in 1990. He only batted .246 and he led the club with 150 strikeouts, but he also produced 25 homeruns and his OPS was the highest on the team.

The number of strikeouts (8.16) per nine innings for Ron Guidry in 1978. He led the club with the second best ratio in the league. Guidry struck out 248 batters, but gave up only 187 hits in 273 innings as he won his only career CYA.

The number of strikeouts (8.17) per nine innings for Melido Perez in 1993. He struck out 148 batters in 163 innings, and he led the club with the second best ratio in the league. Not much else went well for Perez though, as he posted a 6-14 record.

The winning percentage (.818) for pitcher David Wells in 1998. He led the league with the eighth highest winning percentage in franchise history. Wells posted an 18-4 record and pitched a perfect game against the Minnesota Twins, but he only placed third in league CYA balloting.

The number of walks (819) allowed by Allie Reynolds as a member of the Yankees. His total is the fifth highest in franchise history, but his tendency to give up a free base was offset by his ability to win. Reynolds is tenth in franchise history with 131 wins and he won six World Series titles with the club.

The number of runs (820) for the Yankees in 1980. It was the second highest total in the league behind Detroit, but it was the Tigers that trailed the Yankees by 19 games when the season ended. Dick Howser managed the club to 103 wins and a division title, but a little post-season success would have made the season even better. The Kansas City Royals shut down Reggie Jackson and the Yankees offense, giving up only six runs in a three game sweep of the league championship series, and Dick Howser was out as manager. Of course the Royals then lost the World Series to the Phillies, and Kansas City did not claim the first World Series title in their franchise history until former Yankees skipper Dick Howser guided the club to the Promised Land in 1985.

The number of strikeouts (821) as a member of the Yankees for Tony Lazzeri. His total is the sixth highest in franchise history, but he is also among the top 15 in franchise history for both games and at bats. Lazzeri struck out a career high 96 times as a 22-year-old rookie in 1926, but only twice the rest of his career did he strike out 80 or more times in a season.

The number of strikeouts (822) for the Yankees in 1958. It was the highest total in the league, led by Mickey Mantle who struck out 120 times. Mantle and the offense may have missed on a few swings, but it mattered very little in the end. The Yankees led the league in hits, homeruns, average, runs, slugging percentage, and wins. They won the pennant and another World Series title.

823 The number of runs (823) for the Yankees in 1923. It was the third highest total in the league, but in terms of the most important numbers the Yankees came out on top. Miller Huggins managed the club to 98 wins and a third consecutive pennant as five pitchers won 16 or more games, and then the Yankees beat the New York Giants to win the first World Series title in franchise history.

824 The number of strikeouts (8.24) per nine innings for David Cone in 1999. He led the club with the third best ratio in the league, and the ninth best ratio in franchise history. Cone was only 12-9, but his numbers were much better than his record indicates. He gave up only 164 hits in 193 innings for the second lowest ratio of hits per nine innings in the league. Cone was also second in the league in ERA, and fourth in strikeouts.

825 The OPS (.825) for Mickey Mantle in 1967. He was a 35-year-old veteran who led the club in games despite playing in constant pain. Mantle only batted .245, but he led the club with a .391 on-base percentage that was the fifth highest in the league. He also led the club in slugging, homeruns, walks, times on base, total bases, and the tenth highest OPS in the league.

826 The number of hits (8.26) allowed per nine innings for Randy Johnson in 2005. He gave up 207 hits in 225 innings for the best ratio on the club. Johnson gave up the most hits on the staff, but he also pitched the most innings and he led the club with 17 wins.

827 The number of runs (827) for the Yankees in 1961. Roger Maris and Mickey Mantle anchored a line-up reminiscent of 1927, and the duo tied for the league lead with 132 runs each. Maris also led the league with 61 homeruns and 142 RBI, Mantle was second with 54 homeruns and fifth with 128 RBI, and the Yankees hit a major league record 240 homeruns. The record lasted until 2004 when Alex Rodriguez and Gary Sheffield led a Yankees offense that hit 242 homeruns.

828 The number of strikeouts (8.28) per nine innings for Roger Clemens in 2000. He struck out 188 batters in 204 innings and led the club with the fifth best ratio in the league, but his ratio is also the eighth best in franchise history. Clemens posted three of the top eight ratios in the franchise record book in only five seasons from 1999-2003.

829 The number of hits (8.29) allowed per nine innings for Sterling Hitchcock in 1995. He was only 11-10, but he gave up just 155 hits in 168 innings and led the club with the tenth best ratio in the league.

830 The number of walks (830) as a member of the Yankees for Tony Lazzeri. His total is the seventh highest in franchise history. The HOF infielder set a career high with 97 walks in 1936, and he was among the top ten league leaders five times from 1927-36. Lazzeri is also among the top 20 in franchise history with a .379 on-base percentage and 952 runs, a direct result of his high number of walks.

831 The number of runs (831) for the Yankees in 1977. Graig Nettles, Chris Chambliss, Willie Randolph, and Reggie Jackson all scored at least 90 runs. Nettles led the way with 99 runs as the club scored the fourth highest total in the league, posted a 100-62 record, and beat the Los Angeles Dodgers in the 1977 World Series.

832 The number of strikeouts (832) as a member of the Yankees for pitcher Vic Raschi. He never struck out more than 164 batters in a season, but he pitched more than 1,500 innings in eight seasons, and won 21 games three consecutive years from 1949-51. Raschi also posted a 2.24 ERA in the post-season and won six World Series titles.

833 The winning percentage (.833) for pitcher Spud Chandler in 1943. He posted a 20-4 record and led the league with the seventh best winning percentage in franchise history. Chandler also won the MVP, something no other Yankee pitcher has done.

834 The number of RBI (834) as a member of the Yankees for Graig Nettles. He batted only .253 during 11 seasons in the Bronx, but he could hit the long ball. A long time fan favorite in New York, most of those fans can recall at least one of his tape measure shots. He hit 250 of them for the Yankees, the seventh highest total in franchise history.

835 The number of singles (835) as a member of the Yankees for Bobby Murcer. He was a 19-year-old shortstop when he hit his first single in 1965. Murcer was a 37-year-old veteran outfielder when he hit his last single in 1983, and his career total with the club is among the top 30 in franchise history. It would be a mistake though to confuse Murcer with a light-hitting shortstop or outfielder, because he also ranks among the top 30 for hits, slugging percentage, and runs, and he is among the top 20 in franchise history for homeruns.

836 The number of strikeouts (836) for the Yankees pitching staff in 1959. It was the highest total in the league, led by Whitey Ford who struck out 114 batters. Bob Turley was second on the club with 111 strikeouts and the team ERA was the third best in the league. New York won four consecutive pennants from 1955-58, but the Yankees struggled on offense in 1959. Pitching alone could not get the job done as the club fell to third place with a 79-75 record.

837 The number of batters (837) Scott Sanderson faced in 1991. He walked only 29 batters in 208 innings for a 1.25 walks per nine innings ratio that was the second best in the league. Sanderson struck out 130 batters for a 4.48 strikeouts to walk ratio that was also the second best in the league. It was his first season in the Bronx, and he led the club with 16 wins.

838 The number of strikeouts (838) for the Yankees pitching staff in 1962. It was only the sixth highest total in the league, but the Yankees also gave up the second lowest hits, walks, and runs totals. Ralph Terry led the club with a 23-12 record and 176 strikeouts, and with a 96-66 record the Yankees won the pennant.

834 The winning percentage (.839) for pitcher Lefty Gomez in 1934. He was 26-5, and he led the league in wins, strikeouts, and ERA to win the pitching Triple Crown. Gomez only placed third in MVP balloting, but he is one of only seven players in franchise history to win 26 or more games in a season.

840 The number of strikeouts (840) for the Yankees in 1969. It was the second lowest total in the league, but despite having the ability to put the ball into play, the club lacked the ability to get guys on base and across the plate. New York scored only 562 runs, also the second lowest total in the league. The club was 80-81 on the season for a distant fifth place finish in the division standings.

841 The number of batters (841) Ron Guidry faced in 1984. He was a 34-year-old veteran who let 267 batters reach base against him as he struggled to a 10-11 record. The New York media said he was done, but Guidry silenced his critics in 1985. Guidry came back and led the league in wins with a 22-6 record, and he placed second in CYA balloting after letting just 285 batters out of 1,033 he faced get on base.

842 The winning percentage (.842) for pitcher Ralph Terry in 1961. He posted a 16-3 record for the fifth highest winning percentage in franchise history, but his percentage was not even the highest on the club in 1961. Whitey Ford posted a 25-4 record for the fourth highest winning percentage in franchise history.

843 The winning percentage (.843) during blowouts for the Yankees in 1927. New York was 43-8 in games decided by five runs or greater and outscored their opponents during those games 464-174. The Yankees scored 975 runs for the highest total in baseball, and were shutout only once all season.

844 The number of singles (844) for Tony Kubek. His total is among the top 30 in franchise history despite the fact that he was only 28 years old when injuries forced his retirement. Kubek was a shortstop who won the 1957 ROY, and he also ranks among the top 40 in franchise history for at bats, runs, hits, doubles, and games.

845 The number of RBI (845) for the Yankees in 2003. New York scored 877 runs for the third highest total in the league. Alfonso Soriano led the club with 114 runs, Soriano, Jorge Posada, and Jason Giambi all hit 30 or more homeruns, and Posada, Giambi, and Hideki

Matsui all picked up 100 or more RBI. New York posted a 101-61 record and claimed the pennant in the post-season.

The slugging percentage (.846) for Babe Ruth in 1921. He led the league with the second highest slugging percentage in franchise history. Ruth batted .378, and in only 152 games he hit 59 homeruns with 171 RBI.

The slugging percentage (.847) for Babe Ruth in 1920. His slugging percentage is a franchise record, and it was also the major league record until 2001 when Barry Bonds hit 73 homeruns for a .863 slugging percentage. Ruth batted .376 in 1920, and he hit 54 homeruns in only 458 at bats.

The number of strikeouts (8.48) per nine innings as a member of the Yankees for Roger Clemens from 1999-2003. Clemens struck out 946 batters in 1,004 innings during his first tour of duty in the Bronx, and his ratio is the third highest in franchise history.

The number of batters (849) Javier Vazquez faced in 2004. His total led the club, and he also led the club with 198 innings, 14 wins, and 150 strikeouts.

The number of batters (850) Ron Guidry faced in 1977. His total was only third highest on the club, but Guidry tied Ed Figueroa for the team lead with 16 wins. It was his first full season in the Bronx, and he was also fourth in the league with a 2.82 ERA. Guidry was only seventh in CYA balloting, but he got his first ring when the Yankees beat the Dodgers in the 1977 World Series.

The number of batters (851) David Wells faced in 1998. He gave up only 195 hits in 214 innings, and he led the league with a 1.05 WHIP. Wells gave up only 29 walks as he posted an 18-4 record and led the club in ERA, but he was only third in CYA balloting.

The OPS (.852) for Derek Jeter from 1995-2006. He was only 20 years old when he made his major league debut on May 29, 1995. Jeter has been the starting shortstop for the club since 1996, and he will go down in history as one of the most popular and productive players to wear pinstripes. His numbers at the end of 2007 place him among the top 30 in franchise history for slugging percentage, in the top 20 for OPS, in the top 15 for on-base percentage, in the top ten for games, and in the top five for at bats, batting average, and runs.

853 The number of RBI (853) for the Yankees in 1933. The club scored 927 runs for the highest total in the league. Lou Gehrig's 139 RBI led the club, and both Tony Lazzeri and Babe Ruth also surpassed the 100 RBI mark. It was pitching that hurt the Yankees in 1933, as the club gave up the fifth highest runs total in the league. The result was a 91-59 record that left the club sitting at home in October.

854 The number of hits (8.54) allowed per nine innings for Fritz Peterson in 1970. He gave up 247 hits, but pitched 260 innings for the best ratio on the club. Peterson also led the league with a 1.10 WHIP as he posted a career best 20-11 record, and he made his only career All-Star team that season.

855 The number of walks (855) allowed by Bob Shawkey as a member of the Yankees. He is in some pretty elite company in a dubious category as only three players in franchise history gave up more walks: Lefty Gomez, Whitey Ford, and Red Ruffing. Shawkey gave up a lot of walks though because he tossed the fifth highest number of innings in franchise history. Shawkey won 20 or more games four times with the club, and he is also fifth in franchise history with 168 career wins.

856 The number of runs (856) allowed by the Boston Red Sox in 1927. It was the second highest total in the league behind the St. Louis Browns, and the team that scored the most runs against the Red Sox was the Yankees. New York posted an 18-4 record and scored 171 runs against Boston, and the Red Sox trailed the Yankees by 59 games when the season ended.

857 The WHIP (.857) for Mariano Rivera during the 1999 World Series. He was 1-0 with three saves against Atlanta. Rivera gave up three hits and a walk in four plus innings of work, and he struck out three batters. He was so dominant that he broke three of Braves slugger

Ryan Klesko's bats in just one plate appearance—that's as many broken bats as the Braves got hits off of Rivera. The Yankees won the title, and Rivera earned series MVP honors. Rudy Giuliani, the mayor of New York City, presided over a victory rally at City Hall where the team arrived after a celebratory parade through downtown—a parade in which Rivera was given a float of his own.

858 The number of batters (858) Andy Pettitte faced in 2001. He was 15-10, but he gave up a lot of base runners. Pettitte allowed 274 of those batters he faced to get on base, but it was a different story completely in the post-season. He was 2-0 against the Mariners during the league championship series. He faced 54 batters, but gave up only 11 hits and 14 base runners. Pettitte won MVP honors for the series as the Yankees won the pennant.

859 The OPS (.859) for Earle Combs. The HOF outfielder hit only 58 homeruns during 12 seasons in the Bronx, but he is second in franchise history with 154 triples. Combs is also in the top 15 in franchise history for OPS, in the top ten for on-base percentage and hits, and in the top five for average.

860 The number of hits (8.60) allowed per nine innings for Roger Clemens in 2002. He gave up only 172 hits in 180 innings for the best ratio on the club. Clemens was 13-6, and he also led the club with 192 strikeouts.

861 The OPS (.861) for Snuffy Stirnweiss in 1945. His OPS led the club and set a career high, as did his .476 slugging percentage. Stirnweiss batted .309, and he also led the club with 32 doubles and 22 triples. He placed third in league MVP balloting.

862 The winning percentage (.862) for pitcher Whitey Ford in 1961. He led the league with the fourth highest winning percentage in franchise history. Ford set a career high for victories when he posted a 25-4 record, won his only career CYA, and then picked up two more wins against the Cincinnati Reds as the Yankees won the 1961 World Series.

863 The number of RBI (863) for the Yankees in 1921. The club scored 948 runs for the highest total in the majors. Babe Ruth, Bob Meusel, and Roger Peckinpaugh all scored 100 or more runs. Ruth led the club with 171 RBI, and Meusel added 136 RBI as the club posted a 98-55 record for the first pennant in franchise history.

 864 The slugging percentage (.864) for Derek Jeter during the 2000 World Series. He batted 9 for 22 against the New York Mets and scored six runs in only five games. Jeter hit two doubles, a triple, and two homeruns in the series. He also won his fourth ring, and series MVP honors.

865 The number of strikeouts (8.65) per nine innings as a member of the Yankees for Goose Gossage. He struck out 512 batters in only 533 innings during his tenure in the Bronx, and his ratio is the second highest in franchise history.

866 The number of strikeouts (866) for the Yankees pitching staff in 1961. It was the fourth highest total in the league, led by Whitey Ford who was second in the league with 209 strikeouts. New York also gave up the second lowest number of hits and posted the second lowest ERA in the league, but with an offense that scored better than five runs a game, the Yankees posted a 109-53 record and easily won the pennant.

867 The number of strikeouts (8.67) per nine innings as a member of the Yankees for David Cone. He struck out 888 batters in 922 innings for the best ratio in franchise history.

868 The OPS (.868) for Bill Dickey. He set a record for catchers when he batted .362 in 1936, and he hit a career high 29 homeruns in 1937. Dickey is sixth in franchise history with a .313 career average, and he is also among the top 15 in on-base percentage, slugging percentage, and OPS.

869 The OPS (.869) as a member of the Yankees for Paul O'Neill. He set career highs with a .460 on-base percentage and a .603 slugging percentage in 1994, and his career OPS is among the top 15 in franchise history.

870 The winning percentage (.870) for pitcher Roger Clemens in 2001. He won his sixth CYA and led the league with the third highest winning percentage in franchise history. Clemens beat Kansas City 7-3 on opening day, and he did not lose a game until May 20. He was 4-1 after that loss, but when the Yankees met the Tampa Bay Devil Rays four months later on September 25, Clemens was 20-1. Tampa was the worst team in baseball that season, but the Devil Rays beat Clemens twice during the last two weeks of the season, and he finished the year 20-3.

871 The number of runs (871) for the Yankees in 2000. It was only the sixth highest total in the league, led by Derek Jeter who scored 119 runs and placed fifth in the batting title race with a .339 average. Jorge Posada led the club with a .417 on-base percentage that was also the eighth best in the league, and Bernie Williams led the club with a career high 121 RBI. New York won only 87 games for the lowest total under manager Joe Torre from 1996-2007, but the club still won the division title, league pennant, and the World Series.

872 The number of batters (872) Tiny Bonham faced in 1942. His total led the club, as did his 21-5 record and 2.27 ERA. Bonham made his first All-Star team in 1942, and he placed fifth in league MVP balloting. His best seasons came in the Bronx, but Bonham was traded to the Pirates after 1946. He died tragically after his appendix ruptured while pitching a game in Pittsburgh in 1949.

873 The OPS (.873) for Tommy Henrich. He was among the top ten league leaders for OPS four times, and his career OPS is the tenth highest in franchise history. Henrich hit a career high 31 homeruns in 1941, and posted a career high .554 slugging percentage in 1948 when he led the league with 81 extra-base hits. He also posted a .452 slugging percentage in the post-season and won four World Series titles.

874 The number of earned runs (874) allowed by Ron Guidry. He gave up 98 earned runs in 1984 to set a career high, and he posted a 10-11 record for his first losing season since he was 0-1 as a 24-year-old rookie in 1975. Guidry's career total is the sixth highest in franchise history, but he is also sixth in innings and fourth with 170 career wins.

875 The winning percentage (.875) for pitcher Ron Davis in 1979. He was a 23-year-old rookie relief pitcher who posted a 14-2 record for the second highest winning percentage in franchise history. Davis placed fourth in ROY balloting, and though he played nine more years in the majors, he won only 33 games the rest of his career.

876 The number of strikeouts (8.76) per nine innings for Al Downing in 1963. He was a 22-year-old rookie who led the league with the fourth highest ratio in franchise history. Downing was 13-5, and he struck out 171 batters in only 175 innings. He actually set a franchise record with his ratio that lasted until David Cone posted a 10.25 ratio in 1997.

877 The number of runs (877) for Phil Rizzuto. His total is among the top 20 in franchise history. Rizzuto scored a career high 125 runs during his 1950 MVP season, but scored 100 or more runs only one other season, in 1949, when he placed second in league MVP balloting.

878 The number of earned runs (878) allowed by Mel Stottlemyre. His total is the fifth highest in franchise history, and it includes the career high 106 earned runs he allowed during a dismal 12-20 campaign in 1966. Of course, he is also third in franchise history for innings and sixth with 164 wins. Stottlemyre won 15 or more games six times, and he won 20 or more games three times.

879 The number of earned runs (879) allowed by Waite Hoyt as a member of the Yankees. His total is the fourth highest in franchise history. Hoyt gave up 108 earned runs in 1925 to set a career high, and he suffered through his only losing season for the Yankees with an 11-14 record. He gave up a lot of earned runs, but he also pitched a lot of innings. Hoyt is seventh in franchise history for innings, and eighth with 157 wins.

880 The number of batters (880) Herb Pennock faced in 1927. He pitched 209 innings, tossed 18 complete games, and posted a 19-8 record with a 3.00 ERA—but the only statistical category he led the club in was his eight losses. If you think about it though, to lead a club with eight losses means you play on a pretty good club, and Pennock was on one of the best in history.

881 The number of extra-base hits (881) for Joe DiMaggio. His total is among the top 60 in baseball history, but it is the fourth highest in franchise history. DiMaggio led the league in extra-base hits twice, in 1941 and 1950. He set a career high with 84 extra-base hits in 1941, and 35 of them came during his record 56 game hitting streak.

882 The number of batters (882) Whitey Ford faced in 1953. His total led the club, and was a result of the team leading 207 innings he spent on the mound. Ford was only 24 years old and in his second major league season, but it was his first season back after spending two years serving in the military during the Korean War. He also led the club in wins, starts, complete games, and strikeouts.

883 The OPS (.883) for George Selkirk. He was among the top ten league leaders for OPS only three times during his nine year career, but his career OPS is among the top ten in franchise history. Selkirk is also among the top 60 in baseball history with a .400 career on-base percentage.

884 The WHIP (.884) for Mariano Rivera in 1999. He pitched 69 innings and faced 268 batters, but gave up only 43 hits and 18 walks. Rivera also led the league with 45 saves and won his first career Rolaids Relief Award.

885 The number of hits (8.85) allowed per nine innings for Doc Medich in 1974. He was born George Francis Medich, but he earned the nickname Doc because he endured the rigors of medical school at the same time he was beginning his major league career. Medich earned his M.D., and did pretty well on the mound too. He won a career high 19 games in 1974, and his hits per nine innings ratio was the best on the club.

886 The number of runs (886) for the Yankees in 2005. It was the second highest total in the league, led by Alex Rodriguez who scored 124 runs. Gary Sheffield, Hideki Matsui, and Derek Jeter also surpassed

100 runs on the season as the Yankees posted a 95-67 record and won their eighth consecutive division title.

The OPS (.887) for Bobby Bonds in 1975. He led the club with the fifth highest OPS in the league. Bonds played only one season in the Bronx, but he also led the club with 32 homeruns and 61 extra-base hits.

The number of strikeouts (888) as a member of the Yankees for pitcher David Cone. His total is among the top 20 in franchise history, and his 2,668 career strikeouts total is among the top 30 in baseball history. Cone struck out 222 batters in 195 innings in 1997, the third highest season total in franchise history.

The number of hits (889) for the Yankees in 1981. It was the 11th lowest total out of 14 teams in the league during the strike-shortened season. Dave Winfield led the club with 114 hits and 68 RBI, and Jerry Mumphrey was second with 98 hits. Luckily for New York, the club also gave up the fewest hits and the fewest runs among all 14 teams in the league—and after limping into the post-season, the Yankees won the pennant.

The OPS (.890) for Robinson Cano in 2006. The 23-year-old second baseman batted .342 during his sophomore season and placed third in the batting title race. Cano also hit 41 doubles and 15 homeruns for a .525 slugging percentage that was second on the club behind Jason Giambi, but ahead of Alex Rodriguez.

The number of runs (891) for the Yankees in 1997. It was the second highest total in the league, led by Derek Jeter who scored 116 runs. Tino Martinez was second in league MVP balloting after he led the Yankees with 44 homeruns and 141 RBI. Bernie Williams and Paul O'Neill also reached 100 RBI as the Yankees posted a 96-66 record and secured the second Wild Card playoff berth in franchise history.

The fielding percentage (.892) for pitcher Mike Mussina in 2005. He won six Gold Gloves from 1996-2003, and made only 14 fielding errors during his first 16 seasons through 2006. Unfortunately, four of those errors came during his 30 starts in 2005, and they resulted in the lowest fielding percentage of his career.

893 The winning percentage (.893) for pitcher Ron Guidry in 1978. He was 25-3, won the CYA, and led the league with the highest winning percentage in franchise history.

894 The number of runs (894) for the Yankees in 1928. It was the third consecutive season the Yankees led the league in runs. Babe Ruth and Lou Gehrig tied for the team lead with 142 RBI, and Bob Meusel picked up 113 RBI. Gehrig, Ruth, and Earle Combs all scored 118 or more runs as the Yankees posted a 101-53 record to win the pennant. New York then swept the St. Louis Cardinals in the 1928 World Series.

895 The OPS (.895) for Mickey Mantle in 1953. He was only 21 years old but he was already in his third season with the club. Mantle was second on the club in OPS, just behind Gene Woodling who posted a .897 mark on the season. Mantle did lead the club with 105 runs, and 48 of his 136 hits went for extra-bases.

896 The number of batters (896) Andy Pettitte faced in 2003. His total led the club, and he also led the Yankees with the second highest number of wins in the league. Pettitte was 21-8, but he only placed sixth in league CYA balloting.

897 The OPS (.897) as a member of the Yankees for Reggie Jackson. His OPS is the eighth highest in franchise history. Jackson's best season effort came in 1980 when he posted a .995 OPS. He batted .300 with 41 homeruns that season, and placed second in league MVP balloting.

898 The number of runs (898) allowed by the Yankees in 1930. It was the second highest total in the league as the club posted a 4.88 ERA on the season. George Pipgras gave up the most runs with 133, but he also tied Red Ruffing for the team lead in wins with 15. The big problem was defense. Only 741 of the runs were earned, but they all counted, and the season total from 1930 is the highest in franchise history.

899 The number of runs (899) for the Yankees in 1929. The club led the league in runs three consecutive seasons from 1926-28, and won the pennant each time. The runs total in 1929 though was only the third best in the league. The result was an 88-66 record, and no pennant.

900 The number of batters (900) Chien-Ming Wang faced in 2006. His total led the club, as did his 218 innings. Wang, who is a native of Taiwan, posted a 19-6 record to also lead the club in wins and winning percentage. He placed second in league CYA balloting.

Roger Maris and Mickey Mantle

"You kind of took it for granted around the Yankees
that there was always going to be baseball in October."

— *Whitey Ford*

Chapter Ten

The Legends

People either love or hate the Yankees for the same reasons—
because of the franchise's legacy of winning, and the legends who have
worn pinstripes. Other franchises envy the numbers: three Wild Card
berths, 15 East Division titles, 39 American League pennants, and 26
World Series titles. Love them or hate them, the New York Yankees are
the most successful professional sports franchise in the world.

No other franchise can boast as many Hall of Fame members: Frank
Baker, Yogi Berra, Wade Boggs, Frank Chance, Jack Chesbro, Earle
Combs, Stan Coveleski, Bill Dickey, Joe DiMaggio, Leo Durocher,
Whitey Ford, Lou Gehrig, Lefty Gomez, Clark Griffith, Burleigh
Grimes, Bucky Harris, Waite Hoyt, Miller Huggins, Catfish Hunter,
Reggie Jackson, Willie Keeler, Tony Lazzeri, Bob Lemon, Mickey
Mantle, Joe McCarthy, Bill McKechnie, Johnny Mize, Phil Niekro, Herb
Pennock, Gaylord Perry, Phil Rizzuto, Red Ruffing, Babe Ruth, Joe
Sewell, Enos Slaughter, Casey Stengel, Dazzy Vance, Paul Waner, and

Dave Winfield. New York is also the only franchise in baseball with a player in the Hall of Fame from all nine positions.

It does not matter whether you call New York the Bronx Bombers or the Evil Empire, you have to respect the accomplishments of all the legends who have worn Yankee pinstripes.

Two Triple Crown winners: Lou Gehrig (1934) and Mickey Mantle (1956).

Five Cy Young award recipients: Bob Turley (1958), Whitey Ford (1961), Sparky Lyle (1977), Ron Guidry (1978), and Roger Clemens (2001).

Seven league championship series Most Valuable Player award recipients: Graig Nettles (1981), Bernie Williams (1996), David Wells (1998), Orlando Hernandez (1999), David Justice (2000), Andy Pettitte (2001), and Mariano Rivera (2003).

Eight Rookie of the Year recipients: Gil McDougald (1951), Bob Grim (1954), Tony Kubek (1957), Tom Tresh (1962), Stan Bahnsen (1968), Thurman Munson (1970), Dave Righetti (1981), and Derek Jeter (1996).

Eleven World Series Most Valuable Player award recipients: Don Larsen (1956), Bob Turley (1958), Bobby Richardson (1960), Whitey Ford (1961), Ralph Terry (1962), Reggie Jackson (1977), Bucky Dent (1978), John Wetteland (1996), Scott Brosius (1998), Mariano Rivera (1999), and Derek Jeter (2000).

Twenty-two Most Valuable Player award recipients: Babe Ruth (1923), Lou Gehrig (1927, 1936), Joe DiMaggio (1939, 1941, 1947), Joe Gordon (1942), Spud Chandler (1943), Phil Rizzuto (1950), Yogi Berra (1951, 1954, 1955), Mickey Mantle (1955, 1956, 1962), Roger Maris (1960, 1961), Elston Howard (1963), Thurman Munson (1976), Don Mattingly (1985), and Alex Rodriguez (2005, 2007).

Only 11 players have been captain of the Yankees: Hal Chase, Roger Peckinpaugh, Babe Ruth, Everett Scott, Lou Gehrig, Thurman Munson, Graig Nettles, Willie Randolph, Ron Guidry, Don Mattingly, and Derek Jeter.

New York has also retired the most jersey numbers of any major league franchise: Billy Martin (1), Babe Ruth (3), Lou Gehrig (4), Joe DiMaggio (5), Mickey Mantle (7), Yogi Berra and Bill Dickey (8), Roger Maris (9), Phil Rizzuto (10), Thurman Munson (15), Whitey Ford (16),

Don Mattingly (23), Elston Howard (32), Casey Stengel (37), Jackie Robinson (42), Reggie Jackson (44), and Ron Guidry (49).

Don Larsen, David Wells, and David Cone all pitched perfect games for New York. Larsen tossed his during the 1956 World Series for the only post-season perfect game on record, and Joe Torre is the only manager in history to be on the winning side of two perfect games, having been in the dugout for both Wells and Cone. Allie Reynolds pitched a no-hitter for New York on September 28, 1951—to clinch the pennant. It was also his second no-hitter for the club. Dwight Gooden, Jim Abbott, Dave Righetti, Monte Pearson, Sam Jones, and George Mogridge have also thrown no-hitters for the Yankees.

Bert Daniels became the first player in franchise history to hit for the cycle when he pulled it off on July 25, 1912, but Bob Meusel did it for the Yankees three times during his career, and Joe DiMaggio and Lou Gehrig each did it twice. Buddy Rosar is the only catcher to hit for the cycle for the Yankees, and Tony Fernandez, Bobby Murcer, Mickey Mantle, Joe Gordon, and Tony Lazzeri also hit for the cycle.

Lou Gehrig is the only player in franchise history to hit four homeruns in one game, but Andy Phillips, Marcus Thames, and John Miller are the only players in franchise history to hit a homerun in their first major league at bat. Cliff Johnson, Joe Pepitone, and Joe DiMaggio all hit two homeruns in the same inning. On April 23, 2000, Jorge Posada hit a homerun from each side of the plate during the same game—and so did his teammate Bernie Williams, in the very same game.

On June 13, 2003, Roger Clemens recorded strikeout number 4,000 and career victory number 300—in the same game.

Of course we also have George Steinbrenner.

The Boss is synonymous with the New York Yankees and the reaction he gets from people is exactly the same—you either love him or you hate him, but no matter which it is you have to respect his desire to win and his commitment to success, because that is the legacy of this franchise, built by legends who personify the best this game has to offer.

The number of runs (901) for Tommy Henrich. His total is among the top 20 in franchise history, but like many players of his generation, Henrich gave three of his prime seasons to military service during World War II. Henrich led the league with a career high 138 runs in 1948, and he also won four World Series titles with the club.

The number of batters (902) Tiny Bonham faced in 1943. He was 15-8, and he made his second consecutive All-Star team. Bonham was remarkably consistent from 1942-43, as he made 28 starts and pitched 226 innings both seasons. He gave up 199 hits in 1942, and he gave up 197 hits in 1943. Bonham gave up 57 earned runs and posted an identical 2.27 ERA both seasons. He also struck out 71 batters and hit one batter in both seasons. The big difference for Bonham though was the way both seasons ended. The Yankees lost the 1942 World Series in five games to the St. Louis Cardinals, but the Yankees beat the Cardinals in five games during the 1943 World Series.

The number of batters (903) Andy Pettitte faced in 2000. His total led the club, as did his 32 starts and 204 innings. Pettitte posted an unimpressive 4.35 ERA, but he also led the club with 19 wins and placed fourth in CYA balloting. Not to mention, he was 2-0 during the post-season and made two quality starts against the Mets during the 2000 World Series—and won his fourth ring in five seasons with the club. Derek Jeter once said of Pettitte, "Andy is a big game pitcher—that's the bottom line."

The OPS (.904) for Mickey Mantle in 1959. His OPS led the club, but he was second in the league behind fellow HOF outfielder Al Kaline of the Detroit Tigers. Mantle hit 31 homeruns that season, and he led the club in 17 different offensive categories.

The OPS (.905) for Tony Lazzeri in 1932. He was among the top ten league leaders in slugging, on-base percentage, and RBI, but the Yankees offense was so good that the only category he led the club in was strikeouts. Lazzeri posted a .647 slugging percentage and hit two homeruns in the 1932 World Series, but even those totals were second that post-season behind teammate Lou Gehrig. No complaints from Lazzeri though—he won his third World Series title.

906 The number of strikeouts (9.06) per nine innings for David Cone in 1998. He struck out 209 batters in 207 innings for the fifth best ratio in the league, but it is the third best ratio in franchise history. Cone led the N.L. in this category three consecutive seasons from 1990-92 for the New York Mets, but his career high ratio came as a member of the Yankees—though it wasn't in 1998. Cone struck out 10.25 batters per nine innings in 1997 for the best ratio in franchise history.

907 The number of RBI (907) for the Yankees in 1998. Derek Jeter, Chuck Knoblauch, and Bernie Williams all scored 100 or more runs. Tino Martinez and Paul O'Neill both surpassed 115 RBI—and the club scored 965 runs to lead the majors on their way to a franchise record 114 wins.

908 The number of batters (908) Andy Hawkins faced in 1989. His total led the club, as did his starts, innings, strikeouts, wins, and ERA. Hawkins won 15 games, but no other starter for the Yankees won more than six that season.

909 The number of batters (909) Mike Mussina faced in 2001. His total was second on the club behind Roger Clemens, but Mussina gave New York exactly what they were hoping for when they signed him as a free agent in the off-season—innings. Mussina led the club with 228 innings as he posted a 17-11 record. He also led the Yankees in ERA and strikeouts as the club won a fourth consecutive pennant.

910 The number of batters (910) Orlando Hernandez faced in 1999. He led the club with the ninth highest total in the league, and he posted a 17-9 record during his second season in the Bronx. Hernandez was good all year, but he was lights out in the post-season. He gave up only two hits in eight innings against the Rangers in the division series, won two games and series MVP honors against the Red Sox in the league championship series, and gave up just one hit with ten strikeouts to pick up a win against the Braves in the 1999 World Series. He also won his second consecutive ring.

The number of total bases (911) as a member of the Yankees for Wade Boggs. His total is among the top 70 in franchise history, but Boggs only played five seasons and 602 games for New York. He batted .313, and 152 of his 702 hits went for extra-bases.

The number of hits (9.12) allowed per nine innings for Rick Rhoden in 1987. He gave up 184 hits in 181 innings for the best ratio on the club. Rhoden could pitch, but he was also pretty good at hitting things. So good, in fact, that manager Billy Martin used him as the designated hitter for a game in 1988. Rhoden is also a scratch golfer who has won several celebrity golf tournaments since retiring from baseball.

The OPS (.913) for Paul O'Neill in 1995. His OPS led the club as he batted .300 with a .526 slugging percentage. O'Neill also led the club with 56 extra-base hits in only 127 games. He was known throughout his career for an intense emotional desire to win and be successful—but he also understood the dispassionate part of the game, as revealed through comments he once made: "Hitting is a lot more than just picking up a bat and swinging it. You have got to be observant, evaluate the situation, know the pitcher and his tendencies, and know yourself. If you want to be successful, you have to become a student."

The number of hits (9.14) allowed per nine innings for Phil Niekro in 1984. He was a 45-year-old veteran who gave up 219 hits in 215 innings for the best ratio on the club. The HOF knuckleball artist also led the club in starts, wins, innings, strikeouts, and ERA.

The OPS (.915) for Alex Rodriguez in 2006. It was only the second time since 1999 that Rodriguez did not place among the top ten league leaders for OPS, although he did record his ninth consecutive season of 30 homeruns and 100 RBI. Rodriguez responded in 2007 by leading the league with a 1.067 OPS and making it ten consecutive seasons with 30 homeruns and 100 RBI. A-Rod was second in the league with 85 extra-base hits in 2007, but he led the league with 299 times on base, 376 total bases, 54 homeruns, and a .645 slugging percentage. He also averaged one homerun every 10.8 at bats in 2007, just trailing the 10.7 ratio for Carlos Pena of the Tampa Bay Devil Rays.

The number of batters (916) Phil Niekro faced in 1984. His total led the club during his first season in the Bronx. Niekro played only two seasons for New York, but in his career he pitched more than 5,400 innings and faced more than 22,500 batters. Both totals are among the top five in baseball history.

The slugging percentage (.917) for Graig Nettles during the 1981 league championship series. He batted only .244 that season, but Nettles had no trouble seeing the ball against Oakland in the post-season. Nettles hit .500, and he picked up nine RBI in only three games. He also hit two doubles and a homerun as he won series MVP honors.

The number of batters (918) Roger Clemens faced in 2001. His total led the club, and he gave up only 205 hits as he struck out 213 batters. Clemens was 20-3, and he won his sixth career CYA.

The number of times (919) Don Mattingly got credit for a put out in 1994. He made only two errors during 97 games at first base during the strike-shortened season, and he posted a .998 fielding percentage. Mattingly picked up 68 assists and was involved in 95 double-plays as he earned the ninth and final Gold Glove of his career.

The number of batters (920) Randy Johnson faced in 2005. His total led the club, as did his starts, complete games, innings, strikeouts, wins, and ERA. Johnson was 17-8, but he did not receive any votes in the CYA balloting. Bartolo Colon won the award for the Anaheim Angels, but there is no need to feel sorry for Johnson, who won the award five times from 1995-2002. Roger Clemens, who won seven CYA, is the only player in history to win the award more times than Johnson. Part of the success for Clemens and Johnson can be attributed to a shared mindset they both bring with them to the ballpark, as illustrated by comments Johnson has made repeatedly throughout his career, saying, "I expect to win. I've never been content with anything I've ever done."

The OPS (.921) for Charlie Keller in 1943. His OPS led the club, as did his .396 on-base percentage and .525 slugging percentage. Keller also led the club in homeruns, runs, and total bases, and he won his third career title when the Yankees beat the Cardinals in the 1943 World Series.

The number of innings (922) as a member of the Yankees for David Cone. He was 64-40 during six seasons playing in the Bronx, and he won four World Series titles.

The fielding percentage (.923) at third base for Don Mattingly in 1986. It was a bizarre move to put the left-handed Mattingly at third for three games, but manager Lou Piniella was so frustrated with the lack of production from that position that he gave it a try. Mattingly was one of seven players to play third that season. He made 11 assists, turned two double-plays, and made one error.

The OPS (.924) for Mickey Mantle in 1952. He was a 20-year-old outfielder in his second season when he led the league in OPS for the first time and placed third in league MVP balloting. Mantle led the league in OPS five times during his career, and he is among the top 15 in baseball history with a career .977 OPS.

The OPS (.925) for Reggie Jackson in 1977. He led the club with the fifth highest OPS in the league during his first season in the Bronx. Jackson also led the Yankees with 73 extra-base hits and 110 RBI.

The OPS (.926) for Bernie Williams in 1996. He led the club in slugging and OPS, but he only got better in the post-season. Bernie hit six homeruns during the playoffs, and won the first of four career rings.

The number of earned runs (927) allowed by Lefty Gomez as a member of the Yankees. Gomez gave up a career worst 124 earned runs in 1932, but he also won 24 games and his first World Series title that same season. HOF legends Red Ruffing and Whitey Ford are the only players in franchise history to give up more earned runs, but their totals are indicative of extraordinary careers more than anything else. Gomez ranks fifth in franchise history for starts, fourth in innings, and third in wins.

The OPS (.928) as a member of the Yankees for Charlie Keller. His OPS is among the top 50 in baseball history, but it is the seventh highest in franchise history. Keller spent ten seasons playing in the Bronx. He posted a league best .922 OPS in 1943, and a career high .996 OPS in 1941.

The number of batters (929) Andy Pettitte faced in 1996. His total led the club, and he also led the league with 21 wins, but he got lit up during game one of the 1996 World Series against the Atlanta Braves. Pettitte faced just 14 batters in two plus innings, and he gave up seven runs in a 12-1 loss. He got a second chance though in game five. Pettitte made the most of it as he faced 31 batters in eight plus innings, but gave up only five hits and no runs. New York won the game 1-0, and the Yankees went on to take the series in six games for the first World Series title for the franchise since 1978.

The number of runs (930) for the Yankees in 2006. It was the highest total in the league, led by Derek Jeter who scored 118. Alex Rodriguez led the club with 121 RBI, and Jason Giambi led the club with 37 homeruns. But the real star for the Yankees would have to be manager Joe Torre—as he won his ninth consecutive division title, and he made the playoffs for the 11th consecutive season.

The fielding percentage (.931) for Roger Peckinpaugh in 1913. He was a 22-year-old shortstop who made 36 errors in only 93 games. The next season he became just the second team captain in franchise history, but he made 39 errors in 157 games. Peckinpaugh served as captain through his final season with the Yankees in 1921, and the 360 errors he made is the second highest total in franchise history.

The number of batters (932) Andy Pettitte faced in 1998. His total led the club, as did his innings, hits, walks, and runs totals. He had some good numbers, and some not so good numbers, but in the end he was 16-11 and the Yankees were back in the playoffs. Pettitte was at his best when it counted the most. He tossed seven plus shutout innings against the Padres during game four of the 1998 World Series. Pettitte faced 29 batters but gave up only five hits, and he clinched the title for New York.

933 The OPS (.933) for Mickey Mantle in 1954. His OPS led the club, and for the third consecutive season his OPS was among the top five league leaders—but his streak was only getting started. Mantle was among the top five league leaders 11 consecutive seasons from 1952-62. He led the league five times and he came in second four times during that streak. His streak ended in 1963, but Mantle came right back in 1964 and led the league in OPS for the sixth and final time of his career.

934 The number of walks (934) for Roy White. His total is the sixth highest in franchise history, but he never walked 100 times in a season. White walked a career high 99 times in 1972, but he was among the top ten league leaders seven times.

935 The number of strikeouts (935) for the Yankees in 1988. It was the third highest total in the league, led by Jack Clark who struck out 141 times. Don Mattingly struck out only 29 times and was the toughest guy to strike out in the league, but it was a struggle for the rest of the club. New York won only 85 games and placed fifth in the division.

936 The fielding percentage (.936) for Frankie Crosetti in 1933. He was a 22-year-old shortstop who made 43 errors in only 133 games. Crosetti made a staggering 421 errors during his career—the highest total in franchise history—but he also won seven pennants and six World Series titles, and only ten players in franchise history played more games for the Yankees.

937 The WHIP (.937) for Jack Chesbro in 1904. He gave up 338 hits and 88 walks, but he was on the mound 454 innings. His career best ratio was the second best in the league, and it is also the second best in franchise history.

938 The OPS (.938) for Don Mattingly in 1985. He led the club with the second highest OPS in the league. Mattingly led the league with 86 extra-base hits and 370 total bases, and he led the club with 211 hits. He also won a Gold Glove, the Silver Slugger, MVP, and Major League Player of the Year awards in 1985.

The fielding percentage (.939) for the Highlanders in 1912. The club made 386 errors for the worst fielding percentage in franchise history. Jack Martin made 42 errors during 70 games at shortstop; Guy Zinn made 20 errors during 106 games in the outfield; Ed Sweeney made 34 errors during 108 games behind the plate; and ten different players combined to make 51 errors at second base, led by 21 during 88 games for Hack Simmons. Eight players got a shot at third, but they made 72 errors, led by 20 for Roy Hartzell in only 56 games. Hartzell became an outfielder in 1913, but New York won only 50 games in 1912.

The number of strikeouts (940) as a member of the Yankees for pitcher Dave Righetti. His total is among the top 15 in franchise history, but he made only 76 starts for the club. Righetti struck out a career high 169 batters during 31 starts in 1983, but the next season he made the transition to closer. He is second in franchise history with 522 games and 224 saves.

The number of games (941) for Billy Martin as manager from 1975-88. He led the club for all or parts of eight seasons, but his turbulent relationship with owner George Steinbrenner led to five different stints as manager. Regardless of the difficult time they had resolving personal issues, both Martin and Steinbrenner cared more about the team getting the job done on the field. Martin won 556 games, two pennants, and one World Series title during his tenure in New York.

The number of runs (942) for Red Rolfe. He was an everyday player for only seven full seasons, but his total is among the top 15 in franchise history. Rolfe batted .300 and scored 108 runs in 1935, the first of seven consecutive seasons he scored more than 100 runs.

The fielding percentage (.943) for Roy Hartzell as a member of the Highlanders and Yankees. He played six seasons and 680 games for New York, but he made 114 errors and is one of the worst fielders in franchise history. There are more than 1,000 players in franchise history ahead of him in terms of fielding percentage—but he actually did better in New York than he did during five years in St. Louis. Hartzell posted only a .932 fielding percentage overall.

The number of hits (944) allowed by Johnny Murphy as a member of the Yankees. His total is among the top 35 in franchise history, but rather than being a negative, his total is actually a testament to the longevity of his career. He was 93-53 and played 12 seasons in New York, and most of his 383 games came out of the bullpen. Murphy was also 2-0 with four saves in the post-season—and he won six World Series titles.

The OPS (.945) for Alex Rodriguez from 2004-06. He began 2007 with the sixth highest OPS in franchise history, but after leading the league with 54 homeruns and a 1.067 OPS he moved ahead of teammate Jason Giambi into the fifth position.

The WHIP (.946) for Ron Guidry in 1978. He led the league with the third best ratio in franchise history. Guidry faced 1,057 batters, but only 53 reached base and scored an earned run against him.

The slugging percentage (.947) for Bernie Williams during the 1996 league championship series. Bernie led the club with a .535 slugging percentage during the regular season, but against the Orioles in October he was just ridiculous. He got nine hits and six RBI in five games. Bernie hit three doubles and two homeruns, and he got the hardware for series MVP when the Yankees won the pennant.

The number of batters (948) Jimmy Key faced in 1993. His total led the club during his first season in the Bronx. Key played collegiate ball at Clemson University, and he spent nine seasons in Toronto before signing as a free agent with New York. He paid immediate dividends as he also led the club in starts, complete games, innings, strikeouts, shutouts, wins, and ERA. Key only placed fourth in CYA balloting.

The number of strikeouts (949) for the Yankees in 1987. It was only the seventh highest total in the league, led by Mike Pagliarulo who struck out 111 times, but the problem was the offense also scored the seventh lowest run total in the league. Detroit, Boston, Toronto, and Milwaukee all scored more runs than the Yankees, and those were just the teams in their division. New York won 89 games but trailed Detroit, Toronto, and Milwaukee in the standings.

The OPS (.950) for Jason Giambi from 2002-06. He led the club and was third in the league with a 1.034 OPS during his first season in the Bronx. Giambi began play in 2007 with the fifth highest OPS in franchise history, and his career OPS is among the top 15 for all active players in 2007.

The number of hits (951) allowed by Urban Shocker as a member of the Yankees. His total is among the top 35 in franchise history, but he also posted a 61-37 record in less than five full seasons with the club. Shocker won a World Series title with the club in 1927, but he died suddenly from a congenital heart condition in 1928.

The number of extra-base hits (952) for Mickey Mantle. He led the league in extra-base hits three times in four seasons from 1952-56. His career total is among the top 40 in baseball history, but he trails only Lou Gehrig and Babe Ruth in franchise history.

The number of runs (953) allowed by Ron Guidry. His total is the eighth highest in franchise history, but Guidry is also a four-time All-Star who won two World Series titles and a CYA. Guidry also ranks sixth in franchise history in innings and fourth in wins.

The number of hits (954) as a member of the Yankees for Chris Chambliss. His total is among the top 50 in franchise history, but he only played six seasons in the Bronx. He batted .293 with a career high 188 hits in 1976, but his most memorable season had to be 1977. Chambliss hit a homerun in the 1977 World Series and won his first career ring.

The winning percentage (.955) for the Yankees against the St. Louis Browns in 1927. To be fair, New York dominated every team that season—but they especially dominated the hapless Browns. The Yankees posted a 21-1 record against St. Louis, and outscored them 150-65.

956 The number of hits (9.56) allowed per nine innings for Steve Peek in 1941. He was a 26-year-old rookie who made eight starts and nine relief appearances—and that was it for his career, he never pitched in the majors again. Peek gave up 85 hits in 80 innings, but he struck out only 18 batters and was tuned up pretty good for 48 runs. Of course, he did get to play one season of ball—and if that is all you get, do it the way Peek did. He played for the Yankees, and he also won a World Series title.

957 The OPS (.957) for Bernie Williams in 2000. He hit a career high 30 homeruns and led the club in both slugging and OPS. Bernie also led the club in total bases, doubles, triples, homeruns, extra-base hits, and RBI. He placed only 13th in MVP balloting.

958 The WHIP (.958) for Ray Caldwell in 1914. He pitched 213 innings, but gave up only 153 hits and 51 walks. Caldwell was second in the league with the fourth best ratio in franchise history. He was also 17-9, but the club won only 70 games all season.

959 The number of hits (9.59) allowed per nine innings as a member of the Yankees for Tommy John. He is among the top 20 in franchise history for both innings and hits. John played eight seasons in the Bronx and won 91 games for the club.

960 The number of strikeouts (9.60) per nine innings for Roger Clemens in 2002. He was 13-6, and he struck out 192 batters in only 180 innings for the second best ratio in the league, and the second best ratio in franchise history as well.

961 The fielding percentage (.961) at second base for Tony Lazzeri in 1926. He was a 22-year-old rookie who made 31 errors and struggled defensively all season. Lazzeri also picked up 114 RBI during the first season of his HOF career.

962 The fielding percentage (.962) for Roger Peckinpaugh in 1920. He made 28 errors, but turned 56 double-plays. It was actually the lowest number of errors and the highest fielding percentage for the shortstop during his tenure in the Bronx.

The fielding percentage (.963) for Babe Ruth in 1927. He made 13 errors, but he also got credit for 14 outfield assists—both relatively high numbers. Ruth could have booted every ball hit to him though and he still would have made the line-up. He batted .400 and hit two homeruns against the Pittsburgh Pirates in the 1927 World Series for his second title with the club.

The number of runs (964) for Roy White. He scored a career high 109 runs in 1970, and his career total is among the top 15 in franchise history. White played 1,881 games for New York—only Mickey Mantle, Lou Gehrig, Yogi Berra, Babe Ruth, and Bernie Williams played more games for the Yankees.

The number of runs (965) for the Yankees in 1998. It was the highest total in the league, and it led to the best record in baseball: 114-48. Chuck Knoblauch, Derek Jeter, and Bernie Williams all scored 100 or more runs. Tino Martinez and Paul O'Neill both picked up more than 115 RBI, and the club kept scoring runs until they secured the 1998 World Series title with a sweep of the San Diego Padres.

The number of hits (966) for Aaron Ward. He played 12 seasons in the majors, and he spent ten of them as an infielder in the Bronx. Ward played alongside some of the greatest legends in franchise history, and he picked up 840 of his career hits with the club. He also got ten hits and batted .417 against the New York Giants during the 1923 World Series as the Yankees won the first title in franchise history.

The number of earned runs (967) allowed by Whitey Ford. He gave up 108 earned runs in 1961 to set a career high, but that same season he also set career highs with 283 innings and 25 wins, and he also won the major league CYA. He gave up the second highest earned runs total in franchise history—only Red Ruffing gave up more—but he also made more starts, pitched more innings, and won more games than any player in franchise history.

The number of times (968) Frankie Crosetti turned a double-play. All but 24 came while Crosetti was playing shortstop, and his total is the seventh highest in franchise history. The only shortstop in franchise history with more double-plays is HOF legend Phil Rizzuto.

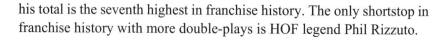The number of hits (9.69) allowed per nine innings as a member of the Yankees for Steve Sundra. His best season was 1939 when he was 11-1. Sundra was not that great the rest of the time, but he was a decent reliever with one very notable accomplishment: he tossed two plus innings of scoreless relief against the Cincinnati Reds during the 1939 World Series. It was the only post-season of his career, and he was used in only that one game, but he contributed to his club winning a World Series title.

The OPS (.970) for Bobby Murcer in 1971. His OPS and 266 times on base both led the league. Murcer also led the club and was third in the league in total bases and extra-base hits, but he only placed seventh in MVP balloting.

The OPS (.971) for Jason Giambi in 2006. He batted just .253 on the season but he reached base at a .413 clip. He also led the team with a .558 slugging percentage and 37 homeruns, and his team leading OPS was the sixth highest number in the league.

The number of strikeouts (9.72) per nine innings as a member of the Yankees for John Wetteland. He was only 3-8 during his two year stint in the Bronx, but it was his 74 saves that earned his paycheck. Wetteland struck out 135 batters in 125 innings, and he gave up only 94 hits.

The number of total bases (973) for Hideki Matsui from 2003-06. He is one of the most respected players in baseball. Matsui came to the Yankees after a successful career in Japan, and he produced 271 total bases in 2003. He improved to 305 total bases in 2004, and 312 in 2005. It took a broken wrist that forced him on the DL in 2006 to slow him down, but he still posted a .494 slugging percentage in 51 games.

The number of hits (974) as a member of the Yankees for Willie Keeler. His total is among the top 40 in franchise history, but he only played seven seasons in the Bronx. Keeler is a HOF outfielder who batted .341 for his career, and he is among the top 35 in baseball history with 2,932 hits.

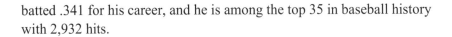

The fielding percentage (.975) for Ben Chapman in 1933. He made only eight errors all season in the outfield—still a relatively high number—but it led to the highest fielding percentage of his career. Chapman earned his paycheck on offense. He batted .315 with a career high 122 RBI in 1931, and he made three straight All-Star teams from 1934-36.

The number of total bases (976) for Alex Rodriguez from 2004-06. He led the club with 308 total bases in 2004, and 369 total bases in 2005. Rodriguez hit 119 homeruns during his first 471 games for New York.

The OPS (.977) for Joe DiMaggio. His OPS is among the top 15 in baseball history, but it is the fourth highest in franchise history. DiMaggio never led the league in OPS for a season, but he placed second among league leaders six times.

The OPS (.978) for Mickey Mantle. His OPS is among the top 15 in baseball history, but it is the third highest in franchise history behind Babe Ruth and Lou Gehrig. Mantle led the league in OPS six times, and he placed second in the league four times.

The OPS (.979) for Joe DiMaggio in 1950. He led the club with the second highest OPS in the league. DiMaggio batted .301, and he also led the team in slugging, triples, homeruns, and extra-base hits.

The number of runs (980) for Hal Chase. He was an infielder who played 15 seasons in the majors, but he scored 551 of his career runs during nine seasons in New York. His total for the Highlanders and Yankees is among the top 40 in franchise history.

The number of total bases (981) for Joe Collins. He played eight full seasons in the Bronx, with his best year coming in 1952. Collins batted .280 with 18 homeruns that season, and he was sixth in the league with a .481 slugging percentage. He never put up HOF numbers, but he was a solid player who also won five World Series titles.

982 The fielding percentage (.982) for Thurman Munson. He posted a career high .998 fielding percentage in 1971, and he made only one error behind the plate all season. Ray Fosse made ten errors and posted a .988 fielding percentage as catcher for the Cleveland Indians, but he won the Gold Glove. Munson did win three consecutive Gold Gloves from 1973-75, but he made 22 errors in 1974, and 23 errors in 1975—giving him the two highest errors totals and the two worst fielding percentages of his career during two of his Gold Glove seasons.

983 The number of hits (9.83) allowed per nine innings as a member of the Yankees for Sterling Hitchcock. He was only 22-24 during parts of seven seasons in the Bronx, and he gave up 439 hits in 402 innings. Hitchcock also suffered from poor timing in terms of who he played for. He was on the Yankees roster when the club lost to Seattle in the 1995 division series, but then he was on the Mariners roster when Seattle placed second in their division in 1996. Hitchcock made it to the 1998 World Series for the Padres, but they were swept by his old club the Yankees. He came back to the Bronx for a second tour of duty and he made it to the 2001 World Series, but the Yankees lost to Arizona.

984 The fielding percentage (.984) for Bobby Richardson in 1963. The All-Star second baseman turned 105 double-plays in 150 games and he made only 12 errors all season. Richardson won his third of five consecutive Gold Gloves.

985 The fielding percentage (.985) for Billy Martin in 1953. He turned 121 double-plays in 146 games and made only 12 errors all season. Martin also came through in a big way during the post-season. He batted .500 with two homeruns against the Brooklyn Dodgers during the 1953 World Series, and the Yankees won a fifth consecutive title.

986 The fielding percentage (.986) for the Yankees in 1995. The club posted the highest fielding percentage in franchise history, but Wade Boggs, who made only five errors at third base, was the only member of the Yankees to win a Gold Glove that season.

The WHIP (.987) for Tiny Bonham in 1942. He led the league with the fifth best ratio in franchise history. Bonham was 21-5, and he also led the club and was second in the league in wins and ERA.

The number of hits (9.88) allowed per nine innings as a member of the Yankees for Ramiro Mendoza. He was 54-34 for the Yankees, and he gave up 768 hits in 700 innings of work. Mendoza found his niche with the club when he became the set-up man for closer Mariano Rivera. He also posted a 2.51 ERA in the post-season and won two World Series titles with the club.

The number of batters (989) Spud Chandler faced in 1943. He led the club with the fifth highest total in the league, and he did better than most at getting them out. Chandler led the league with a 20-4 record and he tossed five complete game shutouts.

The OPS (.990) for Derek Jeter in 1999. He led the club with the fifth highest OPS in the league. Jeter batted .349, and he also led the club in batting, on-base percentage, slugging percentage, runs, hits, total bases, triples, extra-base hits, and times on base. He placed only sixth in MVP balloting.

The fielding percentage (.991) for Roger Maris in 1962. People tend to remember his 61 homeruns and back-to-back MVP seasons, but they overlook that Maris was a great outfielder too. He won a Gold Glove in 1960 when he made only four errors, and in 1962 he made only three errors in 154 games for the second highest fielding percentage of his career.

The WHIP (.992) for Spud Chandler in 1943. He was on the mound for 253 innings, but he gave up only 197 hits and 54 walks. Chandler led the league with the sixth best ratio in franchise history, but he also led the league and set a franchise record with a 1.64 ERA. He closed out the season by winning two games against the St. Louis Cardinals during the 1943 World Series for the second of three career titles.

993 The number of innings (993) as a member of the Yankees for Catfish Hunter. He led the league with 328 innings in 1975, his first season in the Bronx. Hunter was 63-53 during five seasons with the club, and he gave up 1,146 base runners for a 1.15 WHIP that ranks him among the top ten in franchise history.

994 The fielding percentage (.994) for Dave Winfield in 1984. He made only two errors in 140 games as he earned his third consecutive Gold Glove. Winfield is recognized as having one of the strongest outfield arms in baseball history, and his 166 outfield assists back up that claim.

995 The number of RBI (995) for the Yankees in 1936. It was the highest total in baseball, and it also set a franchise record. Lou Gehrig led the club with 152 RBI, but four other players also surpassed the century mark on the season: Bill Dickey, Tony Lazzeri, Joe DiMaggio, and George Selkirk.

996 The WHIP (.996) for Fritz Peterson in 1969. He led the league with the ninth best ratio in franchise history, but the club was so bad that he barely posted a .500 record. Peterson was 17-16, and he also led the club with 150 strikeouts and a 2.55 ERA.

997 The OPS (.997) for Bernie Williams in 1998. His OPS led the club and was the third highest in the league. Bernie also won the batting title with a .339 average, but he only placed seventh in league MVP balloting—and perhaps more surprising still is the fact that his seventh place finish was also the highest of his career.

998 The fielding percentage (.998) for Don Mattingly in 1994. He made only two errors in 97 games and won the ninth and final Gold Glove of his career. Mattingly was one of the best first basemen of his generation—both at the plate and in the field—and he posted a career .996 fielding percentage.

999 The number of hits (999) allowed by Dave Righetti as a member of the Yankees. He took the mound for 1,136 innings wearing pinstripes. Righetti gave up more hits than innings only once during 11 seasons in the Bronx, and his ratio of 7.91 hits per nine innings is among the top 15 in franchise history.

1000 The number of times (1000) mom and dad cheered for us as we rounded the cardboard bases on the sandlot back behind our house, dreaming of wearing pinstripes, and doing our best Babe Ruth homerun trot.

Bibliography

We were lucky that our research for writing this book actually took us to the corner of 161st Street and River Avenue in the Bronx—not just once, but several times. Yankee Stadium is an inspiring sight in itself, and the history that has been made inside the stadium and by all those who have worn Yankee pinstripes is so immense that we could have penned many volumes beyond this one book. It was quite a difficult task to focus on only nine players for the chapter introductions when there are so many current and former players, coaches, and front office personnel who are literally legends in terms of baseball history to choose from. In the end we covered each era in franchise history numerically, but we obviously chose to focus on contemporary stars for the introductory material, though we could just have easily profiled the starting line-up from

1927—and who knows, maybe for a second volume the SBTN Team will do just that.

We do extensive research for all of our titles, and because we know fans like us want to have access to as much material as possible we take great pride in making our own website interactive for our readers—but in addition to that, we also want to make sure we provide a helpful list of all the sources that provide us with information as we write.

Some of the legends featured in our chapter introductions have their own websites that provided us with useful background and anecdotal information:

www.derekjeter.com
www.pauloneill21.com
www.berniewilliams.com
www.joetorre.org
www.donmattingly.com

The SBTN Team has always been committed to supporting charitable organizations and we encourage you to check out our website for ways you can help us to do that—but we also encourage Yankee fans to support the Joe Torre Safe at Home Foundation, Derek Jeter's Turn 2 Foundation, and Paul O'Neill's Right Field Charities.

We also made use of some other valuable websites. Major League Baseball at www.mlb.com has done an amazing job of making statistics available to fans. The individual team sites offer detailed franchise histories, and a virtual clearinghouse of player information from past and present. We also used www.espn.com and www.baseball-reference.com extensively, but we verified all statistics through the MLB site, and when discrepancies arose we always defaulted to the numbers put out by Major League Baseball.

Our preferred method of research is actually to dig through piles and piles of old, dusty copies of *Sports Illustrated* and *Baseball Digest* magazines—and we did that, a lot—but technology being what it is today, we also made good use of LexisNexis to cull through decades of *The New York Times*, *New York Post*, and Associated Press articles via the Internet.

Our personal libraries are filled with books on baseball. *The Team by Team Encyclopedia of Major League Baseball*, written by Dennis Purdy, is one of the best. It proved to be a valuable resource. We also used *The 2005 ESPN Baseball Encyclopedia*, edited by Pete Palmer and Gary Gillette; *100 Years of the World Series*, by Eric Enders; and *Baseball: an Illustrated History*, by Geoffrey C. Ward and Ken Burns.

Of course, any mistakes found in these pages are our own.

We also recommend the following reading list for Yankee fans: *Bat Boy: Coming of Age with the New York Yankees*, by Matthew McGough; *Me and My Dad: A Baseball Memoir, by Paul O'Neill*; and *1941—The Greatest Year in Sports: Two Baseball Legends, Two Boxing Champs, and the Unstoppable Thoroughbred who made History in the Shadow of War*, by Mike Vaccaro. Finally, if you do not own a DVD copy of the Billy Crystal film *61**, add it to your list.

Index